Warfare and Waves

Warfare and Waves

Calvinists and Charismatics in the Church of England

Peter Herriot

☙PICKWICK *Publications* · Eugene, Oregon

WARFARE AND WAVES
Calvinists and Charismatics in the Church of England

Copyright © 2016 Peter Herriot. All rights reserved. Except for brief quotations in critical publications or reviews, no part of this book may be reproduced in any manner without prior written permission from the publisher. Write: Permissions, Wipf and Stock Publishers, 199 W. 8th Ave., Suite 3, Eugene, OR 97401.

Pickwick Publications
An Imprint of Wipf and Stock Publishers
199 W. 8th Ave., Suite 3
Eugene, OR 97401

www.wipfandstock.com

ISBN 13: 978-1-4982-2621-9

Cataloguing-in-Publication Data

Herriot, Peter.

    Warfare and waves : Calvinists and charismatics in the Church of England / Peter Herriot

    xii + 208 p. ; 23 cm. Includes bibliographical references.

    ISBN 13: 978-1-4982-2621-9

    1. Church of England. 2. Evangelicalism—Church of England. 3. Calvinism. 4. Pentecostalism. I. Title.

BX5125 H475 2016

Manufactured in the U.S.A.   12/10/2015

To David Calvert (1940–2015)

Contents

Preface | ix

Chapter 1
Institutions and Movements | 1

Chapter 2
Geneva, Lambeth, Los Angeles, and Toronto | 25

Chapter 3
The Production Line: Calvinist Formation and Leaders | 43

Chapter 4
Trouble and Strife: Calvinist Organizations | 64

Chapter 5
The Power House: Calvinist Congregations and Culture | 85

Chapter 6
Big and Bigger: Charismatic Organization | 104

Chapter 7
The Charismatic Self | 125

Chapter 8
Change: Rhetoric and Reality | 146

Chapter 9
The Days of Miracles and Wonders | 162

Chapter 10
A Global Institution | 177

Bibliography | 195
Index | 201

Preface

THE CHURCH OF ENGLAND (C of E) has featured frequently in the media in recent years. The dominant references have been to its slow and painful progress towards recognizing that women and gays can and should be priests and bishops. Headlines have highlighted predictions of schism, as reactionary elements claim that they cannot remain part of an institution which takes even these faltering steps. Consequently, there is a public perception of an institution being dragged kicking and screaming into the twenty-first century, still hankering after a patriarchal society with misogynistic and homophobic undertones.

I will argue in this book that these perceptions are a consequence of the relationships between the institution of the C of E and certain movements within it. To further their specific aims, the latter have taken full advantage of the institution's relatively democratic structures and procedures, while enjoying the use of its resources. The consequence for the C of E has been a huge expenditure of time and effort to keep movements within the institutional fold, when it could have been doing other much more important things. Furthermore, the compromises that it has made in doing so have resulted in major reputational costs.

How have movements consisting of a relatively small proportion of the regular C of E worshippers and priests succeeded in achieving this impact? Having chosen two movements from the Evangelical wing of the C of E, the Calvinists and the Charismatics, I first briefly outline their origins and histories. Then I explore how they are organized, revealing a dynamic mix of leadership formation, leaders themselves, large congregations, and specific organizations and pressure groups within them. Next I analyze the nature of their respective cultures—their beliefs, values, and norms of behavior—using their talks, articles, practices, and websites as

Preface

examples. These may surprise readers by their aggressive tone, or by their resemblance to contemporary entertainment products.

Why are these two movements the most "successful" elements in the C of E at present (excepting cathedrals)? The Calvinists provide a highly distinctive and dominant social identity that consciously reacts against the C of E's perceived surrender to secularism and heresy. Such an identity provides certainty in an uncertain world, and the self-esteem that comes from knowing that you are right and are one of God's faithful few. The Charismatics, on the other hand, incorporate many of the products, practices, and values of contemporary late modern culture. However, their preference for ecstatic forms of worship, claims of miraculous healing, and pre-modern worldview are sufficiently counter-cultural to limit their attractiveness to many modern people with complex identities.

How will the C of E deal with each of them? I conclude that making concessions to the Calvinists has been disastrous. The leadership, I predict, will in the future concentrate on the world outside the C of E more than on its own internal affairs, addressing issues of justice, poverty, and climate change. It will regain control of the agenda so as to relegate the favorite issues of the Calvinists to a proper place. They may continue politicking in the Anglican Communion, but the C of E will manage its continuing conflict with them so as to reduce their public profile.

The Charismatics, on the other hand, will be more fully incorporated. Their evangelistic skills and motivation and their recently increased concern with community issues render them potentially powerful allies in the C of E leadership's strategic direction. But they will have to moderate their emphasis on individual congregations and personal celebrity "ministries" at the expense of the responsibilities of institutional membership.

There is, however, an elephant in the crypt—globalization. Every social institution now has to take into account the three basic features of globalization (connectivity, "glocalization," and global consciousness) if it is to survive. What are the implications of globalization for the C of E's future direction? I conclude by arguing that the necessary internal reform of organization and finance will not be sufficient. Nor will its laudable attempts to address national injustices. Only a global influence will do.

I am an outsider in many senses to all these issues. I am not a theologian but a social psychologist, and try to wear that hat, taking a social science perspective throughout. And I am not an Anglican but a Methodist, though hopefully retaining some insight into the realities of denominational life

Preface

in an established church. I am deeply grateful to David Calvert and Linda Woodhead for their generous help, advice, and encouragement, without which the book would be littered with theological and sociological errors. The many which doubtless remain are all down to me.

Chapter 1

Institutions and Movements

A NATIONAL INSTITUTION

THE CHURCH OF ENGLAND is a national institution. It is an institution in the everyday sense that it is a part of our national cultural furniture with which most of us are familiar. We may refer to it, with a mixture of affection and exasperation, as the dear old C of E,[1] or we may merely make use of it as a convenience when asked to state our religion for bureaucratic purposes. But it is also an institution in a more formal sense, since institutions can be understood from a social scientific perspective as a category of social system with some unmistakable differentiating features.

Institutions tend to have bureaucratic structures and a long history, but to have survived through many vicissitudes because they have managed to adapt themselves to changing times. The C of E has, over the last half-millennium, survived murderous internal feuds and looming external threats. It has, albeit slowly, adapted to industrialization and post-industrialization, modernity and late-modernity.

Its culture—its beliefs, values, norms, and artefacts—has generally remained sufficiently aligned to the national culture to constitute part of it, but sufficiently distinctive to be able to offer a critique. Consider, for example, the plight of the poor during the Industrial Revolution. Associated with the hierarchical society of traditional rural England to the extent

---

1. Furlong, *C of E: The State It's In.*

that it was almost synonymous with the Tory party at prayer, the C of E was left standing in the blocks by the urgent response to the new industrial society by the Methodists and elements of its own Evangelical wing. However, new parishes were soon set up in the urban slums, the Christian Socialist movement was born, and both the High Church Oxford Movement and the Evangelicals established missions in the cities.

A century and a half later, the Church's same concern for social justice bucked the liberal free market political orthodoxy by producing the powerful report "Faith in the City." Or consider the action of Archbishop Runcie, himself a war veteran, who, in the service at St. Paul's Cathedral in commemoration of the Falklands War, prayed for the Argentinian as well as the British dead. This prayer directly critiqued the dominant nationalistic triumphalism led by Prime Minister Thatcher. In both these cases, the C of E was sufficiently in tune with contemporary English society to be able to give powerful expression to its own values without alienating the majority.

Institutions also have relations with other institutions, acquiring thereby precious social capital in terms of legitimacy and authority. As the established church, the C of E has ties with other established national institutions: the monarchy, parliament, and the legal system, for example. It also derives indirect status from these ties. It is worth emphasizing the continuing extent of the legal involvement of the C of E with the state. For example, the monarch has to be in communion with the Church of England. He or she appoints all of the bishops, and the government appoints the vicars of almost 700 parishes. Prisons and the Armed Services have to have C of E chaplains. And, for the nostalgic, there are still twenty-six bishops in the House of Lords, just as there is honey still for tea at Grantchester. Moreover, while the majority of the English population do not now get christened, married, or buried in their national church, let alone attend it regularly, there is little doubt that it will continue to officiate with great sense of occasion and dignity when, for example, the royal family experiences these life events.

Institutions are supported by their own hierarchical structures of authority and systems of control: rules and regulations, disciplinary procedures, policy-making processes, and so on. These enable them to plan, organize, and coordinate actions across the institution and use human and financial resources effectively. The C of E is no exception. Its hierarchy is based on the episcopal system, with archbishops overseeing the provinces of Canterbury and York, bishops overseeing dioceses such as Chelmsford

Institutions and Movements

or Southwark, clergy overseeing parishes, and uniform governance structures down to and including the level of individual congregations.[2]

Historically it would be true to say that the bishops have exercised a great deal of power both individually and in concert, although the advent of Synod in 1970 curtailed their influence.[3] Synod is, in effect, the C of E's parliament, and consists of bishops, clergy, and laity. Recent reorganization has seen the introduction of the Archbishop's Council in an attempt to centralize decision-making processes and improve the effectiveness of Synod.

So the C of E has all the advantages of being an institution: history, legitimacy, authority, culture, structure, and resources. It also has some of the disadvantages. It can be very slow to change. It has frequently adopted the traditional method of kicking difficult issues into touch by establishing a commission to investigate them. One historic case was the Commission on Doctrine. This was designed to address contentious theological issues between the Catholic and Reformed wings of the Church, which were particularly evident after the First World War. It was established in 1922 and reported in its own good time in 1938. At this point the nation and the Church had certain more urgent concerns.

The C of E, like other institutions, also finds it difficult to innovate, partly because its structure and processes are hierarchical, formal, and established, and discourage radical thought. In the 1960s, for example, when radical social and cultural change was abroad, the Church as a whole discouraged such innovators as Bishops Mervyn Stockwood and John A. T. Robinson (of *Honest to God* fame) and the Reverend Nick Stacey. The very idea that the Church should train its priests, conduct its liturgies, and formulate its stances on ethical issues with a view to engaging with a modern urban post-industrial workforce was at that point a bridge too far for both the Church hierarchy and the laity in general.

And finally, the Church has difficulty in securing a high level of commitment from many of its adherents in terms of time, effort, and money. For, as part of everyone's cultural furniture, it tends to get taken for granted. It has recently, for example, put additional financial responsibility onto individual congregations, instead of relying so much on its income from its investments, but the response has been decidedly mixed. Congregations that are both committed and wealthy support both themselves and the institution generously (although some have used their financial power as a

2. www.churchofengland.org/aboutus.
3. Hastings, *A History of English Christianity 1920–1990*.

political lever to influence diocesan policy). The poorer parishes, and also those individual adherents who perceive the Church as a public institution that provides various services that they need at different points in their lives, are less able, or less inclined, to demonstrate their commitment in financial terms.

So given these pros and cons of its status as an institution, how does the C of E measure up at present? A general conclusion based on two excellent recent reviews of the evidence[4] might run as follows: like most other contemporary institutions, its number of committed adherents is in decline; but it is currently achieving greater public prominence. If we consider membership and regular attendance figures as criteria, then the picture is indeed a grim one.[5] Numbers have been declining over a long period, but especially since the 1960s, with an apparent acceleration of decline in the 1980s and 1990s. Some, however, have detected a recent slowing in the rate of decline, particularly within the theologically Evangelical wing of the church. According to the English Church Census of 2005, in 1998 980,000 Anglicans worshipped regularly, whereas in 2005 the figure had decreased to 871,000. During this same period, mainstream or orthodox Evangelical Anglicans increased from 73,000 to 77,000; Charismatic Evangelicals remained constant at 115,000; and broad church Evangelicals decreased from 121,000 to 105,000. Of the 160 largest churches in the C of E with a membership of over 350, 83 percent are Evangelical. Also, attendance at cathedral services has increased markedly.

On the other hand, at least half of English people still say that they believe in God.[6] This has led Grace Davie[7] to describe the nation as "believing but not belonging." Perhaps, she speculates, English believers (but not belongers) want the minority belongers to act vicariously on their behalf and maintain the institution, to which they are emotionally attached, and upon which they depend in time of personal or national need.[8]

However, the more fundamental question is: by what criteria should a *national institution* be evaluated? Clearly, at the congregational level of analysis, membership and attendance figures are part, but part only, of an

---

4. Woodhead and Catto, *Religion and Change in Modern Britain*; Davie, *Religion in Modern Britain*.

5. www.christian-research.org/religioustrends.html.

6 www.europeanvaluesstudy.eu.

7. Davie, *Religion in Britain since 1945*.

8. Davie, *Religion in Modern Europe*.

appropriate set of criteria. But at the institutional level, success criteria should surely relate to the effectiveness of the C of E within national, and, I will argue, global society.

This response begs some questions, of course: for example, what is it that the C of E has to contribute that is distinctive, and how does it need to relate to other societal institutions? A response to the first question might be that it directs the nation towards a transcendent perspective and its implied ethical imperatives, or, in theological terms, that it presents and represents God within society. In particular, it has consistently spoken for those without a voice, the poor and marginalized. Such a function clearly reflects the differentiation of religion from other social systems and its unique purpose and role. Differentiation of this nature is a central feature of modernity and secularization.[9]

However, the attribution of these functions specifically to religion also implies, as Durkheim and others have argued,[10] that it can be seen as an element of civil society, integrated within it to a degree. Hence the C of E is likely to engage in relationships with a far wider range of social institutions than just the monarchy and parliament, cited above. For example, it is closely concerned with the institution of marriage and the family; the economic system and the distribution of wealth and resources; the provision of medical and social services; the education system; other Christian denominations and other religions and faith groups; and with music and the visual and performing arts.

The fundamental feature of all social systems is that they position themselves somewhere on a continuum between, at the one unsustainable extreme, total *differentiation* from other systems, and at the other, total *integration* with them (and therefore non-existence as a separate entity). By their very nature, institutions are normally likely to be located towards the integration end of the continuum. However, if they are to fulfill a unique role, they will also have to maintain a considerable degree of differentiation. For example, to contribute a prophetic element to the promotion of distributive and procedural justice, the C of E needs to differentiate itself as being more concerned with justice issues than are, for example, commercial corporations or the government of the day; and as having the moral authority to critique existing practice. However, such authority depends

9. Casanova, *Public Religions in the Modern World*.
10. Durkheim, *The Elementary Forms of the Religious Life*; Bellah, *Varieties of Civil Religion*.

upon, among other things, the C of E maintaining a good reputation for justice in its own practices and processes.

This emphasis on moral authority and reputation highlights the importance of public perceptions. In a late-modern and intensely mediated social system, it is difficult to distinguish the actions of a social institution such as the C of E from perceptions of it. Indeed, much of its activity is actively concerned with gaining and shaping media attention. Other activities may not be primarily directed at the media, but because it is a prominent national institution, it always offers a focus for media attention. Hence we see the apparently contradictory situation of increased public visibility at the same time as decreasing membership.

WELBY AND WONGA

A detailed example illustrates both the opportunities for, and the complexities of, social interventions.[11] The whole episode was essentially a media event. The relatively newly installed Archbishop of Canterbury, Justin Welby, who before his ordination worked in the oil industry, was interviewed by the magazine *Total Politics*. He announced that he had told the chief executive of Wonga, the payday loan company that charges 5,853 percent interest per annum, "we're not in the business of trying to legislate you out of existence, we're trying to compete you out of existence." He said that the medium for this commercial assault was to be the credit unions (not-for-profit and usually locally-based loan organizations which are limited by law to charging no more than 26.8 percent interest per annum). He offered the premises of 15,000 churches for use by credit unions, and volunteers to help run them. And, perhaps rashly in hindsight, he said "we're putting our money where our mouth is; we're starting a Church of England credit union."

This announcement did not feature particularly prominently in the national press or broadcasting media. The next day, however, it was the first story in the BBC news and achieved at least a page of coverage in both quality and mid-range newspapers. Why? Because the *Financial Times* had conducted some investigative reporting to the effect that the C of E's pension fund had invested in Accel Partners, a United States venture capital company that has itself invested heavily in Wonga. The headlines included "C of E admits investing £1m in Wonga" (*The Guardian*), and "Welby fury

11. *The Guardian*, 7/26/2013.

Institutions and Movements

as C of E pension fund profits from Wonga" (*The Daily Mail*). The BBC interviewed Welby, who admitted that the episode was very embarrassing. Its religious affairs correspondent suggested that the previous day's announcement had been "a bit of a coup in the Church and the outside world," but that the Church's investment had been "a serious blunder." The story was now the Church's embarrassment, not the Archbishop's initiative—apparently a much more newsworthy event.

The church's immediate task was now one of damage limitation. Welby continued to maintain that his plan was to undercut payday loans by building up the credit union movement, but commended Wonga's professionalism and said that it was better than many other payday lenders. The Archbishop's office, Lambeth Palace, expressed gratitude to the *Financial Times* for bringing to its attention

> this serious inconsistency of which we were unaware. We will be asking the assets committee of the Church Commissioners to investigate how this has occurred, and to review the holding in this pooled investment vehicle. We will also be requesting the Church Commission to investigate whether there are any other inconsistencies [with the C of E's ethical investment policy], as normally all investment policies are reviewed by the Ethical Investment Advisory Group (EIAG).

The implication of this statement is that one arm of the C of E structure, Lambeth Palace, had been let down by another, the Church Commission, and was seeking to shift the blame away from the Archbishop.

The field was now open for a wide range of parties to seek to benefit from the Church's and the Archbishop's discomfiture. The coalition government, and its Chancellor of the Exchequer, George Osborne, were responsible for the policy of austerity that resulted in a greater demand for payday loans. Yet they had consistently refused to legislate a cap on interest rates on loans, but rather made the government's social fund for those in dire need more difficult to access. Osborne, however, affirmed a "huge amount of respect for Justin Welby," recalling that he had appointed him to the parliamentary Banking Standards Commission, and asserting that he agreed with much of what he was proposing. Vince Cable, the Business Secretary, said "The Archbishop of Canterbury has hit the nail on the head." The chief executive of Wonga said that Welby was an exceptional individual and that they had had a meeting of minds on many big issues. He himself was, he stressed, "all for better consumer choice," to the extent that he cheekily published Wonga's version of the Ten Commandments.

This mixture of patronising praise and affirmations of basic agreement indicates that those standing to lose money or power were convinced that they now had nothing to fear. The Archbishop could not now respond feistily to Wonga's chief executive that there was no consumer choice to be made when you did not know where your next meal or the week's rent was coming from, and when the banks either would not lend to you, or else charged exorbitant overdraft rates. Moreover, the financial commentators agreed that credit unions would be no match for the payday lenders. They are often very local and inadequately capitalized, to the extent that from January 2012 through to July 2013, at least fourteen of them collapsed, many citing bad debts as the cause. Wonga, in contrast, announced revenues of £185 million in 2011 and spent £16 million on advertising.

So the Archbishop was temporarily undone by the failure of the bureaucratic institutional structures of the C of E to anticipate the likely investigative response of the media to his initiative. The government and the loans industry could then safely use their professed agreement with him to ward off criticism and present a sympathetic front while avoiding meaningful action. Further, it is possible that he did not assemble in advance a sufficiently powerful set of allies to support him. As Lord Glasman, a Labour peer, argued,[12] Islam has a strong opposition to usury, and indeed a Muslim Newcastle United footballer refused initially to wear his shirt sponsored by Wonga. The Roman Catholic Church, too, has an ongoing tradition of privileging the poor.

But all was certainly not lost. The C of E held its nerve and supported its Archbishop, who established a Task Group on Credit Unions and the Financial Sector. This is chaired by the eminent financial expert Hector Sants, who pointed out that the C of E "has the best branch network in the country."[13] The Church, if it appreciates sufficiently the mediated nature of its social environment, will demonstrate that it is in tune with a solid ethical strand of mainstream social values and has made a good choice of issue to contest. This will be a valuable antidote to its perceived discrimination against gays and women, where it has recently been differentiating itself so far from other social institutions and public sentiment as to risk its status as a valued societal institution (of which much more in later chapters). But

12. *The Observer*, 2/23/2014.
13. *The Guardian*, 10/3/2014.

success on this issue, and more generally, will require a careful weighing up of the benefits of being part of the establishment on the one hand, and the opportunities for prophetic action and multiple alliances provided by full involvement in civil society on the other.

As a postscript to this story, in October 2014 Wonga was required by the Financial Conduct Authority to write off loans to the value of £220 million for 330,000 borrowers, on the grounds that the company had not checked adequately that these customers were financially capable of repaying their loans. The Almighty certainly moves in mysterious ways.

TWO MOVEMENTS

Movements are very different from institutions. Indeed, they frequently define themselves as being their polar opposite. This is partly because institutions are associated with continuity, whereas movements are about change. Of course, the change they desire is not necessarily progressive. Frequently, movements, especially religious movements, are reactionary, seeking to recapture an earlier golden era in contrast to today's godless secularism, which, they argue, has infected historic institutions, including the Church. Certainly one of the movements which I describe is reactionary in this sense. Calvinists and Charismatics are both movements within the Evangelical wing of the C of E. Both also have adherents who are not Anglicans. Indeed, in the case of the Charismatics, only a small proportion of movement adherents are of that denomination. While this book is concerned with these movements as they operate within the C of E, they are both much more widely distributed than this, a context which I will describe in the next chapter.

Now many of the adherents of these movements are likely to angrily deny this description of themselves. They are in no sense "movements," they may argue, considering the term to have a political, if not devious, connotation. They are merely following God's will and doing what He expects of them. And they will probably also object to the labels that I have unilaterally attached to them. But my perspective is that of a social scientist: to demonstrate the existence of a social movement of any sort requires evidence of more or less organized collaboration of individuals and groups in pursuit of a program of action, and I will provide such evidence in the rest of this book. Movements have their own cultures and their own organization, both of which can be investigated empirically. As for the labels,

Calvinist and Charismatic, they do not claim to do justice to the niceties of theological disputation, but at least they bear some relation to the movements' stated origins and aims.

While I adopt a social scientific approach to defining and evidencing movements within the C of E, the two movements that I identify are also among the three categories described in an influential review of the Evangelical wing of the C of E[14] published ten years ago. Evangelicals are sub-categorized by Graham Kings into conservative (my "Calvinists"), open, and charismatic, and the similes of canal, river, and rapids, respectively, are used effectively. Kings's criteria for distinguishing these three are historical and theological rather than sociological and psychological, but the outcome is the same.

Unlike religious institutions, movements tend to concentrate on one or two clearly defined aims. So, the movement which I have labelled Calvinist has as its stated purpose the preservation and propagation of Reformed doctrinal truth. Charismatics, on the other hand, seek above all else to convert others to certain forms of spiritual experience and vitality. Of course, they would contest these aims, which I have presented in such an over-simplified way. Calvinists insist in their self-presentations on offering lengthy summaries of the doctrines that they wish to preserve, and claim to be the true mainstream. Charismatics express the wish to revitalise the spiritual life of individual Christians, the church, the nation, and indeed the world.

But organized they certainly are. Although they demonstrate less of the hierarchical and rule-governed structures of institutions, the very process of organizing tends towards institutionalization (as Weber emphasized). For example, their appointment of professional staff, registration as charities, establishment of boundaries, and codification of processes and practices all threaten to weaken the "fire in the belly," the motivation derived from a strong culture and social identity. The experience of the transcendent becomes institutionalized, and people can now be religious by means of ritual, precepts, and tradition. However, the form of organization that both movements have embraced currently remains sufficiently distinct from institutional structures to encourage motivation and commitment. (Please note, I am distinguishing the *form* of organization that the movements take as a whole from organizational *groups* that constitute an element within this form.)

14. Kings, "Canal, River, and Rapids."

Institutions and Movements

The four basic elements of the organizational form common to both movements are as follows: clerical formation, local congregations, leading clergy, and organizational groups. The relationships between these elements constitute each movement from an organizational perspective. First, the *professional formation* of clergy is vital to the movements' success. In many cases, students have been attracted to a particular version of the faith and to a clerical vocation at university, where various student societies and university churches exercise a profound effect on their intellectual and spiritual development. They then receive their theological training at a college that promotes and instills the movement's culture, for example, Oak Hill. There are close ties between these colleges and large and wealthy *local congregations* (e.g., St. Helens Bishopsgate, Holy Trinity Brompton), which provide work experience and starter appointments.

These congregations are often led by *movement leaders*, and also develop future leaders. Movement leaders are nearly all ordained clerics, but may increasingly be professional officers of organizational groups rather than rectors or vicars of congregations. The latter are enabled to spend much of their time on movement activities rather than on parish work by the additional clergy and other paid staff whom the congregation employs. Congregations offer facilities and resources to organizational groups with which they are associated (for example, St. Marks Battersea Rise and GAFCON).

Organizational groups are differentiated from each other in a variety of ways. They may, for example, concentrate upon one element of the movement's main aim (for example, Anglican Mainstream and Soul Survivor), or be particularly associated with a powerful local congregation (Proclamation Trust, Alpha). Some are long-established and have changed their aims and strategies over time (the Church Society). Others have been recently founded specifically to further the movement's purposes (Anglican Mission in England). Most have formal statements of purpose, trustees, and/or a council, and business meetings and conferences. Nearly all have effective websites and media communications. But every one of them is dependent for its survival and success upon the other three elements of the movement: they all need a continuing supply of ideologically committed leaders and wealthy and large congregations.

It is difficult to overstate the complexity of the interconnections within each movement. For example, as I will demonstrate, movement leaders frequently hold office in more than one of the movement's organizational groups. Wealthy congregations support the conferences and festivals of organizational groups. Leaders have shared the same formation and frequently preach or teach at each other's churches or organizational group's conferences. All repeatedly invoke the same past heroes of the movement, and quote the same key verses of the Bible. The web sites of each organizational group cross-reference the others' events and the media headlines they have achieved. This degree of movement integration is particularly evident in the Calvinists.

Other noteworthy common features are, first, the extent to which the movements are clerically led. It is not surprising, then, that their aims are internally focussed on the church, for Calvinists on doctrine and governance, and for Charismatics on worship. Second, the degree of flux within each movement is considerable. In particular, organizational groups are formed or re-formed and then fade away, while leaders rise and fall. And third, as I will elaborate in the next section, the impact which these movements can have on the institution to which they both belong, the C of E, is considerable.

While their organizational form is common, however, their culture and strategy certainly are not. Different aims and different histories ensure a wide variation. With their aim of preserving and propagating Reformed doctrine, it is hardly surprising that Calvinists have developed a culture strongly focussed on *beliefs*. If cultures are an amalgam of beliefs, values, norms of behavior, and artefacts, then the first of these constituent elements is culturally dominant for Calvinists. Their values, norms, and artefacts are, they consider, all derived from, and driven by, their doctrinal beliefs, in particular by their emphasis on the final authority of the Bible. Charismatics, on the other hand, emphasize *practices*, in particular their mode of ecstatic worship. This informs their doctrinal emphasis on the Holy Spirit, and the high value they place upon spontaneity and spiritual gifts. The leaders of both movements, however, would probably wish to argue that their values, norms, and artefacts are all derived from their belief in the Bible, the Word of God.

In terms of strategy, the movements again differ fundamentally. Returning to the basic social dialectic between differentiation and integration, Calvinists seek to differentiate themselves as sharply as possible from other movements, especially those that are somewhat similar, and with whom they might sometimes be confused. For example, they are usually dismissive of Charismatics, even though these, like themselves, are on the Evangelical

Institutions and Movements

wing of the C of E. At the same time, they seek to be as homogeneous as possible within their movement—diversity is not encouraged, especially of belief, but also of values and practice. This combination, of differentiation without and homogeneity within, is a recipe for an extremely strong social identity.[15] Movement adherents have clear models, in the persons of their fellow adherents and leaders, of who they are and should be; and they have equally clear examples in other movements of who they are not, and should not be. The potential for conflict based upon an us-versus-them worldview is clear, as is the strength of motivation, deriving from a single dominant social identity, to pursue it.

The strategy of Charismatics is not nearly so close to the differentiation end of the scale. They are not so concerned to establish boundaries between themselves and other movements, but, rather, to enlarge and enliven the spiritual experience of their adherents, and to make such gifts of the Spirit available to others. For example, they welcome charismatic Roman Catholics into the movement. They do not particularly stress their social identity as belonging to the movement. Rather, they are much more concerned with the personal identity and uniqueness of each adherent in their very intimate relationship with God, especially in those moments of ecstasy which are such a central feature of their worship. On the other hand, identification with the local congregation with whom these experiences are enjoyed may be strong ("I'm an HTB [Holy Trinity Brompton] person," they might say). Thus they enjoy the benefits of both a personal and unique individual identity, and also congregational and small group social identities.

Compared to institutions, then, movements in general, and these two in particular, have contrasting strengths and weaknesses. They are flexible enough in their organizational form to be able to adapt rapidly and innovatively to changing situations. They are focussed in their aims, and continuously develop a powerful supporting narrative with which to attract and inspire adherents.[16] Their strategies differ in terms of their relations with other social systems, and so they provide different forms of identity for their followers which both, nevertheless, give a strong sense of an "us," united in making change.

However, movements tend to lack the resources of legitimacy and authority that institutions typically possess, and also the more concrete

15. Brewer, "Social Identity Motives in Evolutionary Perspective."
16. Ammerman, "Religious Identities and Religious Institutions."

resources of financial and organizational structure, processes, and policies. Hence Calvinists, for example, strive for reputational credit by gaining a media profile through engineered conflict and drama. The media are consequently saturated with threats of schism and pleas of persecution. Or they may engage in protest or symbolic actions, such as establishing a "Third Province" in the UK, to gain visibility and sustain morale. In so doing, they may alienate potential allies, adding to the inherent difficulty that they all experience in compromising the purity of their aim by collaborating with others whose priorities may differ from their own. Calvinists run the risk, in other words, of finishing up in sectarian isolation.

INSTITUTIONS AND MOVEMENTS

So what is the range of possible relationships between institutions and movements? The most obvious relationship from a rational perspective is one of mutual support. Clearly, the two types of social system have different strengths, which taken together are complementary: structure, legitimacy, and resources allied to innovation, focus, and commitment. Not only are their strengths complementary: they also address each other's weaknesses. However, it is seldom easy for institutions, entwined in their national or regional culture and associated with continuity, to collaborate effectively with movements, whose *raison d'être* is change. This problem was clearly evident even at the very beginnings of Christianity, when the Church of Rome rapidly formalized the flames of inspired enthusiasm.[17]

One possible outcome is that the movement achieves its desired effect while remaining within the institution, and then slowly becomes incorporated and domesticated within it, becoming institutionalized itself. Thus the movement gains its objective, at least to a degree, and the institution probably benefits thereby. The Jesuit Order within the Roman Catholic Church is an example. Alternatively, the movement outgrows the institution where it originated, becoming impatient with its parent's failure to change in the desired direction. Christianity itself was a sect of this nature, driven primarily by St. Paul despite others' efforts to incorporate it into Judaism. Instead, it became in time a separate institutionalized religion. The separation of Methodism from the C of E represents another example.

---

17. Von Campenhausen, *Ecclesiastical Authority and Spiritual Power in the Church of the First Three Centuries.*

Institutions and Movements

Both of these outcomes, incorporation or separation, appear relatively benign to the religious social system as a whole, since either existing institutions change and adapt, or else new movements and institutions are added. In the ubiquitous language of modern management, they are both win-win outcomes. Other forms of relationship may be less favorable, however. A frequent habit of institutions has been to label movements heretical, and actively persecute them. This deprives institutions of possible innovative and adaptive changes, and discourages future innovation, since very unpleasant things have often happened to "heretics." Alternatively, institutions seek to neutralise movements by agreeing with them regarding their aims, but doing little or nothing to help them succeed. In the early days of the movement for women's ordination, the C of E adopted this tactic.

Or else the boot is on the other foot, with a movement parasitically using an institution as a resource to support its aims, a convenient base from which to operate, without regard for the institution's integrity or survival. Movements may simply use an institution as the battleground on which they can engage with other movements that they treat as hostile. Or they may treat the institution itself as the enemy, sometimes even while using its resources and remaining in its employment, professing that their objective is really to save it from itself. The Calvinists, I will argue, have just such a relationship with the C of E.

Which of these forms of relationship best describe that between the C of E and the movements within it in the past and at present, and which are likely to predominate in the future? Any convincing answer to this question may serve to predict the longer term prospects of both institution and movements. The story of the past is vigorously contested, because different parties wish to represent and justify the present situation in terms of a mythical history. An informed construction of the present, on the other hand, will require a detailed investigation of the movements and how they operate within the institution, which is the topic of the main body of this book. And speculation about the future must rest, if it is to have any legitimacy at all, on our views of the past and the present.

VERSIONS OF CHURCH OF ENGLAND HISTORY

So how do the different parties represent the history of the C of E and its relationships with the movements within it? *The C of E itself* likes to construct its story in institutional terms, portraying itself as a unifying national spiritual influence and bulwark. Admitting the turbulent beginnings of its Protestant phase of existence, it nevertheless presents its main story as that of a tolerant, moderate, and peaceful 'Broad Church,' maintaining the balance between its two historic wings, the Catholic and the Reformed, both of which it values, and out of which it was born. Its heroes are such unifying figures as Hooker, who gave theological justification for the Broad Church by proposing that its authority came from Scripture, tradition, and reason. Archbishop William Temple is its twentieth-century iconic figure. Its favorite periods in its history were, perhaps, the eighteenth century, when its parochial system provided the essential social glue for a largely rural nation; and the mid to late nineteenth century when its Evangelical wing in particular was heavily involved in social reform.

The movements, on the other hand, each cherish a very different historical account of the C of E. The *Calvinists* see Reformation London as a colony of Geneva, and the English Reformation as basically unfinished business. Their early heroes are Calvin, Cranmer, and John Knox, together with the martyrs Latimer and Ridley. A landmark in the Calvinist version of the history of the C of E is the publication of the Thirty-Nine Articles in 1571, which were based on Cranmer's earlier Forty-Two Articles, and were essentially a statement of the C of E's doctrinal position as distinguished from that of the Roman Catholic Church. Their Calvinist insistence on predestination (the idea that God chooses His followers rather than the reverse), and their discarding of such Catholic sacraments as ordination of the clergy and marriage, render the Articles an ideal flagship for today's Calvinists (but a difficult inheritance for the C of E itself). The Calvinist account concentrates on the early history of the English Reformation and the Puritans, who sought to complete it. It represents the following centuries in terms of a faithful few keeping alive the true Reformed flame. Their recent heroes are John Stott, Jim Packer, and Dick Lucas, all Anglican clergymen who are essentially the fathers of the UK movement in its present form, its previous generation of leaders.

The *Charismatic* version of C of E history[18] emphasizes, as one might predict, the freeing up of worship from the control of the rituals of the Catholic Church in the Reformation. However, Charismatics have a major difficulty in that, like the Roman Catholic church from which they were to separate, the Reformers, both Calvinist and Lutheran, believed that the charismatic gifts of apostolic days were unnecessary now that the

---

18. Hilborn, *Charismatic Renewal in Britain.*

Institutions and Movements

institutional Church was in place. True, some of the Puritans of Oliver Cromwell's Commonwealth embraced a "baptism of the Spirit," but they soon left the Church of England to form dissenting congregations. Other groups that included ecstatic forms of worship, the Huguenots, Quakers, Moravians, and Methodists, had relatively little impact on the C of E. Rather, the Charismatic movement in the C of E emphasizes its origins in the second half of the twentieth century, and claims as its heroes stalwarts of the immediately previous generation to the present leadership: Michael Harper, David Watson, and David Pytches, who were influenced primarily by their personal experiences of American preachers, congregations, organizations, and denominations. The basic theme of their story is spiritual revival, especially the revival of church institutions.

Thus, in marked contrast to the Calvinists, whose emphasis on Anglican doctrine necessarily leads them to formulate an historical account of the English Reformation, the Charismatics looked back to apostolic times for legitimacy, but to much more recent history for their foundation story. Rather than emphasizing a historical base in the Reformed C of E, they treat that institution merely as the home in which they find themselves.

It is hardly surprising that movements each construct a historical account that accords with, and promotes, their own aims and preoccupations. *Professional historians*, however, present a different version. While the Tudor and Stewart periods in particular are subject to a great deal of scholarly dispute, there is considerable agreement that the Reformation in England was in no way a short period of turbulence followed by a long calm voyage of moderation and peace.[19] On the contrary, the bishops of the newly formed C of E destroyed the products of "popery" just as eagerly as did the Puritans later. The English Reformers actually killed more Catholics than any other Protestant church in Europe, all in the name of truth. The response in kind under the Catholic Queen Mary, and subsequent further iconoclastic retaliation by the regicidal Puritans, demonstrate that England was just as violent in its religious conflicts as was continental Europe.

Even the Restoration of the monarchy and the institutionalization of the C of E did not stop persecution of those of the Roman Catholic faith or of a more general Catholic disposition if they failed to conform to its strict requirements regarding liturgy and doctrine. The late eighteenth century brought the social upheavals of the Industrial Revolution, and the ultimate secession of the Methodists. Next, the powerful response of

---

19. MacCulloch, *Thomas Cranmer*; Maltby, *Prayer Book and People*.

the nineteenth-century C of E Evangelicals to the injustices of industrial capitalism and Empire[20] stimulated an equally powerful reaction to modernity in the Oxford Movement. Its leaders, steeped in Romanticism, saw the C of E as part of the historic Catholic church (not the *Roman* Catholic Church). It was certainly not a mere Reformed church introduced and sponsored by the state. The Oxford Movement found the Thirty-Nine Articles impossible to accept, and reintroduced many historic practices into the liturgies in their churches.

The clashes between the two movements, Evangelical and Catholic, were of course derived from the compromises of the seventeenth century which had gradually brought the era of violent persecution to an end. They continued into the twentieth century, and were made more public by the increasingly democratic structures of the C of E. Efforts at compromise were defeated, for example, in the case of the proposed revision of the Book of Common Prayer, where both Evangelicals and Catholics allied to get the proposal defeated in Parliament in 1928 because it satisfied neither of them. And, as I will describe more fully later, the same alliance of convenience has been used more recently to contest the ordination of women clergy and bishops. If these activities are construed as a case of the tail wagging the dog, then it is an extremely powerful and politically engaged tail.

So overall, the history of the C of E has to be seen as a story of internal conflict. Movements with incompatible aims and beliefs have sought to dominate the institution at each other's expense. The recent conflicted term of office of Archbishop Rowan Williams, then, should not be seen as in any sense atypical.

THE ELEPHANT IN THE CHURCH OF ENGLAND CRYPT

The historical context is not, however, the only perspective important to the understanding of the C of E. Its present positioning vis-à-vis the elephant in the crypt, *globalization,* is also of profound importance. In what sense, if any, is the C of E a global institution? To what extent are the Calvinists and Charismatics within the C of E also adherents of global movements? And why does it matter what the answers are to these questions? To stretch a metaphor to breaking point, can we quietly continue to feed and water the elephant in the crypt, or will it stamp its feet, trumpet loudly, and bring

---

20. Edwards, *A Concise History of English Christianity.*

Institutions and Movements

the whole historic edifice crashing to the ground as it breaks out into the wider world?

The nature of attempted answers to these questions depends upon the perspective from which one approaches the continuing process of globalization. If that perspective is primarily based on a *political/economic* worldview, then we might continue, with Francis Fukuyama,[21] to expect the ultimate universal triumph of liberal democracy, accompanied by free-market capitalism and consumerism. Ideological struggle will be replaced by economic calculation, Fukuyama predicted regretfully, imagination and idealism by "centuries of boredom."

Other political/economic scenarios have naturally been proposed, for example, the continued increase in power and wealth of corporations, but this time at the expense of liberal democracy, rather than as its consequence. But all such political/economic perspectives necessarily construe other social systems as of secondary importance, mere outcomes of these more fundamental processes. Religion and nationalism, for example, were, for Fukuyama, merely reactionary and dying convulsions against the inevitable growth of universal democracy and freedom.

A properly social scientific perspective rejects such a privileging of political and economic ideology. However, it also dismisses any attempt to construe the world entirely in terms of *culture and cultural difference*. One prominent such account is that of Samuel Huntington,[22] who argued that civilizations are the largest and most important social and cultural unit in existence. Civilizations are deeply historically rooted, and religion is their principle defining feature. Indeed, Huntington's names for two of his seven civilizations are religious: Hindu and Islamic. So profound are the differences between civilizations that conflict between them frequently occurs at their points of contact. Twenty years ago, Huntington characterized the global scenario as follows: "A West at the peak of its power confronts non-Wests that increasingly have the desire, the will, and the resources to shape the world in non-Western ways."[23] The most profound conflict of our times, he argues, is between the Western and Islamic civilizations.

Both of these still influential perspectives privilege particular social systems, political/economic or cultural/civilizational, in their accounts. As a consequence, *religion* occupies a secondary position for both of them. For

---

21. Fukuyama, *The End of History and the Last Man*.
22. Huntington, *The Clash of Civilizations and the Remaking of World Order*.
23. Huntington, "The Clash of Civilizations," 26.

Fukuyama it is a reactionary spasm against liberal democracy. Clearly, in a democracy people have the freedom of religious choice, but this is a private and personal matter, runs the argument. Religion is, from this perspective, another consumerist option. For Huntington, on the other hand, religion is typically a justification of and a motive for conflict between civilizations. It provides the opportunity for the divisive identities of "us versus them," which underpin sectarian strife.

The basic dynamic of social systems, however, is the dialectical opposition of differentiation and integration. Every system maintains some sort of equilibrium between these poles. The story of modernity, of which globalization is the culminating and powerful expression, is partly one of increasing differentiation of social systems. Science, religion, nation states, economics and commerce, the arts, the law, and other social systems too, have all established their separate identities. They all have their own assumptions and beliefs, values, and norms of behavior, and specialist languages. They each concentrate on a primary purpose. None of them has any privileged position from an analytic perspective. A proper analysis of globalization is therefore theoretical and descriptive rather than ideological.

At first, this process of differentiation occurred at more local levels, but today all of these systems may be considered global in scope.[24] There is, for example, no longer Chinese science and Western science, just science. Clearly, then, while differentiation is continuing apace (e.g., more scientific disciplines are continually being created), integration has also occurred (e.g., the professed assumptions, values, and practices of science are now the same everywhere). Differentiation is into ever more specialized social systems; integration, ultimately, is now into global ones. The dialectical poles, the "local" and the global, are now further apart than they have ever been.

So one characteristic of globalization is that it is a process that continually oscillates between *the global and the local*,[25] between the processes of integration and differentiation. The ecstatic experiences of the Toronto Blessing were a partially new form of charismatic worship (differentiation), but they soon influenced practices in a wide range of religious settings throughout the world (integration). This continuous dialectical process has been immensely facilitated by the second feature of globalization: its

---

24. Beyer, *Religions in Global Society*.
25. Robertson, *Globalization, Social Theory, and Global Culture*.

Institutions and Movements

connectivity.[26] People are socially connected worldwide as information, ideas, symbols, goods, money, jobs, and indeed, people themselves, move across national and geographical boundaries. It is this connectivity that permits highly differentiated social groups to create and maintain themselves, but at the same time allows global movements to develop based on disparate groups sharing a common agenda.

A final feature of any adequate social scientific account of globalization has to be its *reflexive* nature. People are now aware of the world as a single system, of the great global sub-systems such as religion, and of themselves as social participants in, and reproducers of, these social systems. Such notions as universal human rights, religious freedom, human security, the common good, and the rule of law could not be popularly held unless this (self)-awareness were present. People are also aware of an important implication of a global social system: that it depends upon relationships between its sub-systems if it is to function. Capitalist corporations, national governments, science and technology, and religion, for example, are perceived to need to collaborate in addressing issues of resource scarcity and distributive injustice.

IS THE CHURCH OF ENGLAND GLOBAL?

Against this global context, the account earlier in the chapter of the C of E and two of the movements within it appears at first sight to be irredeemably local and parochial. The sense of place and of particularity feels overwhelming. To what extent, we may ask, has the C of E recognized its new context and entered the globalization process?

As an institution, it was reconfigured in a unique historical situation (the English Reformation) and retained features peculiar to itself: a very local "beginning." However, as part of the subsequent imperial project, it engaged in missionary activity throughout the British Empire. This may have given the impression of a global reach for a local church, but for all its breadth ("wider, still, and wider"), the Empire was still not truly global. Moreover, while the British missionaries of the nineteenth century sought to retain control over the establishment and development of Anglican churches in the colonies, locals fought hard to have their traditional religious beliefs and practices incorporated into their new colonial churches. This resulted in frequent local practices such as polygamy, miraculous

26. Scholte, *Globalization*.

healing, and exorcism from demonic possession becoming accepted, or at least tolerated in the missionary church, particularly in Africa.

However, while the colonial Anglican churches of the Empire were each ultimately established separately and with their own constitution, all of them were episcopal in their governance and parochial in their organization. As the Empire gradually disappeared, they became members of the *Anglican Communion,* in fellowship with each other but led by the Archbishop of Canterbury as "first among equals." Today their archbishops represent churches from rural, industrializing, and post-industrial nations located wherever the British Empire left its deep footprint. There are thirty-six member churches in the Anglican Communion, comprising around eighty million members, and their leaders meet every ten years at the Lambeth Conference.

Thus, in the everyday usage of the term, the Anglican Communion, though not the C of E, might be considered global in its extent; it is at least represented in every continent. But from the social scientific perspective outlined above, it clearly is not global. Neither its ideas nor its people are truly connected worldwide, since membership and organization is largely limited to the former Empire. This historic limitation is associated with an established church still tied to the original imperial power. And there remains a reminder of that imperialism in the historic but changing superior status of the C of E and its archbishop within the Communion.

Moreover, another feature of globalization seems to be missing. Any equilibrium between differentiation and integration, the global/local dynamic, currently seems difficult to achieve in the Anglican Communion. The cultures of the national member churches each reflect elements of their national culture, and this differentiation is not compensated for by a corresponding integrative process as they share their practices with others. The "reverse missions" from the ex-colonies back to the "mother churches" in Britain and America tend to minister to immigrants. And, as I will describe, the recent rapprochement of English and American Calvinists with African Anglicans is a marriage of political convenience rather than any truly integrative process. Indeed, the Anglican Communion is being pulled apart by sectarian divisions.

The contrast of the C of E with the Roman Catholic Church is instructive. The latter has come to be recognized as a truly global institution. It realized that the nation state was a basic tool with which modernity had challenged the church (witness the constitutional separation of church from state in France and the USA). It therefore explicitly abandoned any pretence of established national status and embraced Enlightenment principles of human dignity, religious freedom, and self-determination. In a word, it represented itself as an element of global civil society,[27] with the right to hold modernity to its promises. From the Second Vatican Council of 1962, and through a variety of Declarations such as *Dignitatis Humanae* and *Gaudium et Spes* (Joy and Hope), it has addressed ethical issues generally perceived as universal and global in their scope. These documents directly challenged governments and, sometimes, corporations. The Roman Catholic Church was thus acting as part of global society, since it was engaging with these other major global social sub-systems regarding global issues.

On the other hand, these Declarations were literally *ex cathedra* pronouncements. They did not involve much dialogue with other social systems, but rather made unilateral statements, ignoring the general modern distrust of institutions, particularly those of an authoritarian bent lacking in participation and accountability. Moreover, the Church's integrative efforts within the global sub-system of religion, and the sub-sub-system of Christianity, have neither been conspicuous nor successful. On the contrary, the Church's idea of "re-Christianizing" Europe still seems to have some currency, and it still demonstrates occasional authoritarian and even apparently dismissive attitudes towards other Christian institutions. It fails to participate fully in the World Council of Churches or more local examples of Christian unity such as the United Church of South India. This isolationist stance renders its global integration, at both the general religious and also the specifically Christian levels of social system, difficult to imagine. Thus while the Roman Catholic Church may itself be a global institution in its own right, its major contribution towards the globalization of the social systems of religion and of Christianity is less evident.

Nevertheless, the example of the Roman Catholic Church gives pause to the currently popular thesis that institutions are in general and terminal decline. Using the institutions of democracy as his canvas, Moises Naim[28] argues that there is an ongoing redistribution of power away from institutions to more fluid, accountable, and democratic social forms such as social movements, with their high level of connectivity. But this view may reflect an insular late-modern or post-modern Western perspective, privileging

27. Juergensmeyer, "Religious Antiglobalism."
28. Naim, *The End of Power.*

political social systems. More generally, one might argue that it is not so much the case that one form (institutions) is inevitably yielding place to another (movements) as that the success of each requires their mutual collaboration.

The C of E, then, cannot claim anything like the same degree of progress toward globalization as the Roman Catholic Church. It is demonstrably local in its history and preoccupations. Where it has broadened its horizons, these have largely been limited to the historical bounds of Empire, and integration with the disparate ex-colonial churches has proved very difficult. But what of the movements active within the C of E? How globalized are they? And will the Church's relationships with its movements enable it to firmly establish global connectivity, to achieve a global/local equilibrium, and to develop a conscious perception of itself as global? Alternatively, will they hinder this progress? For success or failure in these definitive tasks will determine its long-term future. To make any such global predictions, we must first examine carefully the local and particular, returning to the global only in the last chapter of the book. But first, we need to consider the recent history of the Calvinists and the Charismatics in order to put the present situation into context.

CHAPTER 2

Geneva, Lambeth, Los Angeles, and Toronto

GENEVA AND AFTER

So if there turns out to be satisfactory evidence for the current and continuing existence of Calvinist and Charismatic movements within the C of E, what are their broader historical roots, their primary emphases, and their global reach? And how have they exercised their influence in recent Anglican history?

The label "Calvinist" stands for one of the two great traditions of the Reformation, the Lutheran Protestant and the Reformed traditions.[1] Calvin was a major player in the latter tradition, but not so dominant as was Luther in the former. Throughout its history, the Reformed tradition has maintained three emphases, although each has carried a greater weight than the other two in particular periods. The first is, as its name suggests, a concern with institutional reform; the second, its theology; and the third, its concern with personal piety and holiness.

Institutional reform was the dominant driver in the first of the three phases of the Reformed movement.[2] The religious institution in need of reform was, of course, the Roman Catholic Church. However, so

---

1. MacCulloch, *The Reformation*; McGrath, *Christianity's Dangerous Idea*.
2. Hart, *Calvinism*.

undifferentiated were the social systems of the day that any reform of the Church necessarily involved reform of other social and political institutions as well. Calvin's famous attempts to introduce the singing of psalms in taverns in Geneva is the popular caricature of the pervasive nature of reform.

The corollary was, however, that radical reform could only be achieved with the support of other institutions, when city states such as Geneva and Zurich collaborated. Alternatively, small countries such as the Netherlands and Scotland permitted the independence of a Reformed church, proving more amenable to its presence than the powerful kings and nobles in other parts of Europe. The pure flame of Reform burned brightly in these few centers.[3] However, in larger countries there remained a feeling of uncompleted business, as powerful rulers compromised with radical reformers (as, for example, did Elizabeth I of England), or persecuted them with the support of Rome (as in France).

In terms of *doctrine*, Luther's emphasis on justification by faith alone, or perhaps more correctly, by grace alone, was paralleled by Calvin's on the authority of the Bible. Both were aimed at discrediting various requirements and practices of the Roman Catholic Church which implied salvation by "works," and which were not mandated in Scripture. Calvin's insistence on the doctrine of *sola scriptura*, the supreme authority of the Bible in all matters of belief and practice, is a cornerstone of conservative Reformed teaching to this day. It was radical in the extreme, since it denied the Church and its traditions any ultimate authority.[4] It was God, through His Word, who had authority, not the pope or his bishops.

However, despite these Herculean political and theological efforts, it became clear to the Reformed movement that complete institutional reform was unlikely. Even within their strongholds in Northern Europe, they faced dissent and opposition, and they lacked the authority to impose their own orthodoxy. They started to concentrate more upon personal spiritual reformation than on institutional reform, more upon piety than polity.[5] They gave their attention to their own souls and to the souls of the local congregation of the saints.

When the commerce and empires of the British and Dutch spread across much of the known world, the Reformed faith that they took with

---

3. Benedict, *Christ's Churches Purely Reformed*.
4. Gordon, *Calvin*.
5. Ward, *The Protestant Evangelical Awakening*.

Geneva, Lambeth, Los Angeles, and Toronto

them was thus pietistic as well as doctrinal and reformist. They were still constrained by imperial control from the home country, and they still frequently had to deal with the power of the Catholic missionaries who had sometimes preceded them. Moreover, their Puritan zeal proved too demanding for the majority of the colonists, just as it had ultimately failed to retain power back in England.

Nevertheless, once independence from England was achieved in America, freedom to establish Presbyterian and Reformed churches independently of the state was exploited to the full. The contrast with Switzerland, the Netherlands, Germany, and Scotland, the original homes of Reformism, was painful, since these and other Reformed churches had had to make compromises with the political establishment in order to survive. The requirement to compromise was entirely understandable: governments did not want a return to the destructive religious wars of the seventeenth century.

The freedoms experienced in North America were soon to be enjoyed in other continents, as missionaries and colonists from Europe brought their faith with them during the late eighteenth and the nineteenth centuries.[6] In particular, Scottish settlers in Canada, Australia, and New Zealand, and Dutch in South Africa, took with them their Reformed convictions. Not only did they establish their own churches, but indigenous churches developed alongside, and often relatively independently. The Reformed faith thus enjoyed a major expansion in the nineteenth century. How would it fare in the twentieth?

In the Protestant power-house of the United States, the main enemy was now no longer the Roman Catholic Church, nor yet the devil in the form of personal sin. Rather, it was liberal theology and the social gospel. Reformed responses to these movements ranged from the conservative theology of such as J. Gresham Machen through to the fundamentalist dogmas of the Reconstructionist theologians towards the end of the twentieth century.[7] Personal and congregational piety and doctrinal orthodoxy were emphasized, but institutional foundation and support were not so forthcoming.

In the continents that received Reformed settlers, radical Reformist traditions remain. In Australia, for example, the so-called "Sydney Anglicans"

---

6. Wuthnow, *Boundless Faith.*
7. Herriot, *Religious Fundamentalism: Global, Local, and Personal,* ch. 7.

are more Calvinist than were the Genevans themselves.[8] However, in comparison with the Charismatics, the Calvinists are few and dispersed. There is a very basic reason—they lack one of the three fundamental features of globalization: connectivity. Their several areas of geographical spread have relatively little to do with each other, even when proximate: Canada and the USA, the Netherlands and Scotland, Australia and Asia, for example.

Nor do the three different groups into which Darryl Hart[9] differentiates contemporary Calvinists collaborate with each other. Hart distinguishes, first, ecumenical Calvinists who are interested in dialogue with other Christians and faiths, more liberal in theology, and to be found in the remaining established churches or those with a strong sense of involvement in society. They tend to belong to the World Council of Reformed Communions. The second grouping is committed to maintaining the forms of doctrine, ministry, and church governance that they trace back to the original reformers. They are not necessarily concerned to be part of an established church or denomination. Finally, Hart refers to large numbers of ex-colonial churches, whose emphasis is on personal piety and local congregational life, not social involvement or institutional development. Nor are these latter Calvinists very concerned with doctrinal niceties as expressed in the historic European confessional documents.

These groups are differentiated by history, belief, values, and practice: they have, in other words, markedly different cultures. There is little connectivity between them, just as there is little connectivity between geographical neighbors. Given this connectivity deficit, there is unlikely to be much of a global/local dialectic, nor any conception of the movement as global. The first of Hart's three groups (above) has the potential for such global development, but is clearly limited in breadth and numbers of adherents. We may conclude that Calvinism is not likely to become a truly global movement any time soon. Its continued success, such as it is, may be partly attributable to the increasingly global spread of Roman Catholicism, to which it is the most obvious dialectical opposite.

What, then, of the Calvinists within the Church of England? Clearly, they belong to the second of Hart's three contemporary groups. They continuously hark back to original Reformed doctrine and congregational governance, especially to the supreme authority of the Bible. They retain the Reformers' hostility towards the doctrines, practices, and authority of the

---

8. Porter, *Sydney Anglicans and the Threat to World Anglicanism*.
9. Hart, *Calvinism*.

Geneva, Lambeth, Los Angeles, and Toronto

Roman Catholic Church. They believe that the Reformation, in England and elsewhere, remains incomplete. And they are indisputably local. Like the C of E itself, their connexions are limited to allies in the Anglican Communion, the former Empire. Their story is that of an absolutist tendency, striving to impose purity of doctrine and practice, but finding it just out of reach. On the few historic occasions they achieved power, for example, as Puritans, they rapidly alienated the country and lost it again.

LAMBETH AND AFTER

Having located the Calvinists within their historical and cultural context, what is the recent history of their relations with the C of E and with the Anglican Communion? In the immediate post-war decades, conservatives enjoyed a powerful position within the church, but soon lost out as they factionalized over doctrinal disputes and ignored the cultural revolution of the 1960s. Since the 1960s, however, and particularly since the 1990s, the story is one of conflict with the institution of which they are formally part,[10] and of their development of complex organizational forms to help them fight these battles. They chose a series of issues on which to take positions, almost all of which relate to sexual or gender issues: whether clergy and bishops should be appointed who were actively gay, for example, or whether women should be appointed as parish priests or bishops. They also play a prominent part in more general debates about civil partnerships and gay marriage. Throughout their recent history, they have sought to portray themselves as the defenders of the historic doctrines and rules of Anglican (and Christian) orthodoxy, and as the victims of persecution for their pains. And they have argued that, if they were to fail to win their battles on behalf of biblical doctrine and practice, then alternative arrangements had to be made so that they did not have to fellowship with the "heretics" currently in positions of ecclesiastical power.

There were two key events that introduced this period of sharp internal conflict. The first was the decision to ordain women in 1992, a milestone that was only achieved because it was supported by many Evangelicals, who historically had opposed it. However, many Anglo-Catholics voted against, some of whom left the C of E to join the Roman Catholic Church, while others were bought off with a compromise. They could be ministered to by Provincial Episcopal Visitors ("flying bishops"), that is, by bishops from

---

10. Herriot, *Religious Fundamentalism and Social Identity*, ch. 5.

other dioceses who were themselves not in sympathy with the ordination of women. Thus their theological conscience could permit them to remain within the C of E. The Calvinists were certainly not among the Evangelicals supportive of women's ordination, however, believing that the Bible teaches the headship of men over women where ministerial authority is concerned. They determined to select their next battle carefully.

The next major conflict[11] concerned gay clergy and bishops, of whom there were many in the C of E, especially among Anglo-Catholics. Historically this fact had been tacitly accepted, but it became an issue when both the Calvinists on the one hand, and the Lesbian and Gay Christian Movement on the other, refused to let sleeping clergy lie. The former wanted clerical sin confronted and punished, the latter sought to celebrate it publicly. The tabloid press recognized a good story when it saw one, and so pressure increased on the C of E to "take a stand" on the issue. As was its custom, it commissioned a report. However, it refused to publish the draft, perhaps because it suggested that the quality of the relationship was the important moral issue, not the gender of the partners. Instead, under Archbishop Carey's guidance, in 1991 it published *Issues in Human Sexuality*. This document argued that where their intention was a lifelong partnership, it was acceptable for a gay couple to have a physical relationship. However, the distinctive nature of the clergy's vocation made this an unacceptable course for them to take.

Shortly after the decision to ordain women and the publication of this advisory document, the organization Reform[12] was founded. Its foundation purpose was "to uphold, defend, and spread the gospel of Jesus Christ according to the doctrine of the Church of England." However, its focus is always powerfully directed onto the current issue at dispute. For example, of its forty-three archived monthly news bulletins between 2008 and 2013, twenty-nine deal prominently with women bishops. Reform played a major lobbying role in the Lambeth Conference of 1998. Lambeth is a meeting of the bishops in the Anglican Communion that occurs every ten years, and that is numerically dominated by bishops from Africa. The Conference passed a resolution, "Lambeth 1.10," which was a hardened up version of *Issues in Human Sexuality*. It rejected all homosexual activity as contrary to Scripture, opposed the blessing of same-sex unions, and rejected the ordination of clergy engaged in such unions. Although Conference resolutions

---

11. Bates, *A Church at War*.
12. www.reform.org.uk.

Geneva, Lambeth, Los Angeles, and Toronto

have advisory status only, and different provinces can moderate their terms in practice, Lambeth 1.10 was treated by the Calvinist movement as a clear and unambiguous indication of the Church's teaching.

However in 2003 Anglican clergy in Vancouver blessed a gay union in church, an event to which the Archbishop of Canterbury, Rowan Williams, responded with a statement expressing regret that this was going further than the teaching of the Church could justify. He was then put under severe pressure by the UK Evangelical press and Evangelical bishops, and by African and Australian archbishops, to rescind the appointment of Jeffrey John, a celibate gay man, to be Bishop of Reading. Facing the threat of a split in the Anglican Communion, Williams did so. From his perspective, however, things went from bad to worse in 2004, when Gene Robinson, a practising gay man, was appointed Bishop of New Hampshire. After his consecration, thirteen provinces of the Communion announced that they were "out of communion" with the Episcopal Church in America. Many American parishes that voted against the consecration now enjoyed the pastoral oversight of doctrinally sound flying bishops, some from African dioceses, who were only too pleased to oblige.

Despite the C of E's best efforts, in which yet another commission criticized both sides in the dispute and urged a moratorium on the consecration of more gay bishops, the Communion remained hopelessly divided. In 2005, nearly half of the Communion's archbishops rejected Williams' plea for dialog, and urged him to act against gay clergy in accordance with what they said was the Bible's and the Church's clear teaching. And most important, a new grouping independent from the Communion, the Global Anglican Future Conference (GAFCON), met in Jerusalem in 2008 and published the Jerusalem Declaration, an affirmation of traditional conservative doctrine. GAFCON spawned the Fellowship of Confessing Anglicans, which has a UK branch and an offshoot, the Anglican Mission in England.

Throughout all these developments in the disputes regarding gays and women, the Calvinist movement played a prominent part. New organizations, for example, Anglican Mainstream,[13] founded in 2004, placed an overwhelming emphasis on a single issue; in their case, sexuality. Powerful pressure groups, such as Reform and Anglican Mainstream, formed part of a tightly knit movement in which formative training colleges such as Oak

---

13. www.anglican-mainstream.net

Hill College[14] develop young, ideologically committed clergy. These will ultimately succeed such presently dominant figures as Revs. Rod Thomas, Chris Sugden, Vaughan Roberts, and Paul Perkin, who mobilize large and wealthy congregations and/or administer organizational pressure groups.

In the recent tortured political history of the C of E and the Anglican Communion, the Calvinist movement has "punched above its weight." Although the movement is not globally connected, it does have links between the UK, Australia, Canada, and the USA. Its power is partly a consequence of its sophisticated organization, and of its readiness to spend time and effort in exploiting to the full the Church's democratic decision-making processes. So, for example, it fought a successful rear-guard action at the C of E Synod in 2012, gaining in prior diocesan elections enough seats among the laity element of Synod to delay the introduction of the ordination of women bishops, contrary to the overwhelming desire of the Church as a whole. Success in fulfilling the C of E's preference was only finally achieved in the Synod of July 2014. The Calvinist story overall is one of well-organized, counter-cultural, aggressive political activity. The Charismatics, however, are a very different kettle of fish.

LOS ANGELES AND AFTER

So what characterizes the Charismatic movement as a whole (and in particular the Pentecostal denominations that played such a large part in its development)? Harvey Cox distinguishes three definitive features: primal speech, primal piety, and primal hope. "Primal" denotes that Cox believes that the Pentecostals "reached beyond the levels of creed and ceremony into the core of human religiousness, into what might be called primal spirituality, that largely unprocessed nucleus of the psyche in which the unending struggle for a sense of purpose and significance goes on."[15] Clearly, in Cox's view, charismatic practices reflect a more genuine and fundamental spirituality than do other forms of worship.

"Primal speech" refers to speaking in tongues, praying in the spirit, or glossolalia: in other words, ecstatic utterances that do not form part of any known language. These are considered to enable prayer without the limitations of formal speech. It is the Holy Spirit who is inspiring the believer. *"Primal piety"* denotes a variety of other forms of ecstatic religious

14. www.oakhill.ac.uk.
15. Cox, *Fire from Heaven*, 81–82.

Geneva, Lambeth, Los Angeles, and Toronto

expression, including trances, visions, healing, dancing, and exorcism. Primal speech and primal piety, Cox insists, are taken as signs of the Spirit, not as ends in themselves. The aim is not merely to enjoy a spiritual experience. Finally, *"primal hope"* is the millennial belief that a new age is about to burst out; ecstatic experiences are signs and foretastes of this new age. God's kingdom is almost here, and the present age with all its sin and suffering will pass away. This world will give way to the next—a heavenly city is at hand.

These three features particularly characterize the Pentecostal church, the early beginnings of which are usually located in Azusa Street in Los Angeles in 1906. However, both ecstatic experiences and millennial hopes have characterized Christianity at periodic intervals from its earliest days, as St. Paul's letter to the Corinthians demonstrates.[16] What was unique about the beginnings of Pentecostalism in America was its powerful blend of Afro-American Spiritual and Wesleyan Holiness traditions. The latter contributed a fourth original feature, which has profoundly affected the Charismatic movement subsequently—a literalist and *"common sense"* view of the Bible. This accepts the pre-modern supernatural thought forms of the biblical narratives as appropriate to today's world. The ecstatic expressions in worship, the Afro-American heritage, are thus foretastes of the kingdom as described in God's Word. They reflect the cosmic struggle between spiritual powers, God and Satan, angels and demons. But, as the Holiness tradition insists, this struggle is played out in believers' lives, and God expects believers to live by the unequivocal moral requirements expressed in His Word[17].

And perhaps there is even a fifth distinguishing feature of early Pentecostalism: the extraordinarily powerful *combination* of the individual believer's unique and direct relationship with God, and the strong communal bonds of the local congregation, a source of spiritual and practical support. Each individual believer has his or her individual testimony to tell, the tale of their own experiences of the Holy Spirit throughout their lives. Such testimonies feature common themes: a desperate need, personal redemption, a frequently resisted call to holiness and service, spiritual peaks and troughs, miracles of healing, and an intimate personal relationship with Jesus Christ. And the believer has a supportive audience, who have similar stories to tell, and who are united with them in both ecstasy and suffering.

16. 1 Cor 14:2–19.
17. Lehmann, *Struggle for the Spirit*.

Warfare and Waves

The European missionaries of the nineteenth century had often tried to contain or suppress the ecstatic tendencies of the indigenous folk religions which they encountered. However, the Americans of the twentieth, especially if they were Pentecostals, were more likely to incorporate such elements into the local churches. After all, their ecstatic African heritage informed their own faith, and they too were poor and dispossessed. The history of the astonishingly rapid spread of Charismatic Christianity over the last hundred years[18] is one of continuous exchange between the common globalizing Charismatic culture and local indigenous religious practices. The contrast with the more austere Reformed faith and its missionary emphasis on doctrine and belief rather than on experience, on the Word rather than on the Spirit, is only too clear.

So the Pentecostal and Charismatic congregations in South America, West Africa, East Africa, and Asia have each incorporated elements of their indigenous religions. In Korea, for example, the traditional faith was shamanistic: polytheistic, polydemonic, and ecstatic. However, it had come to exalt one of the Spirits, Hananim, to a supreme position within the pantheon. This existing combination of ecstatic worship, the existence of demons, and a supreme deity was considered a godsend by the American missionaries,[19] so congruent was it with their own faith.

Or consider the case of South America.[20] Here the Roman Catholic Church had long been the dominant Christian presence, assisted by its willingness to accommodate elements of the indigenous religions into such structures as the black brotherhoods and cults of healing. In the early twentieth century, it attempted to control these unorthodox manifestations of folk religion, using European clergy to Romanize the church. Later the Second Vatican Council enforced further reform. These unpopular "colonialist" interventions allowed Pentecostal religion to fill the gap, particularly since it was introduced more by South Americans returning home from the United States than by "colonizing" American missionaries. After all, healing and exorcism are integral parts of Pentecostal practice. The rapid rise of such denominations as the Universal Church of the Kingdom of God (centered on Brazil)[21] is the outcome.

18. P. Jenkins, *The Next Christendom.*

19. Kim, "Pentecostalism, Shamanism, and Capitalism within Contemporary Korean Society."

20. Martin, "From Pre- to Post-modernity in Latin America."

21. Furre, "Crossing Boundaries."

Geneva, Lambeth, Los Angeles, and Toronto

In Africa, the fastest growing Christian churches are Charismatic and independent of mainline denominations. Before the Pentecostals sent their missionaries in the early twentieth century, some independent churches had already been formed in protest against the mistreatment of native Africans in some of the denominational missionary churches. The continued dominance of established churches, for example, the Anglicans in Uganda,[22] points, however, towards the successful accommodations often achieved. Protest nevertheless continued against what was perceived as colonialism, and elements of folk religion such as ancestor worship were adapted and incorporated. More important, the Holy Spirit, whose importance Africans felt had been concealed from them by the missionaries, was released to lead them out of slavery and into freedom, both spiritually and politically. The East African Revival Fellowship exemplified this approach.

These three cases from Korea, South America, and Africa are but examples of how the globalizing thrust of the Charismatic movement both formed, but also was formed by, local cultural differences. But the global/local dialectic was not only at work between the Charismatic movement and its local manifestations. In addition, throughout the twentieth century, the central core of the Charismatic movement was itself gradually adapting and changing its emphases in tune with other elements of the globalization process. In this form of the dialectic, the movement is the "local" pole, and global society itself the "global" one.

Several profound changes in global society accompany globalization, first among them the movement from the rural agrarian economy to urban industrial or post-industrial production. This has resulted in the growth of huge shanty towns, lacking social services and structures and depending on a hand-to-mouth informal economy, or on a criminal one. The outcome is grinding poverty and the breakdown of family relationships, often replacing equally grinding rural poverty, but replacing also a working kinship and patronage system. Pentecostalism with its early emphasis on the hope of millennial deliverance, the present enjoyment of an ecstatic foretaste of the kingdom, and the support of a community of similarly displaced persons, spoke to these very poor people. An additional serendipitous benefit in Latin cultures was the increase in family security and employability resulting from the more holy, less macho, behavior of the man of the family.

But another consequence of globalization has been the growth of far wealthier consumerist societies based on employment in either industrial

---

22. Noll, *The New Shape of World Christianity*.

or post-industrial modes of production. For these billions, the Pentecostal contrast between this world's suffering and the joys of the world to come cannot carry the same weight of meaning as it does for globalization's victims. Instead, they have to develop a worldview which explains how it is that they are now relatively wealthy, and what choices they should make now that they are presented with so many alternatives.

Again, the Charismatic movement has adapted by placing emphasis on different aspects of its beliefs, values, and practices. The new-found wealth is seen as God's blessing on His obedient children, and the moral precepts relate to how it should be used. But a supernatural worldview in which the Holy Spirit works His miracles of healing and deliverance still prevails. It is important to note in attempting to understand this paradox that, first, the Enlightenment was primarily a European process; and second, for many, the transition from a pre-modern to a late-modern society has taken place within one or two generations (as, for example, in Brazil). Hence it is possible for the Charismatic movement to retain the cosmic worldview of spiritual warfare and signs and wonders typical of agrarian societies for use by the newly enriched urban classes. At the very least, the movement's supernatural worldview and behavioral strictures help to provide continuity with their cultural heritage, while their local church becomes their new extended family in the potentially alienating urban setting.

It is clear that the Charismatic movement is now global in terms of our three criteria.[23] It has developed to its present position through successful practice of the *global-local dialectic*. It is *connected worldwide*, with denominations and organizations characterized by their global reach and international organization and united by a common core of belief and practice. And it has a very strong *reflexive view of itself* as a growing movement inspired by the Spirit to save the world.

But what of those long-term progenitors of modernity, those wealthy late-modern societies of "the West" whose more secular cultures surely argue against a supernatural worldview typical of pre-modern societies? Much more specifically, why should the Charismatic movement be one of the least declining Christian groupings in the United Kingdom, and in the Church of England,[24] and how has it achieved this prized position within recent years? The next section explores its recent local history.

23. Coleman, *The Globalization of Charismatic Christianity*.
24. Brierley, at www.eauk.org/church/research&statistics.

TORONTO AND AFTER

Before reviewing the recent history of the Charismatic movement in the UK, it is important to reflect on the use of metaphor and terminology in the accounts which have been given of Charismatic Renewal. This preferred label for the movement's development within the C of E, for example, itself carries the implication of a church that needed renewing. The metaphors of fire, wave, and inspiration permeate the existing accounts, hardly a surprise when the movement is based on ecstatic experiences that are described as spontaneously "bursting out all over." So, for example, the phrases "Third Wave" and "Toronto Blessing" are commonly used to describe crucial developments in the movement's history. Moreover, a range of labels are used for the varieties of ecstatic behavior which are prominent in this history: "baptism in the Spirit," "being slain in the Spirit," "resting in the Spirit," "words of knowledge," "prophecies," "prayer ministry," "deliverance," and "healing."

All of these terms are employed from a theological perspective. They are used to express a particular theology of the Holy Spirit as spontaneous, uncontrollable, and immediate. They stress in particular the intimacy of individual believers' relationship with God and the importance of their unique experience of the Spirit's working within them. The focus is on the individual's experience of God, although this frequently occurs in the social setting of worship and has as its stated purpose the empowering of the church for evangelism.

However, this book is written from a social scientific, not a theological, perspective: the two forms of account are not mutually exclusive, nor is the social science an attempt to "explain away" the theology. It therefore analyses the development of the movement in terms of the development of its culture, structure, and process. So, for example, the ecstatic behavior defined theologically as experiences of the Spirit can be construed in social psychological terms as practices prescribed by sub-cultural norms of behavior, and informed by the culture's beliefs and values. And the development of the Charismatic sub-culture within the C of E may be attributed in large part to the increase in number and coherence of its clerical leaders, powerful congregations, organizations, and clergy formation, factors that, in dynamic relationship with each other, constitute the movement. This is not, of course, to deny the influence of broader cultural changes, such as the growing social trends of individualism, therapy, and consumerism.

Warfare and Waves

There is a regular pattern throughout the twentieth century of the C of E's relationship with the Charismatic movement.[25] It consists initially in contacts between C of E clergy and American Pentecostals and Charismatics. The English are initiated into ecstatic practices by Americans, and then introduce them into their own congregations back home. Clergy who have had these experiences form networks, and their churches become centers for Charismatic practices, continuing even when they themselves have left or died. Organizations, conferences, and communities are established, and relationships are formed with other elements of the C of E, and with other denominations. Elements of charismatic theology are introduced into some of the theological colleges. However, the momentum tends to be lost after a while, although the basic movement structure remains in place. Some movement organizations fade away, others survive. Then the next impetus ("wave") occurs. In each wave, the forms of ecstatic behavior become more unusual and intense, but the format of worship in which they occur becomes more structured and predictable. Overall, the historical scenario is of the uneven but continuing development of the organizational form of the movement within the C of E, and of the spread of some of the less unusual of its practices into the worship of many congregations who would not label themselves "Charismatic."

The first Pentecostal influence in the C of E occurred very soon after the Pentecostal Church started in Los Angeles in 1906, but was limited to one Durham clergyman, Alexander Boddy. Although three Pentecostal denominations took root in the UK in the 1920s, it was only in 1962 that the first steps towards a movement took place in the C of E. Michael Harper, a curate at the conservative Evangelical London church All Souls Langham Place, was facilitated in his "baptism of the Spirit" by, among others, Larry Christenson, an American Lutheran, and by 1963 he was "speaking in tongues." However, the Rector of All Souls, John Stott, a hero of the Calvinist movement in the C of E, rejected these developments on biblical grounds in 1964, and Harper left All Souls and concentrated on leading and developing the nascent Charismatic movement. His early associates were predominantly Evangelical C of E clergy, and they encouraged him to found the Fountain Trust to support the movement. These developments were supported by American Episcopalian visitors.

The Fountain Trust published the magazine *Renewal*, which called for renewal for individuals and congregations, and for the expectation of

---

25. Steven, *Worship in the Spirit*, ch. 2; Hilborn, *Charismatic Renewal in Britain*.

worldwide revival. It likened the Charismatic Renewal to the Reformation, in that it too was a protest against a spiritually corrupt church that was formalistic, over-organized, bureaucratic, over-intellectual, and in denial of the possibility of miracles and wonders. The Trust also ran conferences throughout the 1970s, which followed a regular pattern and concluded with Holy Communion; other regular conferences, which have continued to the present, are New Wine and Soul Survivor. In addition, and again with American Episcopalian input, Charismatic Communities were formed, which sent out travelling teams to run workshops on worship for Anglican parishes. All this time a network of leaders in key congregations was developing, including David Watson at St. Michael-le-Belfrey, York; David Pytches at St. Andrews, Chorleywood; Tom Walker at St. John's Harborne, Birmingham; and John Collins, and later, Sandy Millar, at Holy Trinity, Brompton. Furthermore, at least one theological college, St. John's College, Nottingham, strongly affirmed the Charismatic movement. Thus, in summary, the basic organizational architecture of the movement was in place

However, the initial enthusiasm of the 1960s and 70s was beginning to wane. The Fountain Trust closed down in 1980, perhaps as a result of disagreements. A new service organization, Anglicans for Renewal was formed, which held conferences and published a magazine. However, growth and innovation were now to be found more in the independent charismatic congregations which were springing up in the UK, known initially as House Churches[26].

At this point, a new "wave," or phase of development, began in the UK. It was initiated by Charismatic Renewal's leader, David Watson, who invited to the UK in 1984 a Californian, John Wimber, at that point the leader of a network of churches called the Vineyard. The emphasis of Wimber's teaching was on the kingdom of God, expressed in terms of the Spirit driving out devils in a cosmic struggle. The kingdom was here and now, with supernatural signs and wonders indicating that the age to come, the "next world," was already partly present. Such Charismatic Renewal leaders as David Pytches spoke of many cases of demon possession being conquered by exorcism, and rumors of Satanic cults were rife in Charismatic circles. Supposed cases of permanent medical healing of physical conditions were also reported, and attributed to the Holy Spirit.[27]

26. Walker, *Restoring the Kingdom*.
27. P. Jenkins, *God's Continent*.

Warfare and Waves

Perhaps more influential in the longer run, however, was the pattern of Wimber's conferences.[28] These consisted of three parts: sung worship, teaching, and "prayer ministry." The theme of the first two was often the kingship of God, who is proclaimed to be worthy of praise, and mighty and to be feared by His spiritual enemies, but at the same time intimately related to each believer as Lord of his or her life.[29] The third part of the conference was, Wimber maintained, a demonstration of God the Spirit's power in action, with the worship leader indicating how the congregation would experience, there and then, and often in physical terms, the cleansing and release that the Spirit bestows. Sometimes the leader spoke "words of knowledge," that is, he referred to (unnamed) individuals in the congregation and to a specific problem or sin which he said that they had brought with them. Ecstatic behavior frequently ensued, and members of "ministry teams," or "prayer leaders," moved among those who were affected in this way.

Thus a change of emphasis in the belief system and a somewhat different model of practice indicated a cultural shift in the Charismatic movement in the UK as a result of Wimber's influence. His impact gave a new impetus to the movement, and the appointment of Archbishop of Canterbury George Carey, who was a Charismatic Evangelical, gave further encouragement. On the other hand, many UK Charismatics were critical of the very specific prediction of a large-scale revival in Britain, like the eighteenth- and nineteenth-century "Great Awakenings" in America, by Wimber's associates, the Kansas City Prophets. Others, however, were confident that the usual ecstatic phenomena, the "signs and wonders," were foretastes of revival itself. Nevertheless, the divisions thus engendered slowed the momentum which Wimber's "Third Wave" had restored.

The impetus was soon regained, however, when yet another transatlantic event enthused the UK Charismatics. In January 1994 the entire Vineyard congregation at Toronto Airport exhibited a wide variety of ecstatic behavior, including unstoppable laughter, animal noises such as barking, and various uncontrolled physical movements. These activities were clearly more intense than the ecstatic phenomena that were regularly to be observed in Charismatic churches. A large number of C of E Charismatics visited the Toronto Airport congregation and themselves participated in this hyper-ecstatic worship. They included two bishops and the vicars of

28. Steven, *Worship in the Spirit*, 26–27.
29. Percy, *Words, Wonders, and Power*.

key Charismatic parishes, and the experience became known as "receiving the Toronto Blessing." By 1996, there had been 300,000 visitors to Toronto for this purpose.[30] When they returned to the UK in June 1994, the Anglican clergy, led by David Pytches and Sandy Millar, introduced the experience in their own churches and helped other clergy to do so.

While the Toronto practices proved very popular in the UK, their intense nature alienated many C of E clergy and adherents, especially conservative Evangelicals who failed to find biblical support for them. But more important for the Charismatic movement, many Charismatics themselves criticized the overwhelming Toronto emphasis on ecstatic experiences at the expense of evangelism, teaching, and piety. Wimber's Association of Vineyard Churches even expelled the Toronto Airport congregation from membership. On the other hand, it is probably on the back of the enthusiasm generated by the Toronto Blessing that the famous Alpha course received such support when it developed at Holy Trinity, Brompton.

In summary, the recent history of the Charismatic movement in the C of E is unique. Charismatic Renewal in the UK seems to be much more dependent on continued connexions with America, and on the stimulus of increasing novelty and intensity of ecstatic experience, than is the case with other parts of the global Charismatic movement described earlier. Moreover, the associated evangelistic campaigns and conferences sponsored by the Evangelical Alliance, such as Spring Harvest, did not fulfill inflated expectations. The decline in the numbers of churchgoers during the 1990s was lower in the Evangelical churches than in other traditions, but it was still a decline.[31]

The recent UK histories of the two movements, Calvinist and Charismatic, are thus interwoven.[32] The loss of dominance of conservative orthodoxy in the 1960s allowed the Charismatics to take advantage of some of the contemporary cultural changes, especially during the last two decades of the twentieth century. However, their over-optimistic promises of extensive revival paved the way for a resurgence of Calvinism, critical of their "pandering to the world." One historical juncture is favorable for a movement with a greater degree of integration with its social environment, the Charismatics; another favors one that is extremely differentiated, the Calvinists.

30. Methodist Church Faith and Order Committee, *The Toronto Blessing*.
31. Brierley, *The Tide is Running Out*.
32. Warner, *Reinventing English Evangelicalism, 1966-2001*.

Warfare and Waves

So much for the recent historical context for both movements sketched briefly in this chapter. The main part of the book that follows analyzes the current organization and culture of each in turn, starting with the Calvinists.

CHAPTER 3

The Production Line
Calvinist Formation and Leaders

THE UCCF

WHAT, THEN, IS THE current condition of these two movements, Calvinist and Charismatic, which have succeeded in exercising so much influence on the C of E in recent years? How are they presently organized, and how do their specific cultures differentiate them? For it is their organizational effectiveness and their cultural distinctiveness that give them their power today, however much they may think they owe to their historical heritage. I start with the Calvinists and their organizational form.

The basic form contains four elements: the *formation* of movement leaders; the *leaders* themselves; important *congregations*; and formalized *organizations*. But the movement itself is essentially process more than structure; in other words, it consists in how these four elements are related to each other in terms of the connectivity between them. First I consider each element, then their inter-relations.

The first major formative process, other than having been brought up as a child in a Calvinist congregation, occurs when students enter universities and colleges. The major elements of Calvinist formation concentrate on students. Those students who arrive at UK institutions as practising Christians are a minority, and of course come from a wide variety of Christian backgrounds and perspectives. The movement's task of formation is therefore one of converting both Christian and non-Christian students into the Calvinist form of the faith. A more general evangelistic aim than this—"To advance the evangelical Christian faith amongst students, graduates, and former members of universities"—forms part of the charter of the University and Colleges Christian Fellowship (UCCF), which used to be known as the Inter-Varsity Fellowship (IVF)[1]. This organization supports the Christian Unions in universities in the UK. The Christian Unions are often the largest Christian societies, and in a few universities constitute the only Christian society.

In its highly professional website,[2] UCCF, in the language of management theory and practice, concisely presents its mission, vision, values, and strategy. Its *mission* is "making disciples of Jesus Christ in the student world"; its *vision* "to give every student in Great Britain an opportunity to hear and respond to the gospel of Jesus Christ." *Values* imply being confident in the truth, urgent in evangelism, passionate about unity, committed to the local church, motivated by grace, and generous in world mission. Finally, *strategy* requires Christian Unions, led by students, to act as missional communities living and speaking for Jesus. They should be "bringing together Christians of all backgrounds and uniting around the core truths of the gospel."

The heavy emphasis on evangelism evident from these statements of intent is borne out in practice. In 2013 there were over 100 Christian Union mission weeks held near the beginning of the autumn term, the biggest of which was promoted by the Cambridge Inter-Collegiate Christian Union (CICCU). This national effort is supported by a full-time UCCF leadership team, and by many professional staff workers, who have normally received a four-year training. There is also a wide range of training programs available for student members, enabling them to more effectively evangelize their fellow students.

In 2013, the emphasis was particularly on one-to-one evangelism. UCCF bought in a program developed and owned by an American evangelist, Rebecca Manley Pippert, founder of Salt Shaker Ministries, called "Uncover." No fewer than 80,000 of the Uncover versions of Luke's Gospel were distributed. The finances of UCCF are very healthy, mainly as a result of individual giving and trust income. In 2011/12, for example, income was

1. www.en.wikipedia.org/wiki/Universities_and_Colleges_Christian_Fellowship.
2. www.uccf.org.uk/about/mission-vision-values.htm.

The Production Line

£4,168,000, providing a surplus of £852,000. Thus the programs of such American ministries can be afforded. In his annual Director's Review, Richard Cunningham comments: "We have never seen fruit like it in our time in UCCF." In an interview,[3] Pippert argues that techniques do not work in one-to-one evangelism, but nevertheless provides a mnemonic to help would-be student evangelists: CPR—Cultivate curiosity, Proclaim truth, and Reap a harvest. Cunningham[4] likewise favors a three element mnemonic: IPI—Identification with the target, Persuasion by reasoned argument, and Invitation, which should be "pastoral, evangelistic, warm and winsome."

The immediate impression of UCCF is therefore of a keenly proselytizing but fairly inclusive organization, "bringing together Christians of all backgrounds and uniting round the core truths of the Gospel." Indeed, the very name "Christian Union" implies inclusivity. It is, however, in the phrase "uniting round the core truths of the Gospel" that the sting lies. When we examine the Doctrinal Basis to which members subscribe, it becomes clear that UCCF is much closer to the Calvinist movement than appears at first sight. The Bible, we are told, "is the inspired and infallible Word of God. It is the supreme authority in all matters of belief and behaviour." This is a succinct statement of *sola scriptura*. And "Sinful human beings are redeemed from the guilt, penalty, and power of sin only through the sacrificial death once and for all time of their representative and substitute, Jesus Christ, the only mediator between them and God" (a classic summary of the doctrine of penal substitution). Thus "uniting round the core truths of the gospel" in fact involves accepting a particular conservative Evangelical account of the gospel. To demonstrate its adherence to this orthodoxy, UCCF withdrew from collaboration with the Charismatic organization Spring Harvest because it did not agree with the doctrine of the atonement espoused by Steve Chalke, one of its leaders.

A more general impression of the worldview favored by UCCF may be derived from the Annual Review for 2013 presented by the Director.[5] Cunningham describes the New Atheists (e.g., Richard Dawkins) as the "new mainstream." Christianity, he alleges, is considered to have "the extreme, edgy, and morally suspect worldview," and to be "totalising, judgmental, homophobic, and threatening to the harmony of our secular state.

---

3. www.youtube.com/watch?v=IGis22MU994.
4. www.bethinking.org/what...../identification-persuasion-and-invitation.htm.
5. www.uccf.org.uk.

Christians who wear crosses to work or who publicly express the historic, biblical view on homosexuality may find themselves arrested by the police or dragged in front of employment tribunals." Christian Union members, similarly, are the new notorious radicals on campus, for they "insist that Jesus is the only way to God and believe that monogamous, heterosexual marriage is the only legitimate context for sexual activity." This is the classic fundamentalist claim to the status of persecuted minority, and is hyperbolically welcomed by Cunningham as echoing the (only too real) sufferings of the first-century Christians.

However, UCCF cannot be portrayed as completely integrated with the Calvinist movement, as the example of OICCU (Oxford University Inter-Collegiate Christian Union), and doubtless that of other Christian Unions, demonstrates. The two main Anglican churches supporting and hosting the OICCU mission are St. Ebbe's and St. Aldate's. The former is orthodox Calvinist Reformed in its perspective, spelling out in similar detail and strikingly similar language to UCCF "what we believe,"[6] and emphasizing that "The chief work of God the Holy Spirit is to draw people to faith in Christ" (not, by implication, to inspire ecstatic worship). St. Aldate's, however, is more Charismatic, hosting such Charismatic luminaries as Bishops Pytches and Dow,[7] and engaging in a healing ministry.

Moreover, Richard Cunningham is on record[8] as saying that while "the C of E for certain will break into all sorts of pieces," it is vital not to split the Evangelicals at this juncture. They should unite over their core theology, and treat such issues as the women's place in the ministry, the gifts of the Holy Spirit, and the precise nature of biblical authority as secondary. When Bristol University Christian Union recently sought to maintain a ban on women speakers teaching the faith to men, the principle of gender equality in the eyes of God was strongly affirmed from the center.[9] Hence the UCCF is certainly not hoping to send only stern Calvinists out into the world.

However, it does hope to send conservative Evangelicals, and several of the local churches who are its partners are undoubtedly Reformed Calvinist in belief and practice (for example, St. Ebbe's). These churches devote major resources and a large professional staff to their student ministry, and UCCF members are encouraged to participate in their life. It is very

6. www.stebbes.org.uk.
7. www.staldates.org.uk/resources.asp.
8. www.patheos.com/...../adrian-interviews-richard-cunningham.
9. www.huffingtonpost.co.uk/...../bristol-university-chris_n_2246489.html.

probable that the Calvinist culture which is acquired or firmed up in the potent combination of Christian Union and local church will constitute their major religious formative experience for committed members. It may well also result in their experiencing a vocation to the ministry, a ministry that has been modelled for them by the clergy in their university church. It seems likely, therefore, that many of these potential Evangelical leaders will be Calvinist in their allegiance.

OAK HILL

If students do decide to enter the Anglican ministry, either as an ordained priest or as a professional Christian worker, their mentors at the Christian Union and their local university church will be able to give them advice regarding the appropriate theological college to attend. There are several Evangelical colleges available, including Ridley Hall Cambridge, Trinity College Bristol, and Cranmer Hall Durham. However, there is only one with a strongly Reformed Calvinist perspective: Oak Hill College,[10] which also houses the Latimer Trust, a Calvinist think-tank. There was for a period a second such college, Wycliffe Hall, Oxford.

Oak Hill is indeed Calvinist. Its trustees, council members, principal, and staff have extensive connections with such organizations as Reform, UCCF, and Moore College in Sydney. Its literal acceptance of the Calvinist doctrine of *sola scriptura* leads it to sponsor an American course on counseling,[11] the outline of which consists entirely of a theological account of the nature of sin and redemption. For "the Bible contains everything we need for life and godliness." Oak Hill spends a lot of time on the divisive sexuality and gender issues, giving the Calvinist hero Jim Packer, the opportunity to define Anglican bishops' attitudes on these matters as heresy.[12] "The world," alleges Packer, now "writes the agenda for the church." If certain bishops are heretical, alternative episcopal oversight is required for the offended faithful. Another visitor to Oak Hill, American Wes Hill, describes himself as "a gay Christian."[13] To avoid any possibility of a Calvinist contradiction in terms, however, he hastens to add that homosexuality is

10. Heinze, *Witness to the World: A History of Oak Hill College 1932–2000*; www.oakhill.ac.uk.
11. www.oakhill.ac.uk/blog/july2013.
12. www.oakhill.ac.uk/people/jim_packer.
13. www.oakhill.ac.uk/people/wes_hill.

a result of the Fall, as sin has broken God's creation of man and woman. He is gladly celibate, being enjoined by God's Word to avoid acting according to his sexual orientation. The Oak Hill position on gender also is Calvinist. C of E inspectors noted the existence of a conflict between the presence of women ordinands among the students and the beliefs of some of the staff.[14]

The positions taken by Principal Mike Ovey are the strongest indicator of where Oak Hill is headed. He wants safeguards for those like himself who will not be able to accept in good conscience the oversight of women bishops, when they are appointed.[15] He considers the doctrine of atonement by penal substitution as a "glory to be rediscovered."[16] And he supports and assists GAFCON and the FCA, schismatic organizations, rather than the Anglican Communion.[17]

Wycliffe Hall Oxford was, for a short period from 2005 until 2012, a second UK Calvinist theological college. Its then-principal, Richard Turnbull, certainly had such a strategic aim in mind. "Capture the theological colleges, and you have captured the influence that is brought to bear" [upon generations in the ministry], he said to the annual conference of Reform in 2006.[18] "Like-minded" parishes should fund "like-minded" colleges by deducting 10 percent of their contribution to the C of E, otherwise these colleges will close within ten years. This prediction appeared only too likely to be fulfilled in 2012, when there were no women applicants to Wycliffe Hall as a result of the known hostility of some faculty and students to women's ordination. Turnbull had himself written (with Mark Burkill) a paper for the Latimer Trust arguing that a woman on her own should not teach men about faith or lead a congregation.[19] After complaints from some staff and students of open homophobia and a culture of bullying and intimidation, together with the discovery of shortcomings in the faculty appointments procedure, Turnbull resigned, and in 2013 was replaced by Michael Lloyd, a Charismatic. It remains to be seen whether Turnbull's attempt to "Reform" the college will have a continuing effect, but Lloyd's statement on his appointment suggests it will not. Lloyd wants Wycliffe Hall to be a "warm,

---

14. www.churchofengland.org/media/...../oak%20hill%20follow%20up.doc.
15. www.churchsociety.org/...../iss_ministry_wombishop_rochester.asp.
16. Jeffery, *Pierced for our Transgressions*.
17. www.gafcon.org/media/video/christ-the-lord.
18. www.thinkinganglicans.org.uk/archives/002411.html.
19. www.latimertrust.org/index.php/publications.

respectful, encouraging, and secure place for women," and wants to train students "who will speak to the wider society and not just to insiders."[20]

WALLACE BENN

Many leaders of local Calvinist congregations are formed in the Christian Unions, university churches, and theological colleges. But what of the leaders of the UK movement as a whole? Leaders of religious movements, like any other leader, have first of all to be *prototypical*.[21] That is, they have to exemplify and demonstrate by their words and actions what it is to be an ideal member of the movement; they have to be models. Having shown themselves to be "one of us," albeit a model "one of us," they can then use the legitimacy and authority which this prototypical status brings to influence the direction of the movement, and to represent it in the media. The five Calvinist leaders in the C of E whom I have selected for this analysis all fulfill this primary qualification: they are all prototypes with the appropriate cultural pedigree.

But, second, they all exercise authority and influence within the Calvinist movement. They are all involved in the organizations which speak for particular constituencies within the movement; they all have connections with powerful congregations; and they were all formed by, and support, the sources of new movement adherents. They are Wallace Benn, Rod Thomas, Vaughan Roberts, Chris Sugden, and Paul Perkin, all ordained clergy of the C of E.

Wallace Benn retired as Bishop of Lewes in 2012, having held that office for fifteen years. However, he is still extremely active within the Calvinist movement, and it is hard to think of a more central player over the last twenty-five years. He has been involved in most of the organizations within the movement, including: Reform, of which he is a founder and council member; GAFCON and the Fellowship of Confessing Anglicans, of which he was a foundational moving spirit, and of which he is now chair of the Council of Reference; the Church Society (vice-president); the Fellowship of Word and Spirit (president); and the Third Province Movement (patron). In addition, he has served as president of the C of E Evangelical Council, a more inclusive organization. The chair of Reform, Rod Thomas, writes in an appreciation on the occasion of his retirement that he played a pivotal

20. www.peter-ould.net/2013/...../new-principal-of-wycliffe-hall-is-mike-lloyd.
21. Haslam, *The New Psychology of Leadership*.

role in the 2008 meeting of GAFCON, and that his retirement "removes the last serving Evangelical bishop who believes in the biblical doctrine of male headship."[22]

Indeed, like his fellow Calvinist leaders, Benn has been busily engaged in ecclesiastical conflict for most of his professional life. Having failed to prevent the ordination of women in 1992, he reports that at the Lambeth Conference of 1998 he "was involved in the thick of the fight, which wasn't easy, but the outcome was tremendous. The Lambeth resolutions were uniformly biblical and orthodox."[23] The passing of Lambeth 1.10 regarding sexuality was an act of God's grace, and a victory for God's truth.[24] It was an affirmation of "the faith once delivered to the saints" (the favorite biblical text of Calvinists). The only thing he had in common with a liberal bishop with whom he disagreed on this issue was the color of his shirt. However, he maintains, he would love not to have to talk about sexual ethics, but it is the presenting problem of a crisis of authority in the church. It is not those who stick to doctrine who cause divisions, but those who seek novelty in doctrine.

Having felt that the issue had been solved at Lambeth, Benn was disappointed when the appointment of Gene Robinson, a practising gay man, as bishop went ahead in America in 2003.[25] He lobbied successfully for Jeffrey John's appointment as Bishop of Reading to be rescinded, but ultimately decided he could not attend Lambeth 2008 as he was out of fellowship with those sixty bishops attending who had selected and ordained Robinson as bishop. He was particularly upset that there was no invitation to the missionary bishops ("flying bishops") who had ministered to those unable to accept the ministry of compromised bishops. And he was "torn-up" for his friend Jim Packer, who had been "persecuted" by some who were attending.

Instead, Benn went to GAFCON in Jerusalem, where he wept tears of joy. "If that's what the Anglican Church can be, who'd want to be anywhere else?" he asked rhetorically. He was delighted with the Jerusalem Declaration, which unanimously re-affirmed the orthodox Anglican gospel as expressed in, among other sources, the Thirty-Nine Articles. Continuing to be politically engaged after retirement, he recommended Glenn Davies to be the next Archbishop of Sydney, a Calvinist Sydney Anglican to succeed

22. www.churchnewspaper.com/27681/archives.
23. www.e-n.org/p-790-What-it's-like-to-be-a-bishop.htm.
24. www.vimeo.com/4674277.
25. www.blip.tv/gafcon-ireland. . . . . ./anglicanism-after-gafcon-Wallace_Benn.

another such, Peter Jensen.[26] "I have hugely benefited from the ministry of Sydney bishops," he avers, "and the whole Anglican world has too."

Although softly spoken, Benn uses robust and uncompromising language. A complaint against him by the diocesan safeguarding advisory group, to the effect that he should personally have informed the police about a paedophile priest, was dismissed in 2013.[27] He claimed that he had been the victim of a "one-sided and unjust process of trial by media . . . orchestrated by unknown people with, it seems, no interest in the truth or the ministry of the church." When speaking at the annual conference of Reform in 2010, he said "We're in January of 1939," referring to the position of opponents of the appointment of women bishops. He later finessed this familiar trope of persecution when taken to task by *The Times*,[28] explaining "I was thinking in terms of the storm clouds being on the horizon." And when addressing a regional meeting of the Fellowship of Confessing Anglicans, he refers to spies in the church, unnoticed in their purple shirts and dog-collars. Like his admired Sydney colleague Dean Phillip Jensen,[29] Benn seems prone to giving the press hostages to fortune when he is talking to the faithful.

Benn is completely doctrinally orthodox as a conservative Evangelical when it comes to the authority of the Bible and the penal substitutionary doctrine of the atonement.[30] His heroes are John Stott and Jim Packer, theological leaders of the previous generation of English Calvinists, an admiration he shares with several other Calvinist leaders. However, he is not averse to a little innovation when it comes to formulating a theological justification for the doctrine of submission of women within the church. Men and women are of equal value, but have different functions, he argues, the function of the latter being to be in submission to the former. This reproduces within the family and the church the relationship within the Trinity, where Father and Son are co-equal, but the Father exercises authority over the Son.

---

26. www.glenndavies.info/uploads/6/7/0/8/6708480/wallacebenn.pdf.
27. www.churchtimes.co.uk/News/UK14May2013-10-23.
28. www.thetimes.co.uk/tto/faith/article2792230.ece.
29. www.guardian.co.uk/uk/2004/oct/13/religion/anglicanism.
30 www.patheos.com/. . . . ./interview-with-bishop-wallace_benn.

Warfare and Waves

ROD THOMAS

So Wallace Benn has been, and remains, an influential leader of the movement. He embodies and expresses its culture: its Manichean worldview, its rigid doctrinal beliefs, its counter-cultural values, and its outspoken stance. He is not alone. Rod Thomas is equally prototypical, but represents a more focussed mode of leadership. He nevertheless still manages to act both as a vicar of a congregation and as an ecclesiastical politician. Like some of the other movement leaders who are also vicars, he enjoys considerable assistance in the form of additional professional staff: two curates, a community minister, a youth minister, a ministry assistant, and an administrative assistant. This should not be taken to imply that he neglects his growing congregation, to which, on the contrary, he preaches on half of the Sundays of the year.[31] However, he also finds the time to act, first as press officer and later as chairman, of the main organization within the movement—Reform. His media output representing Reform, and his political organization within the C of E Synod, are extraordinarily extensive and visible. However, he has still found time to play a major role in formulating GAFCON policies and proclaiming that body's Jerusalem Declaration.[32]

Like Wallace Benn, Thomas is a perfectly prototypical Calvinist. His emphasis on doctrine is heavy. The church, he tells his congregation, should be exclusive in doctrine, while inclusive with people. We are not here in church to debate, but to receive God's revealed Word. That is the basis for a truly unified church, not compromise. The people who cause dissension are not those like himself, regularly called a troublemaker, but rather those who have disobeyed Biblical teaching.[33] Homosexuality, he avers in an interview, "is not at all the main issue—we want to welcome everybody, irrespective of their sexuality. But where the authority of the Bible is undermined, we will stand up for it. We're not a single-issue group—we're fighting the battle wherever the battle is."[34]

And a constant battle it certainly is. Like Benn, Thomas perceives the church as engaged in a cosmic struggle with secularism. No-one has been more determined and steadfast a battle leader than him. Consider, for example, the case of the introduction of women bishops, a dispute that began

---

31. www.elburtonchurch.com.
32. www.churchnewspaper.com?/P=26165.
33. www.elburtonchurch.com/sermons/2012-07-29.
34. www.churchtimes.co.uk/articles/2009/2-january/features/interview-rod-thomas.

soon after the ordination of women in 1994 and has only in 2014 been finally settled. After years of protracted dispute about the sort of provision to be made for those who could not in conscience accept the oversight of women bishops, the matter was finally brought to the vote at Synod in November 2012. Despite the vast majority of dioceses voting in favor, and two of the three sections of Synod, the bishops and the clergy, achieving the necessary two-thirds majority, the proposal failed by six votes in the house of laity, and so, to the dismay of the majority, the proposal was defeated. The will of the church had clearly not been carried out.

Thomas rubbed salt into these wounds. Concluding that the result was very good news for the C of E, he argued that far from making the church more inclusive, the legislation "would have had devastating consequences for the diversity and mission of the Church of England had it been passed. We want the Church of England to continue to be a broad and comprehensive national Church."[35] The implication is that some of those opposed to women bishops would have left had the legislation been passed. Furthermore, when Synod urgently decided in July 2013 to consider new draft legislation which allowed for an alternative male bishop chosen "in a manner which respects their theological convictions," Calvinist and Anglo-Catholic opponents rejected this concession. On the contrary, Thomas said they would suffer "a sense of gnawing anxiety" unless they were given full legal rights to seek alternative oversight.[36] In November 2013, an agreement which appeared to satisfy most of Thomas's anxieties was universally welcomed, presaging a final vote in favor in July 2014. Interviewed on BBC Radio 4, he agreed that the conflict over women bishops seemed to be settled. When asked if this meant that a period of relative agreement would follow the previous ten years' bitterness, however, he happily foresaw issues of sexuality looming which would be of major concern.

It is noteworthy that Thomas regards women bishops as a secondary, not a primary issue. That is, it is not "a gospel issue"; it does not concern salvation, and "is not what we read in the Bible." Since it is a secondary matter of church order, we simply have to put up with one another for as long as we disagree. This, he argues is a good witness. "There must be something that keeps these people together," outsiders will think. If this is only a secondary

---

35. www.anglicanink.com/. . . . ./evangelicalscatholics-lay-out-conditions-women-bishops.

36. www.christianpost.com/world9july2013.

issue, how much time and effort would Thomas be prepared to put into "a gospel issue," we may ask.

The answer is to be found in his continuing and unremitting struggle against the appointment of gay bishops. Consider, for example a recent episode in this conflict. The House of Bishops proposed that the appointment as bishops of those in civil partnerships would in principle be acceptable, but that they would have to be living in accordance with the teaching of the Church on human sexuality and therefore appointed on a case by case basis. "If you thought that was a furore" said Thomas, referring to the conflict over women bishops, "wait to see what will happen the first time a bishop in a civil partnership is appointed."[37] The proposal is "not something that can be slipped out in the news" he complained, "it is something that has to be considered by the General Synod."[38] And as for gay marriage . . . .

Clearly, Thomas is a formidable ecclesiastical politician. But he is characterized not only by determination and conviction, but also by a powerful intellect and a history of employment which gave him a sophisticated appreciation of how the media work. He was a fast-track civil servant, but left for a business career, finishing up as Director of Employment and Environmental Affairs at the Confederation of British Industry. He is not alone among prominent Anglican clergy in having a high-flying secular career before ordination (witness Archbishop Justin Welby), but he is certainly not typical.[39]

However, he is definitely a prototypical member of the Calvinist movement. Not only is he doctrinally orthodox and focussed on those issues that preoccupy the movement, but also he is able to tell a familiar and accepted narrative about his spiritual history. He was converted at the age of seven, growing up in a family of Exclusive Plymouth Brethren. He assisted at the Billy Graham mission at Earls Court when a youth, but then "fell away from Christ" during young adulthood. However, he discovered a C of E church that "opened God's revelation to me," teaching the Bible in a way he had not heard before. After "a long period of discernment" he decided on ordination. This story of conversion, backsliding, repentance, call, and hesitation before ministry is a classic Evangelical testimony.[40]

---

37. www.bbc.co.uk/news/uk-20910100.
38. www.christianpost.com/news/church-of-england-moves-to-ordain-gay-bishops.
39. www.churchtimes.co.uk/articles/2009/2-january/features/interview-rod-thomas.
40. Lienesch, *Redeeming America*.

The Production Line

Also prototypical is his welcome of the status of *victim of persecution*. Preaching to his congregation,[41] he insists that "all those who want to live a godly life will be persecuted." Citing the case of those American clergy who have been legally evicted after objecting to a gay bishop and leaving their denomination, Thomas says that we are to expect the same sort of thing here in the UK. Quoting cases recently in the news, he notes that you cannot now be foster parents if you are anti-gay, and you cannot legally exclude gay people from your hotel. Indeed, people never listen when he takes an interviewer through St. Paul's actual views about women, a refusal which is itself a form of persecution. But the church cannot withdraw from the world, like the Amesh, nor capitulate to it, like theological liberals. Rather, the task is to be both in Christ and in the world, which will always result in persecution since the world will feel accused by our lives. Persecution proves we are living a godly life.

VAUGHAN ROBERTS

Another Calvinist leader who succeeds in heading up an organization as well as being in charge of a congregation is Vaughan Roberts. Rector of St. Ebbe's, Oxford, he is also president of the Proclamation Trust, and a founder member of "9.38," an organization that encourages students to consider the ministry as a career. Roberts, too, is a prototypical Calvinist leader. He was converted at the age of eighteen as a result of reading the Bible, an activity prompted by the amazing faith he observed in a couple whose child had been killed in an accident. He was educated at Winchester and Cambridge University, where he was president of CICCU, the Christian Union that was the original foundation member of the Federation of Christian Collegiate Unions. He then studied theology at Wycliffe Hall, Oxford, before becoming curate (1991) and then rector (1998) of St. Ebbe's. He has thus not been outside a university conservative Evangelical environment since his conversion. A lucid and engaging preacher and writer, he has made the ministry to students a central concern while at St. Ebbe's.

However, there is one aspect of his c.v. which is not prototypical. He does not start his various self-descriptions with the statement that he is married, as do most of the Calvinist leadership. This is because he is not himself married, and indeed "struggles with same-sex attraction."[42] This,

---

41. www.elburtonchurch.com/sermons/2012-10-14.

42. www.e-n.org.uk/p-6028-A-battle-I-face.htm.

he insists, does not mean that he is "gay," since this label implies a social identity as a gay person. Rather, it is one of the eight "battles" that he and others face, which he describes in the second edition of his book *Battles Christians Face*.[43] The other battles are against image, lust, guilt, doubt, pride, depression, and spiritual staleness. He says that he is presently succeeding in winning this struggle, since he upholds "the Bible's teaching that sex is only for heterosexual marriage in teaching and lifestyle." His main purpose in revealing that he himself struggles in all eight areas is basically pastoral. There are many other Evangelical Christians in the same situation regarding same-sex attraction, but the church has not in general provided a loving spiritual family for them, or, more generally for those living single, celibate lives for whatever reason.

Response to this personal disclosure has been positive within the movement, with strong support from Anglican Mainstream for his "clear endorsement of biblical teaching."[44] Battling against temptation, particularly when successful, is a very godly thing to do, argues Roberts, as is being able to recognize the loving hand of God in all we experience, and see it as an opportunity for service, growth, and fruitfulness. Hence Roberts's prototypicality as a movement leader remains unimpaired, and maybe even enhanced.

However, there are other features of his career which make him interestingly different from the others. One is his emphasis on the internal spiritual struggle, as opposed to the external ecclesiastical struggles which mostly preoccupy the other Calvinist leaders. Consider, for example, his book *Daring to be Different in an Indifferent World*. The cover reads "How to respond biblically to the temptations and pitfalls surrounding us." The chapter titles are: "Perspective in a world that lives for the moment; Service in a world that looks after number one; Contentment in a world that never has enough; Purity in a world obsessed with sex; Certainty in a world in which everything is relative; Holiness in a world where anything goes; Wholeheartedness in a world that can't be bothered." Clearly the usual Calvinist emphasis on differentiation from this evil and ungodly world is paramount, but the emphasis is on the individual's personal life, not on the movement's stance. Indeed, generally Roberts is not one of the media's

---

43. Roberts, *Battles Christians Face*.
44. www.anglican-mainstream.net/2012/10/11/vaughan-roberts-interview.

immediate sources of quotes on issues of contention within the C of E, and he criticizes "some people [who] like a theological fight too much."[45]

Moreover, he does not appear to seek to differentiate the movement from other Evangelicals as eagerly as do other Calvinist leaders. In a manifesto[46] first delivered in a colloquium with Open and Charismatic Evangelicals, he argues that its heritage shows that the Evangelical movement has been both dynamic and diverse. Nevertheless, there is "a core of fundamental beliefs which have united Evangelicals. . . . Our diverse movement will only remain united today if we too commit ourselves to the same foundational truths" (the supremacy of Scripture, the seriousness of sin, the substitution of the Savior, and the significance of the Spirit, a list which is nothing if not alliterative). But Evangelicals will only succeed in their mission of proclaiming this word of God if they join together in local action: planting churches regardless of parish boundaries, for example, and stopping "propping up a system in which ineffective churches are subsidised indefinitely and the life in Evangelical churches is prevented from spreading . . . We need to get out of our different ghettoes" he argues, and stop "sniping at each other and fostering little jealousies. . . . It would be wonderful if we Evangelicals were able to unite and work together, not only in what we oppose, but in what matters most to us—the work of mission."[47]

This is clearly Roberts' attempt to be inclusive and statesmanlike, although it has to be said that the doctrinal formulations that he claims to be held in common are typically Calvinist. He has subsequently further risked the criticism of "true Calvinists" by inviting various American "New Calvinists" to speak at conferences run by the Proclamation Trust. The Proclamation Trust consequently is now in error, urge these critics. It "promotes the dogma of theistic evolution," failing to "defend the biblical view of 6-day creation." It is "given over to the contemporary worship scene . . . singing the latest new song produced by the Charismatic movement." It is "wide open to the social gospel." In a word, it is not prepared "to contend for the gospel once for all delivered to the saints" (that favorite text again), or to "separate from false teachers."[48]

---

45. www.conversation.lausanne.org/en/conversations/detail/11452.
46. www.biblicalstudies.org.uk/pdf/anvil/20-3_185pdf.
47. www.theologian.org.uk/pastoralia/messageout.html.
48. www.newcalvinist.com/proclamation-trust.

Warfare and Waves

CHRIS SUGDEN AND PAUL PERKIN

Vaughan Roberts is one of the Calvinist leaders willing to take a risk by supporting a degree of integration, or, at the least, collaboration. He built on his asset of prototypicality by championing an innovation, which is an act of real leadership. Others have followed suit, particularly influenced by the major development of the last ten years, the emergence of GAFCON and its associated organizations. Consider, for example, Chris Sugden and Paul Perkin.

Sugden, although ordained, has for the latter part of his career been a full-time employee of Christian organizations: first, executive director of the Oxford Centre for Mission Studies, heavily involved in lobbying at Lambeth 1998[49]; and then, from 2004, executive secretary of Anglican Mainstream. He retired in 2013, but continues as press adviser to GAFCON and secretary to the Fellowship of Confessing Anglicans in the UK. Educated at Oxford, he presents a prototypical c.v., telling us not only his wife's and children's names but also those of his children's spouses and the number of his grandchildren! This accords well with his concentration on family, gender, and sexuality, issues which preoccupy Anglican Mainstream.

Sugden is the sort of leader every movement needs among its leadership cadre. He is a diligent master of legislative and procedural detail, and hence is a formidable ecclesiastical politician.[50] However, at the same time he has a well-developed appreciation of how to be provocative enough to secure media attention. He also understands the importance of labels for conveying legitimacy, appropriating at every available opportunity such adjectives as "orthodox" and "mainstream" to describe the movement.

Some examples of these skills are to be found in his contributions to the movement's key issues. Realizing that the issue of gay marriage is concerning a wide range of citizens as well as conservative Evangelicals, he has achieved considerable media exposure on the topic. He told a television audience, for example, that gay marriage would de-gender marriage, being a contract between neuter individuals without the issue of children.[51] Seeking the backing of Muslims in Tooting,[52] he argues that it is a threat to real

49. Bates, *A Church at War*.

50. www.blip.tv/anglicantv/canon-chris-sugden-general-synod-women-bishops.

51. www.christianconcern.com/media/itv-day-break-canon-chris-sugden-on-same-sex-marriage.

52. www.youtube.com/watch?v=DR=BU3eMLSg.

marriage, and that their sons will be taught at school to marry boys, and daughters, girls. He helpfully drafts a template letter for Muslims to send to their MPs, characterizing the proposed legislation as "deeply hurtful to our Muslim community." It will be illegal for us to teach about real marriage according to our Scriptures, he predicts, and we risk our tax exemption as charities being removed. In a report for Anglican Mainstream on the progress of the bill through parliament, he demonstrated his sharp appreciation of media priorities:

> Some listening to the debate in the Lords have noted that those arguing for traditional marriage tend to keep the debate at such an abstract, cerebral level that for many, nothing lands. When there is a comparison between the lovely gay couple next door and abstract notions of justice, the former wins hands down. Concentrating upon the damage to children . . . gets attention.[53]

The issue of gay bishops and the appointment of Bishop Robinson was a major impetus for the foundation of Anglican Mainstream, and it is not surprising that Sugden, as its executive secretary, was widely reported on the topic. He took the opportunity of the BBC News, for example, to create some alarming headlines (e.g., "The Church is always within a generation of extinction"), and simultaneously to encourage the movement.[54] The action of the Episcopal Church of the USA (ECUSA) in dropping its ban on the appointment of gay bishops could lead to a motion in the C of E Synod to declare fellowship with the breakaway conservative Anglican Church of North America (ACNA), he predicted, doubtless hoping thereby to increase pressure for such a motion. He was also encouraging the faithful by reminding them of their allies. He reminded them of who the enemy are ("advocates of a gay agenda"), and criticized these enemies for inviting Bishop Gene Robinson to the annual Greenbelt festival. It is they, and not we, who are obsessed with sex, he argued, using the familiar reverse-insult technique. Rejecting the alternative of being in fellowship with both ECUSA and ACNA simultaneously, he argued that the issue is not institutional peace but theological integrity and clarity—fellowship with "those who bless sin" is impossible.

Paul Perkin, unlike Sugden, is, and has been for twenty-six years, "senior pastor" of a parish, St. Marks Battersea Rise, one of the wealthiest in the C of E. Despite having no less than twenty-seven staff members to assist

53. www.fcasa.wordpress.com/2013/06/19/update-from-canon-chris-sugden.
54. www.news.bbc.co.uk/1/hi/uk/8149812.stm.

him,[55] he nevertheless astonishes by the range and extent of his activities. On the councils of Reform and Wycliffe Hall, he is the chair of the executive council of the Fellowship of Confessing Anglicans (FCA) in the UK, and also of the steering group of the Anglican Mission in England (AMIE). He is a trustee of Anglican Mainstream, and represents the New Wine Network on Mainstream's steering committee. With his wife and "associate pastor," Christine, he finds time to write books and conduct training courses on marriage and on the upbringing of teenagers, among other topics. After the riots of 2011, he gave evidence to the House of Commons Home Affairs Committee, and offered some advice on the policing of such disturbances.[56]

An accomplished ecclesiastical politician, his drafting skills are superb.[57] His polemical rhetoric is also highly developed. For example, the House of Bishops advised on the matter of civil partnerships as follows: "Where clergy are approached by people asking for prayer in relation to entering into a civil partnership they should respond pastorally and sensitively in the light of the circumstances of each case." Perkin replied in an open letter to English bishops: "I intend always pastorally and sensitively to decline politely any request for such a prayer affirming a same-sex union. Can you clarify for me 'the light of the circumstances' in which you would feel it necessary to discipline me for such a refusal, before I go any further?"[58] And of course, even in ecclesiastical politics, "follow the money" is always good advice. Perkin fully appreciates the power that wealthy congregations such as his own possess in influencing policy by threatening to withhold contributions to the C of E.[59]

Like Sugden, Perkin's role in the establishment and development of GAFCON, FCA, and AMIE has been considerable, of which more in the next chapter. To conclude this account of some of the leaders of the Calvinist movement, a more detailed analysis of Perkin's widely reported address to the second conference of GAFCON in Nairobi in 2013 follows, demonstrating as it does many of their skills and strategies in operation.

---

55. www.stmarks-battersea.org.uk/home/aboutus/who'swho.
56. www.anglican-mainstream.net/...../update-on-looting-st-marks.
57. www.churchofengland.org./media/38238/gsmisc843a.rtf.
58. www.thinkinganglicans.org.uk/archives/001291.html.
59. www.theguardian.com/world/2012/may/23/church-of-england-money.

The Production Line

A NAIROBI BROADSIDE

Before the UK contingent of over one hundred left for the conference, a preparatory meeting was held, unsurprisingly at St. Marks Battersea Rise. Seeking, perhaps, to influence the media reportage of the conference, Perkin seizes the opportunity to "rebrand" GAFCON: "GAFCON 2 is not a rearguard movement of traditionalists, but a renewal movement for the sake of the Great Commission."[60] In the address itself,[61] under the strapline "Battle for the Soul of Britain," Perkin pictures two opposing sides in the C of E. On the one hand there are "flourishing local churches," one of which has even started its own theological college, "after three years the largest Anglican theological seminary in Europe. . . . So Jesus is the sovereign, risen Lord, miraculously active in the UK, prospering gospel evangelism, pouring out His Holy Spirit, growing the churches and planting new ones, and bringing glory to Himself in it all."

But as well as the church penetrating the nation in this way, there also exists "the nightmare of a secular nation invading the church." And this is "the general climate of the church in the UK today," an issue not of individual disbelief, but of the culture of the church. "At its heart, and in many of its central institutions, and with much of its leadership and style, it is a worldly church—a church that is of the world, that is infected by the world, that is unbelieving like the world, that is as immoral as the world, that is not very present in the world, and is running away from the world."

To back up this somewhat unfavorable analysis, Perkin quotes a survey commissioned by the organization Cost of Conscience in 2002 which, he asserts, shows that "one out of every four male clergy in the C of E does not believe in the Trinity, or in God the Father who made the world, or in the Holy Spirit, or that Jesus died to take away the sins of the world." Almost half do not believe in the virgin birth or the bodily resurrection. The results are even worse for female clergy, and "many of the least believing, male and female, are in central leadership positions in the church." This interpretation of the data is based on the assumption that only those who responded "believe without question" *really* believed. Those who responded "believe, but not sure I understand" were lumped together with those who responded "mostly believe," "not sure I believe this," and "definitely don't believe."

---

60. www.anglican-mainstream.net/2013/09/17/preparing-for-gafcon-2.

61. www.anglicanink.com/article/battle-soul-of-britain-gafcon-address-paul-perkin.

Clearly, only those clergy who believe without question are on God's side of the struggle.[62]

But how is the worldly church opposing the church that "accepts and obeys God's Word"? Perkin is clear about this: "The answer is, in subtle ways. 'Hatred' in Britain is, thank God, not often life threatening but sometimes aggressive, and often very subtle and therefore more difficult to discern." Perkin succeeds in discerning it, however, in restrictions put in the way of the various Calvinist initiatives: church planting, withholding finance, appointing "gospel" clergy, and only having real fellowship in the truth rather than superficial unity and unfaithful leaders. So opposition to the movement's proposals and practices can only be motivated by hatred. "There is a battle for Britain in our own day," he concludes, "a battle for the heart and soul of Britain. The Confessing Anglicans in the UK and Ireland are uniquely placed to support both those who stay in the structures, and those God is raising up beyond them. Both types of initiative are needed in the huge challenge before us."

Perkin's address exemplifies perfectly the leadership skills and strategies of the Calvinist movement. The major task of any leader is to help the movement develop a strong social identity, for without one the movement will not be noticed, and its adherents will not be motivated. One favored strategy is to characterize the situation as warfare, as a battle with an enemy, as "us versus them." And who are "them"? The secular world is the cosmic spiritual enemy, confirmed as such by the exposition of a biblical reference, John's Gospel, chapter 17. But the presenting enemy, the institutional C of E, is associated with this cosmic enemy by the metaphor of "infection"—the world has infected the church. Further, the "frame" of conflict and warfare allows the themes of righteous war, persecution, "hatred," and soulless institutional structures (versus inspired movements) to be marshalled.

Although local congregations provide a direct experience of this social identity, it is primarily through *mediated* perceptions that the movement gains visibility and political influence. The skills of media relations and those of ecclesiastical politics are equally vital, since the former now constitutes the major element of the latter. The words quoted in the media are aimed not primarily at a face-to-face audience, but at the media, and, through them, at adherents and opponents. Highly developed verbal and presentational skills and a clear message are required. It is evident that all of the leaders whom I have described have these attributes. It is also evident

62. www.thinkinganglicans.org.uk/archives/000144.html.

that their formation has contributed mightily to their effectiveness within the movement, since it has provided them with a closed and complex system of thinking with unquestioned assumptions and a concentration on verbal expression. Moreover, the similarity of their formative experiences has enabled them to collaborate within the movement on the same issues, and to constitute a leadership prototype which can be trusted and emulated by adherents. They are, in sum, a capable, energetic, and determined group of driven men.

Chapter 4

Trouble and Strife
Calvinist Organizations

REFORM

The Calvinist movement's visible cutting edge consists of its organizations and their leaders. Yet while the issues which Reform and other organizations contest provide the movement with a high profile, its power also lies in any threat it poses to the authority of the Church of England and the Anglican Communion as institutions.

Reform's stated purpose is "to uphold, defend, and spread the gospel of Jesus Christ according to the doctrine of the Church of England,"[1] a self-evidently worthy Anglican aim until it becomes clear that "the doctrine of the Church of England" is an extremely partial selection of metaphors from the Bible transformed into a rigid theological system. The Calvinist "gospel" includes a particularly penal version of the substitutionary atonement, the infallibility of the Bible, and "the divine order of male headship."[2] The initial statement reads "Established in 1993, Reform is a network of individuals and churches promoting the gospel of Jesus Christ by reforming the Church of England." The implication is that the gospel can only

---

1. www.reform.org.uk/about/what-is-reform.
2. www.reform.org.uk/about/reform-covenant.

be effectively promoted if the C of E is reformed so as to affirm Calvinist doctrines.

Reform is not primarily noted for its general aim of preaching the gospel, however, nor for its particular view of what the gospel consists of. Rather, its public visibility comes from its outspoken opposition to the equal treatment within the church of groups who are now generally considered in late modern culture to have equal rights. Given the historical association of its founding with the C of E's introduction of the ordination of women, it is unsurprising that the issue of women bishops has recently dominated its agenda.[3] When issues such as gay marriage arise in national politics, it seizes the opportunity to raise its profile in opposition. However, its overt success on these issues has largely been limited to slowing down the C of E's gradual progression towards opening up the priesthood and episcopate to women and gays. Having anticipated women bishops as the next big issue, Reform organized its supporters in 2010 to get elected onto the laity section of the C of E Synod, and succeeded in placing thirty-one of them.[4] These were sufficient to defeat the appointment of women in the 2012 Synod vote, with the help of the Anglo-Catholic organization "Forward in Faith." Interestingly, the "gospel" as perceived by this temporary but frequent ally is very different from the Calvinist version.

However, it is likely that the slowing down of the apparently inevitable is not really the prime purpose of Reform. Indeed, it could be argued that Reform's actual political objectives are more likely to be achieved when women and gays *are* finally accepted as bishops. For once they are in place, Reform, and the Calvinist movement in general, can claim further structural changes in church authority in terms of "flying bishops" exercising an alternative supervisory and disciplinary role to any female or gay bishop or to those who consecrated such bishops. Reform insists that their obedience to the biblical gospel does not allow the faithful to have communion or fellowship with such betrayers of the faith, or submit themselves to any supervisory role they exercise.

And this is only one of the ways in which Reform is seeking to weaken the authority of the present C of E structures and processes. It proclaims "the need radically to reform the present state of episcopacy and pastoral discipline, to enable local churches to evangelise more effectively." It has established an alternative method of selecting candidates for ordination.

3. www.reform.org.uk/resources/god's-way-women.
4. www.reform.org.uk/resources/reform-news-update-dec2010.

It has sought to put pressure on bishops by advocating the withholding of wealthy Calvinist parishes' funds to support those poorer churches and initiatives in the diocese that are not properly "gospel."[5] It also supports the decentralization of decisions down from diocesan to parish level, in particular regarding such evangelistic issues as church planting which cross parish and sometimes diocesan boundaries.[6] By taking both of these latter two positions, Reform is seeking to enhance the power of the local and frequently wealthy congregations which constitute its bedrock support. And finally, it sometimes simply shows disrespect for institutional office and its incumbent, as when it refused to welcome the newly appointed Archbishop Rowan Williams to address the Evangelical Council meeting in 2004.[7]

However, despite its assiduous devotion to ecclesiastical politics and media exposure, Reform has had little success on its own, or in association with the other UK Calvinist organizations, in its attempts to appropriate the C of E's institutional authority within the UK. An exception is the impression that it often gives to the general public, as a result of its media profile, that it represents the views of the C of E regarding issues of gender and sexuality. Perhaps its overall lack of institutional authority is partly due to its failure to represent more than a small proportion of clergy and laity, a necessary outcome of its strategy of differentiating itself from a wide variety of errant others.

An examination of Reform's structures and process reveals very little turnover in membership of its trustees and council. At the last count only four of the twenty-five members of council were not ordained, and only three were women (two of whom were lay people). Most of them are the priests in charge of large supportive congregations, but it is not clear how council members are appointed. The member churches are divided into twelve groups, led by the vicars of key Calvinist congregations such as William Taylor of St. Helens Bishopsgate and Vaughan Roberts of St. Ebbe's Oxford. The first professional director of Reform was appointed in 2013, and she is a woman. However chairman Rod Thomas indicated that the appointment did not contradict the doctrine of male headship, as this applied only in the church context.[8] "Rather, it is a role which needs considerable

---

5. www.reform.org.uk/about/council.

6. www.cranmercurate.blogspot.co.uk/2013/06/conservative-evangelical-network-reform.

7. www.anglican-mainstream.net.

8. www.reform.org.uk/about/council.

administrative gifts—and these are shared among men and women. As chairman, I will continue to speak publicly on behalf of Reform and Susie [Director Susie Leafe] will report to me[;] . . . she will be able to consult in depth with members and help us in formulating a strategy that genuinely engages everyone in working towards the reform of the Church." Clearly, Reform's leadership is aware of a lack of engagement by the membership.

Within the UK, then, Reform's challenges to the C of E's institutional authority have not been notably successful. But the authority of the C of E is bound up to a considerable degree in its role in the Anglican Communion. Hence, it is no accident that Reform and its chairman Rod Thomas, together with the other Calvinist organizations and leaders, have all committed considerable time, effort, and resources to GAFCON and its associated organizations, over and above their work in the UK. For GAFCON may yet offer bigger challenges to existing Anglican institutions than the UK Calvinist movement could ever have imagined or hoped.

ANGLICAN MAINSTREAM

Just as Reform chose its name carefully to point to a legitimating tradition, so too Anglican Mainstream sought to put itself at the center of C of E Anglicanism with its label. Indeed, it boasts a banner on its website which reads "Anglo-Catholic, Evangelical, Orthodox, Charismatic, *Mainstream*."[9] It is, in fact, as fringe as Reform, the real UK "mainstream" starting with the moderate Evangelicals and reaching across to the liberal Catholics. And just as the founding of Reform was prompted by women's ordination, so the stimulus for Anglican Mainstream (founded 2004) was the appointment of the gay bishop, Gene Robinson, in the United States. Moreover, just as issues of gender are foremost among Reform's favorite issues, so those of sexuality are dominant for Anglican Mainstream.

Indeed, the similarities continue. Mainstream states that it "is a community within the Anglican Communion committed to promote, teach, and maintain the Scriptural truths on which the Anglican Church was founded. These also guarantee its fellowship with Christians down history and throughout the world."[10] Since the contrast between this unimpeachable and inclusive aim and Anglican Mainstream's concentration on a single divisive issue is immediately evident, the website adds a justificatory quota-

9. www.anglican-mainstream.net.

10. www.anglican-mainstream.net/anglican-mainstream-who-we-are.

tion from Luther: "If I profess with the loudest voice and clearest exposition every portion of the truth of God except precisely that little point which the world and the devil are at the moment attacking, I am not confessing Christ, however boldly I may be professing Christ. Where the battle rages, there the loyalty of the soldier is proved. To be steady on all fronts besides is mere flight and disgrace if he flinches at that point." Indeed, perhaps the only distinctive feature of Mainstream relative to Reform is its greater emphasis on its international dimension, although this only extends structurally to the USA, Canada, and South Africa to any real extent.

This is not to say that Anglican Mainstream concentrates solely on the issue of sexual orientation, however. It supports other Calvinist organizations, especially Reform, on the other issues that they have chosen to contest; for example, women bishops, same-sex marriage, and so on. But its main concern is with homosexuality, a concern that is best explored by the following extended account of its support for "therapy" for those "experiencing same-sex attraction."

There is a long history of construing homosexuality as an illness or disability, and an even longer one of castigating it as a sin. As I noted in my picture of Vaughan Roberts in the previous chapter, *experiencing* same-sex attraction is regarded by Calvinists as an unfortunate consequence of mankind's fallen state, but *acting upon it* is a sin. Hence, Christians such as Roberts have two alternatives if they are to remain "godly": to embrace celibacy, or to seek to decrease or discard their homosexual orientation and move into a heterosexual one. In the latter case, they may seek the services of a variety of therapists who provide a category of treatment called conversion or reparative therapy.

Here, then, we have a clash of two global social systems: religion and medicine. The belief system of the former (in its Calvinist form) construes homosexual practice as a sin to be repented of and delivered from, and homosexual orientation as a burden to bear. For medicine (in its psychotherapeutic form), on the other hand, homosexuality is not now considered to be any sort of pathology. Any problems individuals may experience in living with their sexual orientation are, of course, open for consultation and advice, but there is no question of assisting anyone to change it. Conflating and confounding the categories and assumptions of religion and medicine is therefore treading on very thin ice. Such category confusion may offer opportunities for struggle and publicity, but is fraught with danger. How, then, does Anglican Mainstream fare as it eagerly joins battle on the contentious issue of conversion therapy?

It has recently fought two related campaigns. The first is in support of two "Christian therapists" (note the immediate category confusion) who have been expelled from their professional associations. The second concerns its thwarted plans to place a provocative advertisement on the side of London buses responding to a similar advert by the gay advocacy group Stonewall. The therapists remained expelled, and the advertisement has never appeared. But while the former battle took the organization into deep waters as it faced a combination of professional power and the general public's support for gay people, the latter reaped some rewards.

Conversion therapy has had a long history, having been very popular in the UK in the two decades after the World War II, when many gay people were referred for treatment by a variety of social agents: teachers, doctors, and the law, for example. In 1973, however, homosexuality was removed from the psychiatrists' bible, the Diagnostic and Statistical Manual of Mental Disorders, implying it should no longer be considered a disorder to be treated. The World Health Organization finally removed it from its international classification of diseases in 1992. However, a survey conducted in 2009, the so-called King Report,[11] found that 17 percent of the 1,848 UK mental health professionals surveyed responded that they had helped at least one patient to reduce or change their homosexual or lesbian orientation.

In response to this finding, three of the professional bodies related to psychotherapy, the UK Council for Psychotherapy (UKCP), the British Association for Counselling and Psychotherapy (BACP), and the British Psychological Society (BPS), stated that homosexuality and other sexual orientations were not pathologies, from which it follows that "no responsible psychotherapist will attempt to 'convert' a client from homosexuality to heterosexuality" (UKCP). Further, they supported clients' "freedom from harassment or discrimination in any sphere, and a right to protection from therapies that are potentially damaging, particularly those that purport to change or 'convert' sexual orientation" (BPS). The much more powerful British Medical Association passed a motion calling for the Royal College of Psychiatrists and other mental health bodies to ban the use of conversion

---

11. Bartlett, "The Response of Mental Health Professionals to Clients Seeking Help to Change or Redirect Same-sex Sexual Orientation."

therapy in their codes of practice.[12] The model of sexual orientation now accepted by the medical, therapeutic, and scientific world is of a continuum ranging from totally male to totally female response.

Such statements as those quoted above position professional bodies unequivocally against conversion therapy, and hence provide authoritative support for those seeking to prevent its practice. However, they fail to make a more general public aware of its methods and claims. This omission was dramatically rectified by investigative journalist Patrick Strudwick of the *Independent*,[13] who attended a conference of conversion therapists. There he approached two therapists for help, posing as a gay man (true), and seeking to deal with his same-sex attraction having rediscovered his faith (false). At the therapy sessions one therapist, Lesley Pilkington, agreed that she perceived homosexuality as a mental illness, an addiction, and an anti-religious phenomenon. She explained his same-sex attraction in terms of a developmental abnormality, and said that his love for his boyfriend "needs to be broken . . . a darkness that's very real . . . but of course our God is more powerful than that." Among the possible causes for his "wounds," she adduces a difficult birth leading to loss of attachment to his mother, contact with Freemasonry, low self-esteem, bullying, and sexual abuse. The courses of action which she suggests are to distance himself from his gay friends, take up rugby, and above all, pray.

As a result of Strudwick's complaint, the BACP, of which Pilkington was a member, struck her off their register on the grounds of professional malpractice. She decided to appeal on the basis of faulty process, arguing that only the two session tapes were considered as evidence, not her prior agreement with Strudwick that the therapy would be conducted "within a biblical Christian framework."[14] Before her appeal was heard, a letter supporting Pilkington was sent to the BACP by a large number of supporters, including Wallace Benn, George Carey, Mike Davidson (of whom more later), Michael Nazir-Ali, Paul Perkin, Chris Sugden (described as Executive Secretary, Anglican Mainstream), and Lisa Nolland (described as co-editor of the book *God, Gays, and the Church*, but also an employee of Anglican Mainstream).[15]

12. www.independent.co.uk/life-style/health-and-families/health-news/bma. . . . .

13. www.independent.co.uk/news/uk/this-britain/the-exgay-files.

14. www.anglican-mainstream.net/2011/06/10/joint-statement-on-lesley-pilkington.

15. www.christianconcern.com/press-release/senior-clergy-back-christian-counsellor.

Trouble and Strife

The letter confidently asserts that "Psychological care for those who are distressed by unwanted homosexual attractions has been shown to yield a range of beneficial client outcomes, especially in motivated clients." It goes on to list several research scientists supportive of this statement, and affirms "Such therapy does not produce harm despite the Royal College of Psychiatrists and others maintaining the contrary." Clients, the signatories argue, not practitioners, "have the prerogative to choose the yardstick by which to define themselves. . . . .The mental health profession, which professes to be sensitive and respectful towards diversity and equality, should beware of taking a paternalistic line that says, effectively, not all clients know what is best for their lives." Furthermore, competent practitioners, including those working with biblical Judaeo-Christian values, should be free to assist those seeking help. Despite this appeal to the freedom of the consumer/client to treat and be treated in whatever way they desire, Pilkington lost her appeal.

Anglican Mainstream was involved in the Pilkington episode, and has also championed conversion therapy in several different ways. First, by way of providing an alternative to the medical/scientific definition of terms, Mainstream presents a Glossary on Sex,[16] which it hopes "will prove useful in defining and clarifying important terms and concepts from a traditional Western historical and religious perspective." Mainstream, after all, "stands squarely in the historic orthodox stream of Christianity, and we perceive things accordingly. Others from different moral or philosophic starting points will call things differently." One such different starting point, it might be suggested, would be the belief that questions of the validity and outcomes of psychotherapeutic practices can only be answered by empirical scientific investigation. This response stands squarely in the historic orthodox stream of science. Mainstream's definition of the Ex-Gay Movement in the glossary runs as follows: "Individuals, groups of individuals, organisations, and networks which promote the possibility of change in sexual orientation and facilitate the processes by which this change can occur." Two primary approaches are distinguished, "the overtly Christian/psychological realm of 'inner healing,' . . . and the scientific, secular psychotherapeutic realm of 'reparative therapy.' Both are equally valid and important."

On its website, Mainstream lists a large number of providers of conversion/reparative therapy and their contact details,[17] nearly all of them

---

16. www.anglican-mainstream.net/glossary-on-sex.
17. www.anglican-mainstream.net/resources-for-same-sex-and-transgender-issues.

American in origin. One which is British is the Core Issues Trust,[18] a vehicle for its director, Mike Davidson, with whom Mainstream has developed a close collaborative relationship. Davidson is a trainee psychotherapist, and was a member of the British Psychodrama Association, a relatively minor professional body, until it expelled him. In an interesting take on the persecution of minorities, Davidson argued that he and others "are being discriminated and are being forced into a gay-affirming worldview."

Davidson has collaborated with Mainstream in at least three different projects, in addition to supporting Lesley Pilkington. The first was the distribution of the Core Issues leaflet *Gay Myths*[19] at the Conservative Party Conference of 2012. In its introduction, this document states: "[Kids] are told 'SMOKING KILLS.' Though not universally true, we know it damages and at times does kill. So too does gay sex." The second was a conference at first entitled "The Lepers Among Us: Homosexuality and the Life of the Church."[20] This title was later emended to "The Pastoral and the Prophetic in Conflict? Homosexuality and the Church," after complaints by gay activists to the police. Chris Sugden chaired the conference, and Paul Perkin interviewed the key speaker, a Texan called Jim Reynolds. Reynolds advocated healing homosexuals in church, rather than, as is the Texan way, sending them away to reparative therapists until they are "cured" and can safely be welcomed back into the church. The most remarkable conference contribution was from Lisa Nolland of Anglican Mainstream, who described in considerable detail a range of unlikely sexual acts which, she alleged, LGTB organizations are teaching in schools, and others even more recondite to which ordinary homosexual behavior subsequently leads.[21]

The most widely reported collaboration between Mainstream and Core Issues, however, was the attempt to place an advertisement on the side of London Transport buses.[22] In response to the advert sponsored by Stonewall "Some people are gay. Get over it," they proposed "Not gay! Ex-gay, post-gay, and proud. Get over it." This was initially accepted, but was subsequently pulled by the mayor of London, Boris Johnson, and by Trans-

18. www.core-issues.org.

19. www.image.slidesharecdn.com/gaymyth-121019162852-phpapp01/95/slide-2-638.jpg.

20. www.changingattitude.org.uk/archives/5057.

21. www.exgaywatch.com/2012/02/more-homophobia-from-anglican-mainstream.

22. www.independent.co.uk/news/uk/home-news/christian-group-to-sue-boris-johnson.

port for London, on the grounds that "It is clearly offensive to suggest that being gay is an illness that someone recovers from." However, Core Issues sued for breach of contract and for violation of Human Rights Article 9 (freedom of religion and belief) and Article 10 (freedom of expression). The judgment[23] found that Article 10 was relevant, but that the advertising policy of Transport for London was justified and proportionate, and protected the rights of others from serious offence. Article 9 was not relevant, since rights to freedom of religion and belief could not be enjoyed by trusts, and since the advert expressed a moral issue, not a religious belief. However, Transport for London had been inconsistent in allowing the Stonewall advert but not the Core Issues one, despite the fact that both were highly offensive to many. Nevertheless, this inequality of treatment was not considered sufficient grounds for finding in favor of Core Issues, since the avoidance of offence was of greater importance.

This conversion therapy case study illustrates well the campaigning strategy and priorities of Anglican Mainstream. Every opportunity is taken to provide a story for the media (and thence to adherents and opponents) which represents themselves, or those whom they are championing, as a persecuted minority. The restrictions on some employees regarding the wearing of crosses, and the prosecution of hotel proprietors for refusing gay visitors are recent examples. "Ex-gays" are perfect examples of persecution. They are, we are told, people who want to change their sexual orientation, but who are being prevented from doing so. Their human right to choose is being denied them, as is that of their therapists. And it is they who are the true minority, not gays, who are a "powerful lobby," instrumental in maintaining and developing the current "cultural bias" in favor of homosexuality.

So the ban on the advertisement was a gift. Not only was the gay lobby seen to have been unfairly favored, but the ex-gays' freedom of expression (displaying the advert) was denied them through an excess of "political correctness." No wonder that Mainstream spokesperson Alan Craig remarked "Thanks to Boris we have been given lots of extra publicity for our side...."

PROCLAMATION TRUST

The Proclamation Trust is quite unlike Anglican Mainstream and Reform. It is not a campaigning organization, but, rather, sits more easily within the

23. www.thirdway.eu/2013/04/03/was-anglican-mainstream-advert-ban-judgment-right.

"formation" element in the process model of the Calvinist movement (see pp. 43–49 *). Its main aim is "to teach the Bible to preachers in order that they can in turn teach it to others. A further aim is to provide a fellowship of like-minded Evangelicals across the denominations for encouragement in an exacting work."[24] Its emphasis, then, is on teaching biblical theology and its exposition to ministers, both Anglican and nonconformist. This, for Calvinists, is the central activity of worship and of the ministry—the preaching of the Word.

The Trust primarily uses two instruments for this purpose: a portfolio of annual conferences, and a training course. There is also an extensive resource center, PT Media, producing books, CDs, and DVDs. The most important conference is the Evangelical Ministry Assembly (EMA), attended by around a thousand delegates. Speakers have included Jim Packer and John Stott, Church of England movement heroes; John Chapman and Phillip Jensen, from the Calvinist Sydney Anglicans; and John Piper and Tim Keller, leading American "New Calvinists." There are also conferences for particular constituencies, for example, for younger ministers and for ministers' wives (sic).

The training course is known as the Cornhill Training Course (CTC), and gives instruction in biblical theology and theoretical and practical training in preaching to about ninety students per annum. It offers only one course, entitled "Oral exposition of the Bible," validated by Middlesex University. It allocates students for work placements to "likeminded" churches for a considerable proportion of the course. In 2012 an external review required by the UK Border Agency was overwhelmingly favorable in its evaluation.[25]

Although it is not a campaigning organization, however, Proclamation Trust is nevertheless strictly orthodox Calvinist. It was started at one of the powerhouse churches of the movement, St. Helen's Bishopsgate, by one of the movement's modern heroes, the then Rector Dick Lucas, in 1986. Its doctrinal basis emphasizes the two cornerstone Calvinist beliefs, the infallibility of the Bible and the substitutionary atonement. It considers local congregations to be the fundamental building block of the church, and its own function to be that of supporting them and helping them to keep on faithfully proclaiming God's Word.

24. www.proctrust.org.uk/about-us/what-we-believe.

25. www.bridgesschoolsinspectorate.co.uk/files/the-proclamation-trust_cornhill-training-course.

A review of its conference offerings in 2013[26] indicates that it maintains the movement's cultural beliefs and values enthusiastically. Consider, for example, the address to the ministers at the EMA, entitled "Living among the Pagans: Engaging with Culture," by Dan Strange, Vice-Principal of Oak Hill. Strange argues for the dualist fundamentalist worldview of two ways only of living in the world: rooted in Christ vs. everything else (including in the latter category even the archetypical lovely kind old neighbor). Even the binary distinction "people of faith vs. people of no faith" is false, because faith that is not rooted in Christ is false faith. Thus even doubts are false. "I am," affirms Strange unsurprisingly, "a hardcore five-point Calvinist."

In a seminar entitled "Engaging with an Alien World: Same-sex Attraction," a speaker who admits to same-sex attraction says that we should not tell people that they will be healed. He argues that some do change but some don't, and nowhere in the Bible does it say that one's besetting sins will disappear. There is little point in seeking to address the causes of same-sex attraction, since nowhere in the Bible is anything said about them. Rather, it's a suffering issue, a matter of constant suffering and struggle from which the godly Christian can emerge stronger. But it has to be addressed from the start, so we have to tell non-believing gays that if they are to become Christians, they will have to leave their partners.

In contrast to the theological depths that the ministers enjoy at EMA, the ministers' wives are winsomely addressed by Carrie Sandom (Associate Minister for Women and Pastoral Care at St. John's Tunbridge Wells, council member of Reform, and author of *Different by Design: God's Blueprint for Men and Women*) at their own conference. She humorously takes delegates through the typical hectic day of a minister, with clear implications for their supportive and nurturing role.

So in sum, Proclamation Trust is straight down the line on the current bellwether issues for the movement: sexuality and gender. Vaughan Roberts, its president, may come in for some criticism for talking to Charismatics and Americans, but in reality Proclamation Trust is a powerful tool for retaining and maintaining clergy in the movement's culture and ambit. It makes a lot less noise to the outside world than Reform and Anglican Mainstream, but it serves to enhance the internal cohesion of the movement. All three organizations help to strengthen the movement's and its adherents' unique identity. Reform and Mainstream do so mostly by emphasizing who they are not—"a bureaucratic and secularised denominational institution,"

---

26. www.proctrust.org.uk/resources/EMA-2013.

for example. Proclamation Trust tends to stress who they are: "the faithful preachers of the true Word of God."

GAFCON: A HISTORY

This book is about the Church of England and movements within it, and the three organizations that I have reviewed so far in this chapter all originated in the UK and operate mainly within the C of E. However, it is impossible to complete the account without expanding our horizons to the Anglican Communion. For what is happening within the Communion has important consequences for the C of E, not least the establishment of new Calvinist organizations specific to the UK.

The historical context can be satisfactorily reviewed by a consideration of the last fifteen years, in which radical changes have been occurring in the Communion, in marked contrast to the seemingly interminable efforts required to achieve equal treatment for women in the C of E. The stimulus for these changes was without doubt the success of the international alliance between conservative dissidents from ECUSA (the Episcopal Church of the USA) and bishops from Africa at the Lambeth Conference of 1998. The Americans provided funding and organization at Lambeth,[27] and the Africans numbers and legitimacy. The Calvinist movement in America, the UK, and Australia immediately recognized the potential power of "the sleeping giant" within the Communion, if action could be organized and coordinated. Work soon started on this project, with financial resources from the USA and Australia, and with strategic help from such UK leaders as Wallace Benn and Mike Ovey. These contributions, however, do not imply that African leaders did not also play a major role in the project's development.

The first major fruit of these plans was the GAFCON (Global Anglican Futures Conference) assembly of 2008 in Jerusalem, timed to occur close to the decennial Lambeth Conference. Many bishops did not accept their invitation to Lambeth, since they did not wish to be in fellowship with those who had been invited to Lambeth who had supported the appointment of Bishop Gene Robinson. The Jerusalem Declaration, agreed at the Conference, affirmed "We recognise the orders and jurisdiction of those Anglicans who uphold orthodox faith and practice, and we encourage them to join us in this declaration . . . . We reject the authority of those churches and leaders

---

27. Bates, *A Church at War*.

Trouble and Strife

who have denied the orthodox faith in word or deed. We pray for them and call on them to repent and return to the Lord."[28]

The next major GAFCON event was a "leadership conference," held in London at St. Marks Battersea Rise, Paul Perkin's church. The Chairman of GAFCON/FCA (Fellowship of Confessing Anglicans), Archbishop Wabukala of Kenya, gave the keynote address,[29] characterizing the situation within the Anglican Communion as a continuing crisis. There is, he argued, a "breakdown of the existing governance structures" where "the instruments of unity e.g. the Primates' Meeting, the Anglican Consultative Council, [and] the Lambeth Conference, no longer command general confidence." All attempts to remedy this institutional crisis, such as the proposed Anglican Covenant have failed. "At Lambeth [in 2008] there was a loss of nerve and nothing more than conversation, at Jerusalem we boldly reaffirmed our confidence in the faith we confess."

The Archbishop then goes on to remind his hearers that GAFCON had sponsored the Anglican Church in North America (ACNA), the dissident conservatives from the Episcopal Church, as a new province. This new province was growing remarkably through visionary church planting, he announced. Further, GAFCON had announced itself no longer to be in communion with ECUSA and the Anglican Church of Canada. And finally, he recounted how the Anglican Mission in England had been formed so that "those genuinely in need of effective orthodox oversight in the Church of England could receive it." All this, he stresses, "we do with humility and prayer." In future, given that the instruments of unity in the Anglican Communion have failed us "we have to go back to the basic principles and develop new structures while remaining firmly within the Anglican Communion."

The scene was thus prepared for the second GAFCON conference at Nairobi in 2013. The conference communiqué[30] emphasizes once again the alleged institutional failure of the Communion, suggesting GAFCON as an effective substitute: "We believe we have acted as an important and effective instrument of Communion during a period in which other instruments of Communion have failed both to uphold gospel priorities in the Church, and to heal the divisions among us. . . . The character and boundaries of our fellowship are not determined by institutions but by the Word of God[;]

---

28. www.gafcon.org/the-jerusalem-declaration.
29. www.gafcon.org/news/a-global-communion-for-the-twenty-first-century.
30. www.gafcon.org/news/nairobi-communique-and-commitment.

... the divisions in the Anglican Communion will not be healed without a change of heart from those promoting the false gospel."

However, the communiqué continued, a fellowship network will not be sufficient if GAFCON/FCA is to recognize its responsibilities as an effective expression of faithful Anglicanism. Further organization is required, including a Primates' Council, Board of Trustees, Executive Committee, and regional liaison officers. These will prove especially useful in the task of "authorising and affirming faithful Anglicans who have been excluded by their diocese or province. The main thrust of the work here would be devoted to discerning the need for new provinces, dioceses, and churches—and then authenticating their ministries and orders as Anglican." Such "authentication" may involve ordination and consecration "if the situation requires." Members are urged to contribute to the FCA (now termed the GFCA, the Global Fellowship of Confessing Anglicans) by financing it additionally to, or instead of, "those Anglican structures that are used to undermine biblical faithfulness."

The communiqué makes particular reference to the C of E in this regard.

> We commit ourselves to the support and defence of those who in standing for apostolic truth are marginalised or excluded from formal communion with others in their dioceses. We have *therefore* [italics added] recognised the Anglican Mission in England (AMIE) as an expression of authentic Anglicanism both for those within and outside the Church of England, and welcomed their intention to appoint a General Secretary of AMIE.

This impression that the C of E is the next strategic target of GAFCON was reinforced by Chairman Wabukala's Advent letter for 2013.[31] The first news he mentions after coming down from the mountain-top experience of Nairobi, "in which the Lord Jesus was gloriously present," was the C of E's Pilling Report, which recommends that parishes should be free to bless civil partnerships. Such a developing situation in the C of E

> underlines the need for our Global Fellowship to build on the success of GAFCON 2013 and implement our commitments. As was noted in the Nairobi Communique, the GFCA is becoming an important and effective instrument of Communion during a period in which other instruments of Communion have failed both to

---

31. www.gafcon.org/news/chairmans-advent-letter.

Trouble and Strife

uphold gospel priorities in the Church, and to heal the divisions among us.

In sum, this recent history of escalating statements of intent by GAFCON suggests that its ambition is to undermine the present Anglican Communion, and assume alternative or even replacement authority. It will establish the "structures and instruments" necessary for this purpose, which will presumably not be "man's invention," like the Anglican Communion, but the Almighty's. It also suggests that it regards the "mother church" (the C of E) as the next prominent beneficiary of its reforming zeal.

GAFCON: NEW NARRATIVES

While the above historical account of the last fifteen years is indicative of GAFCON's strategic intent, more may be understood from the *new narratives* which have accompanied its growth.[32] Of course, the original Calvinist narrative of the faithful remnant fighting for the biblical faith against the apostate church and the secularizing world still dominates. However, supplementary narratives derive from the supposedly global nature of GAFCON, and have been promoted at Nairobi and subsequently.

The first such narrative is the familiar tale of the faithful and virile "South" compared with the compromised and tired "West" (or "North," as the terms West and North are used interchangeably, indicating that they are symbolic rather than geographical). Clearly, on this basis, the South can and should help to "re-evangelize the West,"[33] in accordance with the strategic aims of GAFCON. However, the appalling sufferings of Christians from the South were also rehearsed at Nairobi. The numerous murders of Christians for their faith in such countries as Nigeria might therefore reasonably suggest to an observer that GAFCON should be directing its efforts primarily in support of them, not towards the West. By anyone's criteria, this is real persecution, engendering mortal fear and danger.

The *South vs. West narrative* had therefore to be finessed if GAFCON's strategic priority of gaining influence in the West was to be justified. Both South and West faced difficult struggles, but that of the West had to receive prior attention. The rhetorical solution was the old Manichean distinction between the physical and the spiritual. The perils faced by the South

32. Hassett, *Anglican Communion in Crisis*.
33. www.gafcon.org/resources/re-evangelising-the-west.

were physical, ran the revised narrative, but those of the West were more threatening, since they were spiritual. Indeed, it was alleged by an English delegate that this order of priorities was insisted on by the South:

> How could we not be even more challenged therefore, when such people [an archbishop from a truly persecuted Southern province] said that we from the West were at far greater risk than them? More than loss of life or property, they feared that their people would be lost to a faith that has no need for the substitutionary death of the Lord Jesus because it has either done away with a God of principled anger or because it has re-categorised that which is sinful as good.[34]

So the West needs help because its "structures" and "instruments" have compromised with secular culture. Mike Ovey, Principal of Oak Hill, attributed even the West's repentance to the motive of appeasement in his Nairobi address.[35] "It's always difficult to be sure about people's motives," he concedes,

> but when Western churches repent of the history of colonialism and the murder of indigenous peoples, are we doing it because it is offensive to God or because it is—rightly—offensive to the world? I think the acid test of whether our repentance is really towards God is when God and the world disagree. . . . As we all know too painfully, things that the Western world doesn't find offensive, like sexual sins, the Western churches are increasingly disinclined to condemn. Repentance like that: is it really turning to *God*, or acknowledging the *world*?

The Archbishop of Canterbury, Justin Welby, however, could not have been clearer in his message of greeting to the Nairobi Conference.[36] We do indeed all need to be a holy church and holy individuals, he agreed. However, the challenge differs slightly wherever we live. In the rapidly changing cultures of the West, a problem is how to respond truthfully to issues of sexuality. But in other places the dominant issues might be war or corruption. Wherever we are, however, we must be holy and in unity (but not necessarily unanimous, given our different perspectives), concluded Welby.

---

34. www.reform.org.uk/resources/media-downloads/src/article/38title/reflections-from-gafcon2.

35. www.gafcon.org/resources/the-grace-of-god-or-the-world-of-the-west.

36. www.anglicanink.com/. . . ./archbishop-canterbury's-address-gafcon-conference.

After all, we may note, the Nairobi communiqué had admitted disagreement on the issue of the authority of women in the church, but was able to class this as a "secondary" not a "gospel" issue.

This hint of contextualisation and relativism from Welby drew criticism, however, as he counterposed collegial Communion against doctrinal unanimity. He was justified in pointing to such a contrast, given another rapidly developing GAFCON narrative, that of *orthodoxy and discipline*. This narrative clearly underpins Archbishop Wabukala's review of recent Anglican history in his Ridley Lecture in November 2013:[37] "The Anglican story for the past 15 years has been the attempt by the revisionist Provinces of North America, with significant support from the Church of England itself, to undermine the collegiality of the Lambeth Conference's resolution on human sexuality." In the face of such disobedience,

> we should not reject the idea of a body with a more circumscribed authority to exercise the ministry of being "a witness and keeper of Holy Writ" for the Communion as a whole . . . . We may therefore say that the formation of a Primates Council, as agreed at the first GAFCON in 2008 and reaffirmed in Nairobi, is a step towards Conciliar leadership which could be of great value in sustaining and clarifying global Anglican mission.

Wabukala contrasts such a Primates Council, which could hold heretics to account, with the Anglican Communion's Primates Meeting, which he dismisses as no more than "a forum for debate."

These new narratives—of a dominant global orthodoxy, a fragmented and compromised West, and a comprehensive doctrinal disciplinary process—are clearly intended to justify and motivate GAFCON/GFCA moves to gain control of the Anglican Communion by means of alternative "instruments." To what extent have such moves succeeded *within the C of E* so far? How close are we to a "third province" in the UK in addition to Canterbury and York? Is the next organization to be reviewed, the Anglican Mission in England, a means to this end?

THE AMIE

Of the other Calvinist organizations within the C of E, Reform and Anglican Mainstream may best be characterized as campaigning on specific

---

37. www.ridleyinstitute.com/wabukala-gafcon.

issues, while the Proclamation Trust is more geared to maintaining and developing the movement's culture. The adjective that best describes the Anglican Mission in England (founded in 2011), however, is "provocative."

The first provocation is the name itself, changed from the original "St. Augustine Society." The Anglican Mission in America had already facilitated the breakaway of the Anglican Church of North America from the Episcopal Church of the USA. It had permitted ACNA to remain within the Anglican Communion by providing episcopal oversight and clergy membership in the Province of Rwanda, a "mission" from Africa to America. The use of the same phrase for an English organization implies the desire for same outcome.[38]

But the challenge to the C of E lies in more than just a name. AMIE's very purpose carries a threat. Its main aim is to "provide refuge" for those in impaired communion with their bishops by offering alternative episcopal oversight. This in itself is a major issue of ecclesiastical authority. But AMIE also invites support from all Anglicans who "identify with and support" fellow believers in such a plight.[39] In other words, it is trying to build a constituency of those who may not yet be willing to go so far as to declare themselves out of communion with their bishop.

The steering committee of AMIE (chair, Paul Perkin, secretary Chris Sugden) has, without the agreement of the leadership of the C of E, already named a panel of bishops who will exercise oversight on behalf of the Chairman of GAFCON, Archbishop Wabukala.[40] They are all retired bishops, having served in overseas dioceses, apart from Nazir Ali, formerly of Rochester. The panel is chaired by Wallace Benn. Nazir Ali said that while only a few parishes may need alternative oversight at present, "there may be others if bishops . . . teach that same-sex relationships are equivalent to marriage or are in same-sex civil partnerships themselves, and if no provision is made for those who in conscience cannot accept women bishops."[41]

An equally important threat to C of E authority is posed by the ordination of ministers by GAFCON bishops in their own dioceses "for ministry in the wider Anglican Communion,"[42] that is, so that they can take up positions in parishes "out of communion" with their bishop. This has already

38 www.fulcrum-anglican.org.uk/articles/fulcrum-statement on interventionist. . ..
39 www.anglicanmissioninengland.org/about-anglican-mission-england-amie.
40 www.e-n.org.uk/p-5553-new-mission-to-england.htm.
41 www.bbc.co.uk/news/uk-15241528.
42 See 37 above.

Trouble and Strife

happened, when three British men were ordained by Wabukala in Kenya to minister as "missionaries" in the UK. Incidentally, these ordinands might in principle already have been rejected by the C of E as unsuitable for ordination in the UK. They cannot legally become Church of England clergy until they have been licensed, so their employment in an existing parish would be illegal. However, as missionaries and ordinands of the Province of Kenya, they could be provided with permission to officiate as overseas clergy.

Wabukala has requested such permission from the Archbishop of Canterbury, and also asked that the three could be overseen by the AMIE panel of bishops. The Archbishop replied,[43] seeking discussion in a spirit of collegiality, and noting the legal and good practice requirements regarding selection for ordination and deployment. AMIE responded, claiming that the issues had been discussed for four and a half years already, that the ordination had been properly conducted, and that there was a large unmet demand for clergy, especially to unrecognized congregations and church plants. Furthermore, there was no apparent strategy in place to address this shortfall. "Episcopal collegiality within England needs to be matched by both Episcopal collegiality within the wider Anglican Communion, and Episcopal integrity in upholding and teaching the truth of the Christian faith as found in the Scriptures" concludes the AMIE response. The tone was not conciliatory.

Indeed, the most provocative element of AMIE's actions may not in the end be the threats to ecclesiastical authority, but the rhetoric in which these threats are couched: "AMIE is about protecting unity with those Anglicans looking in on the Church of England and assuring them that they can still maintain unity with us" [In other words, GAFCON has the power now, and they support us, so we might be able to keep them on-side]. "It also enables Anglican ministers to remain within the Church of England."[44] [Calvinist C of E clergy could potentially be employed by other provinces.] So protecting unity, and providing refuge to the dispossessed, are favorite rhetorical tropes. But the most provocative of all is the narrative of the fight against the establishment, elaborated in the article "AMIE is a Game-changer" by Vinay Samuel and Chris Sugden.[45]

---

43. www.thinkinganglicans.org.uk/archives/005060.html.
44. www.anglicanmissioninengland.org/about-anglican-mission-england-amie.
45. www.anglicanmissioninengland.org/amie-game-changer.

"The launch of AMIE and the establishment of the panel of bishops indicated that we would no longer play the game of the Church of England politics as defined by the Church of England Establishment," begins the article. Their tactics of divide and rule, and of presenting a "wall of silence" will no longer work. We should learn from the Arab Spring, and stand together, demonstrating a different way of doing things. Mission is about planting churches rather than seeking power and influence in the present system. Anglicanism embraces a global Anglican identity based on the Bible rather than a technical institutional identity. Episcopy is missional and accountable, not prelatical or monarchical. And so on, through the issues of gender and sexuality, contrasting AMIE with the authors' perceptions of the C of E.

All of these issues are not really separate, argue Samuel and Sugden. Rather, taken together, they indicate that "the current malaise [should be analyzed as] a gradual process of destabilising biblically faithful Anglican witness and ministry. . . . The summer ordinations in Kenya were part of the process of saying that we will remain Anglican but not on the current terms of the C of E . . . .We will not be robbed of our Anglican identity. We will not be marginalised. You are the usurpers. We will not allow you to deprive us of our Anglican heritage of faithfulness to the Bible. We will find a way of being faithfully Anglican in being true to the Bible which does not depend on you."

This is fighting talk by any criterion: it is the angry language of revolution. The analogy of the Arab Spring was not idly chosen. What can be its purpose? To conceal internal Calvinist disagreements regarding women's roles in the church? To divert attention from the failure to achieve much of their agenda within the C of E? To provoke a disciplinary response from the C of E that can be represented as further persecution of the faithful? Or is it a sincere expression of the belief that the boot is now truly on the other foot and that the future is Calvinist?

Whatever the answer, this review of organizations within the Calvinist movement indicates that they have noisily and successfully colonized a territory that is both ancient and modern, based as it is on the old empire and the new media. I review in the next chapter the final element of Calvinist organization: the congregations which form its bedrock support.

CHAPTER 5

The Power House
Calvinist Congregations and Culture

CONGREGATIONS THE ENGINE ROOM

THE CALVINIST MOVEMENT SURVIVES and prospers in the UK, despite its minority status, primarily because of its dozen or so key congregations, the movement's engine. These are each powerful organizations in their own right, and in a couple of cases (All Souls Langham Place[1] and St. Helens Bishopsgate)[2] are so iconic for the movement that they could at a pinch be termed institutions. All Souls certainly has recognition in other national institutions, as in 2012 the Rector was appointed a Chaplain to the Queen.

Some of these churches owe their power mainly to the influence they exercise indirectly, through their attraction and development of subsequent leaders (e.g., St. Ebbe's Oxford[3] and St. Andrew the Great Cambridge).[4] Others enjoy the support of the well-connected and wealthy parishioners of central London and the authority which a long history of leadership of the movement has given them. All Souls once had John Stott, a movement hero, as its Rector, while St. Helens was led by another, Dick Lucas. Other

1. www.allsouls.org.
2. www.st-helens.org.uk.
3. www.stebbes.org.uk.
4. www.stag.org.

congregations, too, have prospered in London itself, some in the traditionally wealthy areas (e.g., Christ Church Mayfair)[5] or in an area newly colonized by young professionals (St. Marks Battersea Rise).[6] One of the dozen is located in a predominantly middle-class suburb (Christ Church Bromley),[7] but the wealthy "stockbroker belt" provides a larger representation (St. Nicholas Sevenoaks,[8] St. Johns Tunbridge Wells,[9] and Christ Church Virginia Water[10]). And even the two key congregations outside the metropolis and Oxbridge are located in wealthy suburbs of major provincial cities, Sheffield and Newcastle (Christ Church Fulwood[11] and Jesmond Parish Church[12]).

All of these congregations are *wealthy and well-attended*. For example, All Souls reported an income for 2012 of £1,750,000, St. Ebbes one of £1,140,000, St. Nicholas Sevenoaks £1,125,000, and St. Johns Tunbridge Wells £510,000. The projected 2013 budget for St. Marks was £850,000, and for Christ Church Virginia Water, £570,000, while St. Nicholas even felt able to afford an £850,000 house for its associate rector. Weekly attendances were equally large. Around 2,300 worshipped in the four Sunday services at All Souls, while approximately 500 attended the two services at St. Johns Tunbridge Wells and 950 those at St. Nicholas Sevenoaks. St. Nicholas has in addition offered a Sunday service at 4.00 pm to cater for changes in social habits.

This level of resource provides Calvinist congregations with considerable opportunities. For example, they can afford to employ a large number of professional and administrative staff (relative to most other Anglican churches). At time of writing, All Souls employs twenty-two professional and twenty-four administrative staff; St. Marks, twenty-seven in total; St. Ebbe's, twenty-six (including nine interns); Christ Church Fulwood, twenty-four (ten interns); St. Nicholas Sevenoaks, twenty-two; St. Helens sixteen; and Christ Church Virginia Water, and St. John's Tunbridge Wells, twelve each. One church was even concerned enough for its employees

---

5. www.christchurchmayfair.org.
6. www.stmarks-battersea.org.uk.
7. www.christchurchbromley.org.
8. www.stnicholas-sevenoaks.org.
9. www.stjohnstw.org.
10. www.cc-vw.org.
11. www.fulwoodchurch.co.uk.
12. www.church.org.uk.

The Power House

to appoint a human resources committee. The ministerial staff are mostly male, with females only being employed to minister to families and to women. Every one of the twelve rectors/vicars is male.

Clearly, such a high level of staffing allows these churches to provide an attractively wide range of services to their congregations, and, in some cases (e.g., St. Marks) to their local communities as well. A typical list of activities (e.g., St. Nicholas Sevenoaks) includes a crèche, babies club, one or more activities for carefully graded age-groups right through to adulthood, a student ministry, a young adults group with a social program, weekend breaks, Bible study, a coffee shop and Christian book shop, a mothers' study group, workers' breakfasts, a retired men's group, a fellowship group for the elderly, music groups, orchestra, choir, and drama group.

Interestingly, this church leaves blank the space entitled "Local outreach and community activities" on the "find a church" website.[13] Perhaps this reflects its emphasis, typical of most of the dozen, on the teaching of the Bible in order to make and build up disciples of Jesus Christ. This is the true task of the church, it maintains, not anything that might be called "the social gospel." St. John's Tunbridge Wells, echoes these priorities: "St. John's is a bible-believing church which seeks to glorify God—Father, Son, and Holy Spirit—by:

- Teaching the word of God, to help all ages grow in Christ.

- Praying and Caring *for everyone within our church community* [italics added]

- Sharing the good news of Jesus Christ with our parish, our town, and the world beyond.

St John's exists to know Jesus Christ better, and to make Jesus better known." For Christ Church Bromley, "The central point of the [Sunday morning] service is reading the Bible and having it opened up to us by a speaker . . . the 7pm [Bible Talks] gathering is essentially the same as the 10.30 am Family Gathering." The goal at St. Helen's is "to teach everyone about the life-changing gospel of Jesus Christ, the Son of God."

Clearly the financial resources and staffing levels of these churches permits a range of services designed to meet the varied needs of many different categories of person. As such, they attract not only individuals, but families as a whole, and have surplus resource capacity to seize opportunities when they arise. Most of them have entered a virtuous positive

13. www.findachurch.co.uk/details/sevenoaks/10007.htm.

feedback loop, in the sense that the more adherents they attract, the more resources they accrue, and so are able to attract yet more. This is because, in general, adherents are willing, and can afford, to support their church generously and often sacrificially, some with time, some with money, and many with both.

A major form of mission for these churches is *church planting* (establishing a new congregation). All Souls, St. Helens, St. Marks, and the Christ Churches Bromley and Fulwood have all planted, for example. These initiatives are made possible by the employment of professional staff by the planting congregation to establish the planted one, sometimes together with some volunteer members from the planting congregation. Some of the dozen (e.g., St. Marks) were themselves plants. Another, Christ Church Fulwood, is now a grandparent, in the sense that one of its plants has itself planted an offshoot.

These church plants can become a source of contention between the planting congregation and the Church of England as an institution. Such conflicts follow inevitably from the growing power of Calvinist congregations, and from their belief that the central element of the Christian church is the local congregation, not the national or international denomination. Consider, for example, the case of Christ Church Fulwood, which in 2009 stated its aim of planting a church every two years for the next twenty years. Here the issue of planting without consultation with the diocesan bishop was compounded by the appointment of clergy ordained in Kenya (see p. 83). With the support of Christ Church Fulwood, Christ Church Central, Fulwood's plant in central Sheffield, itself established a plant, Christ Church Walkley, and appointed Pete Jackson as minister. This was done without consulting either the parish church of St. Mary's Walkley, or the Bishop of Sheffield. The Bishop says he will be "entering into correspondence . . . with the various parties . . . to explore their motives and reasons for acting in the way that they have." Graciously praying both for St. Mary's (understandably upset) and for Christ Church, the Bishop nevertheless pointedly affirms that he will "continue in our commitment to mission, to the making of disciples and to joyful and creative church planting *within the order and polity of the Church of England*"[14] [italics added].

Resource power can clearly be used to challenge ecclesiastical authority. Another example concerns the *contributions paid by parishes* to

---

14. www.kiwianglo.wordpress.com/2013/02/26/statement-from-sheffield-on-the-ordination. . . . .

their diocese for the funding of clergy salaries and the support of poorer churches. Back in 2002, for example, William Taylor, Rector of St. Helen's, wished "to make a public, symbolic protest against the new Archbishop's [Rowan Williams'] appointment. . . . We hate it when our politicians believe one thing in private and act differently in public—we call it hypocrisy. It will be awful to have this kind of behaviour in a man who is leading millions of Christians across the world."[15] Taylor decided to short-circuit the system whereby parishes pay contributions to dioceses, and dioceses pass the money on to the Church Commissioners, who then disburse it. He and his clergy colleagues, he determined, would be paid directly by the congregation. Asked by his interviewer whether he thought it ethical for Evangelicals to use their financial muscle in taking their stand, Taylor went on to say he thought it unethical to use money given to support mission for projects where the gospel is not being taught, or on leaders "who will not repent of teaching doctrine and living lifestyles that are not Christian . . . . If he [Rowan Williams] will not renounce his false teaching and repent of his actions, then, regretfully, we need to distance ourselves from him." Taylor was not yet confident enough to explicitly threaten to withhold diocesan contributions, but subsequently Calvinist leaders have not been so cautious.

Move on ten years to 2012, and the ubiquitous Paul Perkin of St. Marks, together with three other conservative Evangelical vicars from the Southwark Diocese, established the Southwark Good Stewards Trust.[16] The "Good Stewards" are those vicars within the diocese "who can genuinely sign the Jerusalem Declaration" (see p. 76–77) [by implication, all the others are bad stewards]. They may then apply for funds from the Trust, which is "simply an alternative mechanism to funding churches within the Diocese. Such churches will still pay their own clergy costs and still pay a contribution towards Diocesan and National Church central costs. Excess monies will be paid into the Trust for distribution."[17] In other words, participating churches will pay *a* contribution to diocesan funds, but not their full required contribution. The money which they should have paid is paid instead to the Trust, which will dispense it to participating churches, in order to "promote orthodoxy rather than subsidise revisionism." This will ensure "the salvation of future generations." Income from Parochial Church Councils as a result of withholding their contributions will be

15. www.e-n.org.uk/p-2015-At-the-heart-of-the-controversy.htm.
16. www.theguardian.com/world/2012/may/23/church-of-england-money.
17. www.evangelicals.org/news.asp?id=1471.

supplemented by individual donors, charitable trusts, and companies. It may be used to part-fund additional staff at participating churches.

It is difficult to know how to interpret this action other than as an overt attempt to exercise resource power to achieve political objectives. St. Marks at present contributes £90,000 per annum to Diocesan funds, constituting 11% of its total budget.[18] However, not all Evangelical churches within the diocese are as wealthy as St. Marks, nor are they all minded to participate in the Trust.

Another use of congregational resources to further the movement's cause is more indirect. It results from the generous staffing of these wealthy Calvinist churches, which *frees up their rectors/vicars* to represent the movement, mostly through their work in the movement's key organizations. Paul Perkin is the outstanding example, being spared by St. Marks to take leadership roles in AMIE, FCA, GAFCON, Wycliffe Hall, Reform, and Anglican Mainstream. Vaughan Roberts has sufficient time away from St. Ebbe's to lead the Proclamation Trust and 9.38, and be heavily involved in AMIE, Reform, and UCCF. Even a medium sized church, St. Matthew's Elburton, can spare Rod Thomas to chair Reform and maintain a prominent media profile.

Others make a more tangential contribution to the movement. David Holloway of Jesmond Parish Church, for example, was one of the founders of the Christian Institute, located in Newcastle. With a group of clergy, he planned to open a school in Newcastle similar to Emmanuel College, Gateshead, noted for its teaching of creationism. He debated creationism with Richard Dawkins on Radio 4, defending Emmanuel College.[19] He also gained publicity for arguing that the new Girl Guide pledge, which does not mention God, is illegal. Stephen Sizer (Christ Church Virginia Water), on the other hand, is freed up to spend two months of the year in international mission, much of it in the Middle East. Sizer obtained his PhD on Christian Zionism from Oak Hill,[20] and is a prominent critic of that movement. The church website invites contributions to his international ministry expenses.

A final contribution of these twelve congregations to the movement is the immense effort that they put into *training, development, and professional formation*. The two located in Oxford and Cambridge treat this as their primary purpose (see pp. 46–47), but it is present in all the others

18. www.stmarks-battersea.org.uk/GivingFinancially.
19. www.angelfire.com/nb/It/docs/called17/htm.
20. www.stephensizer.com/about.

to a greater or lesser degree. The belief that church worship is primarily about expounding the Bible rather than the other sacraments lends itself to a concentration on teaching and learning. Christ Church Fulwood goes so far as to say that the aim of its Bible Training Course "is to train trainers to train God's people to train one another, building the body of Christ in truth and love."[21]

Many of the Calvinist congregations have considerable numbers of students attending (e.g., Christ Church Virginia Water and All Souls), and students are primary, although certainly not the only, targets for training and development. Early additional development is sometimes provided by one-to-one Bible study with an older Christian (e.g., at Christ Church Mayfair and St. John's Tunbridge Wells), a heavy demand on resources. Specific ministers are often appointed to be responsible for training (e.g., at Christ Church Fulwood), and they run courses frequently labelled "ministry training courses." Where these are full-time, trainees can be awarded a bursary by the local church. They spend their time learning from practical service within the congregation, attachment to a specific area of ministry within the church (e.g., youth), and initial training in biblical theology, Bible study, and Christian doctrine. However, these courses are considered to be preparatory for subsequent detailed theological study at colleges such as Oak Hill. Christ Church Fulwood is pleased to "have sent 7 people to theological college, seen 5 of them ordained, and continue to send and support people into mission all over the world."

Thus, although the Calvinist movement treats individual congregations as the relatively autonomous local expression of the Christian church, it is evident that they function as the power house of the movement. In terms of financial clout, number of adherents, iconic status, and above all, connectivity across the movement, they are the engine room of the system.

A CONNECTED AND SYSTEMIC MOVEMENT

I have now reviewed four major elements—formation, leaders, organizations, and congregations—which, I argue, constitute the Calvinist movement in the C of E. However, the movement can only be considered to be a functioning social system if it can be shown that the elements are in dynamic interdependent relationship with each other. At the risk of seeming over-schematic, I will concentrate on the connections between two triplets

---

21. www.fulwoodchurch.co.uk/what-we-do/fulwood-bible-training?ref=nav.

of elements: first, *congregations, formation, and leaders*; and second, *leaders, organizations, and formation*.

In the previous section, evidence was presented of the immense investment in formation that local Calvinist congregations make. Where the congregation consists mainly or substantially of students, specific training and development is provided for them, and close connexions are normally maintained with the local university Christian Union. But even when students are not a major presence, training is provided for young adults in the form of apprenticeships or internships, during which trainees sit next to Nellie (or more usually Norman), and assist with or observe all the activities of conservative Evangelical clergy. This realistic job preview enables them to develop a model of ministry and to further internalize the movement's culture. Thus any subsequent formal theological training puts finishing touches to a formation already well advanced. Vaughan Roberts is an example of a leader's progression from Christian Union and university church through theological training to the ministry. Rod Thomas and Paul Perkin, on the other hand, were attracted to, and formed for, the ministry after a period in secular employment, and attribute their vocation in large part to the congregations which they attended when young professionals.

The training and development effort sponsored by congregations is not limited to those with the potential to become movement leaders, however, nor does it necessarily take the form of sponsored internships and apprenticeships with a view to theological training and ordination. The majority of the training effort is put into developing individuals to minister to others, whether they are going to be ordained or not. The idea of the "ministry of all believers" is given such emphasis in Calvinist theology that Phillip Jensen, Dean of Sydney, felt impelled to correct his interviewer when being questioned about his career when it was nearing its end. He insisted that he started ministering the Word to his friends as soon as he was converted under Billy Graham, not after he was ordained.[22] Christ's Great Commission ("Go ye therefore and teach all nations") applies to all His disciples, and therefore all must be trained to teach and minister the Word according to their abilities.

Nevertheless, the exclusive pathway from universities (especially the elite ones), through large wealthy highly-educated urban and metropolitan congregations, to intellectually able, politically astute, and doctrinally obsessed movement leadership is clearly apparent. However, the relationship

---

22. Herriot, *Phillip Jensen*, ch. 1.

is reciprocal—movement leaders, in their turn, exercise considerable influence on the process of formation. As leaders of congregations they provide role models for aspiring youth. They also ensure that training opportunities are provided by their congregation, and that their content and outcome are consistent with the culture (the beliefs, values, and norms) of the movement. A high degree of uniformity is already likely as a result of the similarity of the formations of the movement leaders themselves (Christian Union, Calvinist congregation, Calvinist theological college). But movement leaders further ensure conformity by their wide-ranging influence over the means of formation. Vaughan Roberts, for example, writes teaching materials for Christian Unions and organizes conferences for young clergy, while Paul Perkin is a member of the council of Wycliffe Hall theological college.

A second triplet of movement elements is *leaders, organizations, and formation*. In several cases, movement leaders have been responsible (usually in collaboration with others) for the foundation and direction of movement organizations. Wallace Benn helped found Reform, for example, while Rod Thomas has played a major role in developing and executing its strategy and tactics. Benn, Perkin, Chris Sugden, and Roberts were all heavily involved in the founding of FCA and AMIE, with Perkin and Sugden continuing to lead them. Benn, Sugden, and Perkin have all been big in Anglican Mainstream, Roberts in Proclamation Trust. Although their foundation was prompted by specific historical events, the movement's organizations reflect the concerns and interests of its leaders, in particular their judgments as to where it was possible to exercise leverage upon the C of E.

I have described in chapter 4 how the organizations have sought to play a role in C of E politics, and how they have achieved a media profile way in excess of their internal power. Indeed, the general public might be forgiven for forming the impression that the C of E as a whole, or at least in large part, is homophobic, misogynist, patriarchal, and judgmental. However, the organizations' campaigning activities have also fed back into the movement, in particular into the element of formation. During the course of their formation and incorporation into a movement, individuals are likely to experience social insecurity and uncertainty. While they may be taught what to believe doctrinally, and be given role models of what it means to live a godly life and truly minister the gospel, they may still feel uncertain about their own identity as movement members. Are these problems of sexuality and gender really the issues that matter to me or to the rest of the world, they may ask themselves, and does the movement's position on them have to be so counter-cultural?

Organizations' media pronouncements and profile can reduce this social insecurity. Young movement adherents continuously see these issues discussed in the media coverage of religion, so they conclude that they must indeed be the ones that matter. Further, what are in fact minority positions on these issues within the C of E are often represented in the media as deserving equal weight and consideration with much more widely held views. And finally, young adherents are given good reasons for being counter-cultural, since Reform and Anglican Mainstream represent the movement and its allies as the only part of the C of E which has not been seduced by secular culture, and is being persecuted as a result. Thus the movement's organizations mediate the outside world to young adherents by their strategic use of the secular media, although this is not their primary aim.

Finally, the relations within this triplet of elements also are dynamic. The organizations and their political and media campaigns may in turn affect their leaders. The regular experience of advocating a particular position is likely to render a leader more rigid and unyielding in his beliefs and less open to new thinking, not least because to retreat from an "orthodox" position, which he has publicly expressed and for which he is the representative spokesman, is likely to damage his reputation in the movement and his self-esteem. And that self-esteem may increasingly come to depend upon his media profile.

Overall, it is hard to escape the conclusion that the Calvinist movement in the C of E is a dynamic social system. Within its ambit, leaders (e.g., Perkin, Roberts, Thomas), congregations (St. Helens, St. Marks, All Souls), theological colleges (Oak Hill, Wycliffe Hall), and organizations (Reform, Anglican Mainstream) constantly circulate and communicate. They feature ubiquitously in any situation or event associated with the movement.

However, while the analysis hitherto may partly answer the sociological question of the existence and nature of the Calvinist movement as a social system, it cannot explain how it succeeds in attracting, retaining, and motivating its adherents. This requires a more psychological analysis in terms of the movement's *culture* and the *social identity* which that culture engenders.

The Power House

BELIEFS, VALUES, NORMS, AND ARTEFACTS

Anthropologists have long analyzed national or tribal cultures, often by participating as far as possible in their practices. More recently, their methods and concepts have been applied to many other social systems, for example, organizations. Hence their application to a religious movement is nothing unusual. The discovery and description of a unique culture would provide added confidence that the Calvinist movement is a social system in its own right. But, more important, it would assist our understanding of the movement's relationship with its members. In particular, it would shed light on how and why the movement's culture becomes internalized as a social identity, and forms so central a part of its adherents' self-concept.

The major elements of a culture are its beliefs, values, norms of behavior, and artefacts. This description makes a culture sound a static and structural entity, whereas it is an ongoing social process of dialog and contestation between social actors. Nevertheless, all cultures, including that of the Calvinist movement, may be analyzed in terms of these four elements, and cultures differ according to their contents. The direction of inference is from the (observable) artefacts of the movement to beliefs, values, and norms of behavior, psychological constructs assumed to be present in the minds of both leaders and adherents.

Artefacts are essentially anything observable that the movement produces. They are not necessarily actual objects, for example, church buildings and what they contain, although these may be important. Where, for example, is the communion table located in church? Is the décor Spartan, or full of color and art? What do the ministers wear? These physical features are symbolic, and carry usually intended meanings. For example, Calvinist ministers wear informal clothing wherever possible, pointing to their belief in the priesthood of all believers. Phillip Jensen, the Dean of Sydney, sometimes wears a severe Geneva gown for formal services to signify his Calvinist persuasion.[23] Most artefacts are not physical objects, however. Rather, they are such "things" as congregational practices, organizational structures, websites, sermons, media interviews, self-descriptions, role-titles (e.g., pastor, minister, vicar, or priest?), and vocabulary (e.g., the Lord's Supper, Holy Communion, the Eucharist, or Mass?). In fact, the previous chapters are stuffed full of Calvinist artefacts, potentially a rich source of inferences to culture.

23. McGillion, *The Chosen Ones*.

The first and deepest level of inference from artefacts is to *beliefs*. Beliefs may be consciously held, and indeed, one ubiquitous Calvinist artefact is the explicit statements of doctrinal beliefs, which almost every Calvinist congregation and organization feels obliged to publish. This is not to deny that these artefacts represent what adherents actually believe. Rather, it is to point to another and deeper level of belief of which they may not be consciously aware, for example, that truth consists of theological propositions. These latter basic assumptions are often so taken for granted that they are rarely made explicit. Many management consultants believe that their most important task is to help their clients to uncover their unspoken assumptions, and to understand how these are affecting their decisions and actions.[24]

Values, the second form of psychological construct within a culture, are a particular evaluative form of belief. While other beliefs concern what is considered true, "a *value* is an enduring belief that a specific mode of conduct or end-state of existence is personally or socially preferable to an opposite or converse mode of conduct or end-state of existence. A *value system* is an enduring organisation of beliefs concerning preferable modes of conduct or end-states of existence along a continuum of relative importance."[25] So, for example, salvation, obedience, and family security probably constitute a far more important cluster of values for the Calvinist culture than an exciting life, independence, and freedom.

Finally, *norms of behavior*, the third psychological element of culture, are social rules, again often unspoken, about how one should act. Because such rules are so often implicit, new adherents are usually uncertain about how they should behave. It is very important for them that they quickly learn, however, since behavior is observable and therefore subject to reward or censure, acceptance or rejection. Norms of behavior may be inferred both from approved behavior, which is therefore likely to be more frequently observed, and disapproved behavior, which may be more rarely displayed by adherents or absent entirely. Calvinists, however, do not leave a great deal unspoken, particularly in terms of which behavior is disapproved.

What, then, may we infer are the beliefs underpinning the Calvinist movement, bearing in mind that the most important beliefs are likely to be the unspoken and implicit ones rather than those expressed in explicit statements of doctrine? Indeed, statements of doctrine may be considered

24. Schein, *Organizational Culture and Leadership*.
25. Rokeach, *The Nature of Human Values*, 5.

artefacts which reveal more fundamental assumptions (or meta-beliefs). Such Calvinist assumptions are about *the nature of knowledge*, that is, how we come to know things, and what form that knowledge takes. In a word, they are epistemological assumptions: first, that we come to know things through divine revelation of the truth, not human discovery; and second, that what we know can be expressed as a set of verbal propositions. The obsessive concern with words such as "substitute" (of Christ) or "infallible" (of the Bible) indicate how important propositional statements and the meaning they express are considered to be.

The predominant mode of Calvinist worship is another significant artefact. Its central feature is the exposition of a passage of the Bible, the purported meaning of which is taught by the preacher and learned by the congregation. For example, in morning worship at Christ Church Bromley, the whole congregation of all ages are taught about two or three verses of the Bible. Then the children leave, and a lengthier passage is expounded. The same teaching and learning model dominates the evening service, although there are no children present and the atmosphere is less formal.[26] The Bible, it is assumed, is the Word of God by which He clearly reveals the truth to us. Provided the preacher has not been seduced by secularism, he will faithfully present God's truth from the passage. Since truth is absolute, and the meaning is clear to "the common man," there can only be one correct view of what the Bible means. This, of course, begs the question of why in that case there is so much need for "teaching."

A final artefact that points to Calvinist beliefs about the nature of knowledge and truth is their account of church history (see pp. 16–17). The gospel was foreshadowed in the Old Testament and revealed by Christ to His apostles, they acknowledge, but it was rediscovered in church times by the Reformers. They gave us God's truth in a propositional form, which we have no reason at all to change. Rather, it is our task to be the faithful guardians of the gospel as they handed it down to us, and to proclaim it tirelessly. Such recent heroes of the movement as John Stott, Jim Packer, and Dick Lucas have kept the faith and guarded the flame, inspiring us to continue in the great tradition. So the truth is absolute, there are no relativities or alternative interpretations, and no variations according to cultural context. Thus we cannot reasonably be accused of failing to dialog with other theological perspectives. Since there is only one true gospel, which has been revealed to us, then everyone who differs from us is in error and

---

26. www.christchurchbromley.org/sundays.htm.

preaching a false gospel. We must avoid fellowship with them, so that we may preserve purity in both doctrine and association.

When we examine the content of Calvinist sermons and articles (for example, Paul Perkin's address to GAFCON in Nairobi (see pp. 61–62)), it becomes clear that another belief system relates to *the nature of the world and of reality*. Calvinists often call this set of assumptions a "worldview." Their reality is expressed in a simple black and white binary model as a constant cosmic struggle between God's revealed truth and secular falsehood, between his true church and "the world." Recent history, present, and future is seen simply as the account of this struggle (although God is always in control and will ultimately rule unchallenged). So, for example, the disagreements between the movement and the institutional representatives of the C of E are construed as part of this same eternal struggle between the true church (themselves) and the world (which has infected the C of E). Since there is only one revealed truth, on behalf of which they themselves contend, then any who oppose them must by definition be contending for falsehood, having been seduced by the secular enemy.

Another significant movement artefact is its organizations, especially the two most prominent, Reform and Anglican Mainstream. These are conflictual and combative in their strategy and tactics, which basically consist of unremitting campaigning on various issues associated with sexuality and gender. The organizations thus point to the inference of a Calvinist worldview of struggle between God's truth and mankind's sin. The immediate reasons for concentrating on these issues may have been opportunistic, but their choice is significant. Issues of sexuality and gender are at the forefront of the struggle for minority human rights, and human rights are, according to Calvinists, a dominant concern of secularists.

Beliefs and assumptions, then, underpin Calvinist culture, an unsurprising dominance given its overwhelming emphasis on orthodoxy. It is the absolutist and (supposedly) unchanging nature of these beliefs which stands out. The truth has been revealed once for all, and handed down thereafter. The idea that truth is defined within a social context is unacceptably relativist. And the possibility that claims to the possession of absolute truth can be construed as social acts aimed at gaining and retaining power is steadfastly ignored.

The other major feature of Calvinist beliefs and assumptions is their *binary nature*. There is always a contrast, between, for example, truth and error, the sacred and the secular, or the church and the world. And the movement always claims exclusive possession of the virtuous alternative. This facilitates a movement identity and strategy that embraces conflict; and it provides a strong social identity for adherents. I will argue that Calvinist assumptions are in this respect fundamentally different from those of Charismatics. The Charismatic belief system blurs many binary distinctions, and facilitates adherents' personal identities as unique individuals and their immediate, congregational, social identities.

Inferences can also be drawn from the examination of other movement artefacts to *values and norms of behavior*. Consider, for example, the brief self-descriptions that ministerial staff provide for their congregation's website. A content analysis was conducted on sixty-five such descriptions derived from the websites of five of the twelve congregations and one theological college. Of the sixty-five, forty-six staff said that they were married, and named their spouse. The remaining nineteen did not say that they were married; nor did any of them say that they were single or partnered. Of the married respondents, thirty-six stated whether they had children, and twenty-nine listed their children's names. Frequently, married status was the first thing that was mentioned, and its citations exceeded in number those of previous work experience, qualifications, and present job description.

Now the writers of these self-descriptions may have had a variety of purposes in concentrating so heavily on marriage. They may, for example, have wanted to portray themselves as just like the young families that they wish to attract and retain in their congregations. But considering this artefact together with sermons, articles, and campaigns, it is reasonable to conclude that the movement places a very high value on family (defined traditionally) and on parenthood.

Incidentally, these self-descriptions may also hint at a degree of unease regarding "secular" pursuits. Such secular enjoyments are instantly followed by sacred virtues. "He enjoys drinking good coffee and reading the Bible with students" reads one statement of interests. "He still enjoys reading History and Politics books (for fun!) but nothing gives him greater joy than seeing someone come to know Jesus Christ as Lord and Saviour." And "he enjoys music, reading, and watercolour painting. He is passionate about church planting."

Other cultural values can be inferred from the descriptions of formation, leaders, organizations, and congregations in earlier chapters. For example, conflict with the world outside the movement is highly valued, especially when it is accompanied by allegations of persecution. Conformity of belief within the movement is equally important, however, with the implied respect for the authority of the teacher by the learner. Overall, the values and norms of behavior are cast within an individualist moral framework. Ethics are seen to concern individual acts, especially in the sexual arena, where sins have to be privately wrestled with. Hence the quality of a gay relationship is considered to be of no relevance—it is the fact of sexual activity that matters. Like beliefs, values and norms are construed without reference to their social context, and with little attention to any social or political dimension. Care for the congregation, the conversion of the unsaved, and campaigns about conservative moral issues seem to define the Calvinist social horizon.

A DOMINANT SOCIAL IDENTITY

In sum, the Calvinist culture is conflictual, doctrinaire, and conformist. But, above all, it is *distinctive*. The movement's leaders take every opportunity to *differentiate* it from other social systems. It is very important to them that it is not confused with other movements or groupings within the Evangelical wing of the C of E, for example the Charismatics. Charismatics are among its primary targets, since they might appear to the outside observer to be most similar to it. At every opportunity they point to the institutional ("bureaucratic," "hierarchical") nature of the C of E itself, but insist that the movement represents its original and pure Reformed state, untainted by the secular world. A variety of differentiating features has been reviewed in this and the preceding chapters, but perhaps the most distinctive are the following. First, its insistence on explicit statements of, and assent to, Reformed doctrine that marks it out from other Christian groups; second, its overwhelming emphasis on a patriarchal model of the family and its opposition to any sexual relationships outside it; and finally, its representation of every situation as one of conflict with a variety of foes, religious and secular.

These features, and many others, directly distinguish the movement from other social systems. But there is another aspect that has a more indirect differentiating function: its *internal conformity*. If adherents were to differ from each other in terms of doctrinal belief, or if their interpersonal relationships were more varied, or if they participated in a wide range of secular activities with people who were not bible-believers, then differentiation would be compromised. It is only when there is uniformity within the movement that its distinctiveness from the rest of the social world can remain crystal clear. Otherwise, there is no clear single model offered by its adherents of what it stands for.

How, then, does such a very distinctive movement, hostile both to other Christians and to the secular world, attract, retain, and motivate its adherents? The answer is that it uses its very distinctiveness to provide a *unique social identity* that dominates the self-concept of adherents, providing them with self-esteem, purpose, and meaning, both for their own lives and for the world in which they are lived.[27]

The movement is counter-cultural in at least two respects. First, in general terms, it is hostile to most of its surrounding culture's late-modern beliefs, values, and norms. For example, it believes that truth is revealed rather than discovered and absolute rather than relative to context; it values obedience to (divine) authority more highly than the universal achievement of human rights; and it favors controlled rather than spontaneous behavior. Second, more specifically, it emphasizes *social* as opposed to *personal* identity. The belief that one belongs to a category of person ("Bible-believer," or "Reformed Anglican," or however the movement is labelled) is far more important than one's personal identity as a unique and authentic individual.

The psychological implications for the individual of this high degree of movement differentiation are profound. Once adherents are committed to the movement, its social identity becomes incorporated into their self-concept, together with its beliefs, values, and norms. These are so counter-cultural as to be incompatible with many of the beliefs, values, and norms of other social identities that they also maintain, for example, occupational ones. It is no accident that Calvinists have sought to establish cross-categories such as Christian therapist (see p. 69) or Christian lawyers.[28] A consequence of Calvinism's counter-cultural distinctiveness and incompatibility is that adherents find it very hard to hold their Calvinist identity in tandem with their other, "secular," social identities. They are likely to need at least a degree of compatibility to be able to hold their self-concept together, so if they commit fully to the movement, its social identity has to become dominant.

---

27. Hogg, "Intergroup Behaviour and Social Identity"; Hogg, "Joining Groups to Reduce Uncertainty."

28. www.lawcf.org.

Now one of the main functions of social identities is to become uppermost in the mind in situations where they are relevant. The appropriate identity can then regulate behavior so that it is in accordance with the cultural requirements of the situation, for example, in a consulting room, court of law, or church. When a particular social identity dominates the self-concept, it tends to become salient in a wide variety of situations. The Calvinist adherent is thus likely to seek to "minister" or "witness" to others in situations where such behavior is not usually considered appropriate. In the Calvinist case, it is the single *social* identity that dominates the self and therefore elicits beliefs, values, and behavior. Where individuals' *personal* identity dominates their self-concept, as it frequently does in late-modern and post-modern societies, a similar disregard for situational norms of behavior may be evident. However, in this latter case it is justified in terms of the requirement of the "heroic" individual to act "authentically" in the face of pressures to conform.

The importance to Calvinists of a conversion experience is significant in this regard. Its explanatory function is evident from the self-descriptions on congregational websites, where turning points, some at an extraordinarily early age, are recounted by twenty-two of the sixty-five clergy reviewed. Conversion signals theologically the expectation that new adherents have turned from "the world" to God. Their old sinful secular allegiances have been jettisoned and the gospel of Christ embraced. From a psychological perspective, it implies that their social identity as Calvinist Christians is now so central a part of their selves that it dominates their beliefs, values, and behavior in most situations.

But why should the Calvinist social identity in particular motivate adherents so effectively? One reason is to be found in the nature of the movement's organizational form. An adherent internalizes the central social identity of movement member, but this is not just a single, simple category. Rather, it embraces a range of related categories, which are "*nested*" in the sense that a lower-order category is incorporated into a higher-order, more inclusive one. Identities in a nested structure socially reinforce the same beliefs, values, and norms. So, for example, having an identity as a member of a Calvinist family reinforces the movement norms for gender roles. These (and other elements of the culture) are also reinforced by sub-identities for demographic groupings such as youth, men, women, young mothers, business people, Bible and ministry trainees, and so on, for whom separate ministries are provided.

The Power House

Congregational membership also reinforces the movement identity, with role models from all generations available, and ministers who have all been formed by a similar developmental process, both those within the congregation and those from other core Calvinist congregations. And while adherents may identify as "Calvinists within the C of E," the recent developments regarding GAFCON and the Anglican Communion allow them to embrace an international movement identity. The nested nature of movement identity, then, strengthens it considerably.

But the most powerful identification with the movement is achieved by means of the *personal narrative* that its culture makes available to adherents. God has chosen us as His soldiers in the war between truth and falsehood, they can tell themselves. I am one of His select band, which keeps alive the pure flame of Reformation truth, ministers the Word to others, and fights the apostate church and the secular devil. God has revealed His plain truth to me through his Word, so I have no doubts about the faith. I know what to believe and how to act, who I am in God's scheme of things, and who I most emphatically am not. God himself confirms that He has chosen me by allowing me to suffer persecution on His behalf, a sure sign that I am fighting the good fight in good faith, and in a select and glorious band.

So here is a source of *self-esteem*—I am "chosen, called, and faithful"; of *certainty* about myself, the world, and the truth; and of *affiliation* to others like myself. These are major motivators for those few who are willing and able to radically downgrade their personal identity and their other social identities in favor of the Calvinist identity. Perhaps this account brings us closer to understanding both the high degree of adherent commitment to the movement, but also its relative weakness in numbers. Adherence is personally rewarding—but it can also initially be socially and psychologically costly.

I now move on to discuss the Charismatic movement within the C of E. The elements of the movement are the same as the Calvinists (formation, leaders, congregations, and organizations), but I will argue that these are related in different ways. Moreover, and most importantly, the Charismatic culture and identity is radically different from that of the Calvinists. Calvinists are different from, and hostile towards, their own denomination and the society in which they live. Charismatics are simultaneously differentiated and integrated, a balance that ensures not only motivated adherents but also potential societal influence.

CHAPTER 6

Big and Bigger
Charismatic Organization

MINISTERS AND THEIR MINISTRIES

THE CHARISMATIC ORGANIZATIONAL FORM consists of the same basic elements as Calvinist: formation, leaders, congregations, and organizations. However, because of recent Charismatic history in the UK, the relationships between these elements are markedly different for the two movements. Calvinist organization, for its part, has had a long history. As a consequence, its four elements are each highly developed, and their interrelationships well established. Formation via Christian Unions, theological colleges, and university churches is via tried and tested pathways, and the leadership controls these elements, as well as the various organizations. Congregations and their members provide most of the resources. In sum, Calvinists in the UK are tightly organized and effective at what they do—perpetuate and publicise a small but cohesive reactionary oppositional movement that punches well above its weight.

The UK Charismatics, however, are the historical product of the sequence of relationships of leaders of major Anglican congregations with American religious entrepreneurs, each introducing a new "wave" of fervent practice (see pp. 37–41). They established Charismatic practices in their own congregations, and persuaded colleagues in charge of other parishes

Big and Bigger

to follow suite. David Pytches, Rector of St. Andrews Chorleywood, rose to particular prominence after the visit to Britain of John Wimber, Californian founder of the Vineyard churches in the so-called "third wave" (1980s). Nicky Gumbel, then Curate of Holy Trinity Brompton (HTB), later gained an even higher profile, partly as a consequence of the introduction to the UK of the Toronto Blessing of 1994.[1]

Pytches established and led New Wine,[2] a conference for Charismatics, which rapidly also became an organization with regional hub churches such as Holy Trinity Cheltenham (Trinity),[3] and St. Thomas Crookes Sheffield (Crookes).[4] He ensured New Wine's continuation after his own retirement by appointing John Coles as director with a professional staff. He also encouraged Mike Pilavachi, a youth leader at St. Andrews, to establish Soul Survivor[5] in 2003. Soul Survivor was the name of a conference for youth, which then became an organization. It was also the name of a congregation in Watford set up by Pilavachi, who became its senior pastor, in the same year. Soul Survivor has now grown into an international "ministry."

At Holy Trinity Brompton[6] there was similar rapid expansion. When the Rector, Sandy Millar, retired in 2005, Nicky Gumbel became Rector. While Curate he had developed the Alpha Course[7] from a teaching and development aid for new Christians into an evangelical tool for the conversion of non-believers. Alpha, which is mainly orthodox conservative in its theology but contains extensive Charismatic elements, gained worldwide prominence, with an estimated twenty million having undertaken it hitherto. Another major impetus was the introduction of elements of the Toronto Blessing into HTB worship and practice. HTB grew so rapidly that it has at a recent count planted sixteen direct congregation plants, which in their turn have produced nine plants from plants, and two plants from plants from plants.

The major difference between HTB and St. Andrews, however, was that HTB retained control over Alpha. While HTB and Alpha now have

---

1. Steven, *Worship in the Spirit*; Warner, *Reinventing English Evangelicalism 1966–2001*.
2. www.new-wine.org.
3. www.trinitycheltenham.com.
4. www.stthomascrookes.org.
5. www.soulsurvivor.com.
6. www.htb.org.uk.
7. www.alpha.org.

separate governance arrangements, Gumbel is still leader of both, and they share many personnel. HTB benefits immensely in terms of new members and influence from its retention of Alpha. St. Andrews, on the other hand, has spun off two major successful independent organizations (New Wine and Soul Survivor).

A common feature of the growth of the Charismatic movement has been its emphasis on learning how to experience and to lead its ecstatic forms of worship. New Wine and Soul Survivor conferences, together with many large congregations, essentially offered the liturgical sequence developed by Wimber: worship, teaching, and prayer. However, these terms have specific meanings for Charismatics. *"Worship"* consists of modern songs, accompanied by a folk/rock band, praising the kingship of Christ and then dwelling on each believer's unique intimacy with Him. *"Teaching"* is an often lengthy and informal address by the leading "pastor" or one of his assistants, or an inspirational talk from an eminent visiting speaker. And *"prayer"* is an opportunity which is provided for ecstatic behavior to be exhibited in a variety of forms.[8] Those who attended conferences learned how to experience and to lead worship and prayer. Many of them became skilled worship leaders and prayer leaders, impresarios of dramatic and highly-charged liturgical events.

This "ministry of all believers" gave opportunities for many adherents, most not having experienced formal theological or pastoral training, to develop prominent roles both within and across congregations. Some of them developed their own "ministries," which have sometimes enabled a regional or national, or even an international, career. So, for example, Matt Redman, worship leader who developed his skills at New Wine, and his speaker and author wife Beth, now have international ministries. This association of a freelance individual with their own ministry, outside denominational structures, is a feature of American Evangelical Protestantism, where a ministry is often handed down the generations within a family. Christy Wimber, for example, daughter of John, is based in his church in California but is a frequent speaker at Charismatic conferences in the UK.

This association of individuals with "their" ministries contrasts with the more popular use of the term, where an individual enters "the" ministry, although both the C of E and the Methodists speak of "the ministry of the whole people of God." It has had two major implications for Charismatic organization in the UK. The first is the issue of *control and*

---

8. Steven, *Worship in the Spirit*.

Big and Bigger

accountability. People with pronounced Charismatic and evangelistic skills have often developed their ministries under the aegis of the C of E. For example, they can pioneer church plants in unusual or challenging contexts; they may establish experimental worship services designed for particular categories of adherent; or perhaps they will develop counseling facilities within a church setting. The innovative nature of these developments, and the entrepreneurial and often dominant character of their "ministers," have proved challenging for the established structures of the C of E to oversee, both at diocesan and at congregational levels. The outcomes have occasionally been extremely damaging to congregations and to leaders.

An unrelated control issue concerns the sheer size and proselytizing success of the major congregations and organizations. The fact that they are succeeding in at least stemming the tide of the loss of attendees is, of course, a major source of their influence and power. HTB with Alpha is the outstanding example, with Gumbel being compared with Welby, Rector with Archbishop, in terms of influence within Anglicanism.[9] But "hub" congregations such as Trinity, Crookes, and The Belfrey (St. Michael-le-Belfrey York[10]) are also major organizational power centers, not only individually within their parishes, but throughout their regions. Crookes, for example, speaks of "evangelizing the North," and an association of three Northern Charismatic congregations from Sheffield, Leeds, and York has established a theological college for the region.[11] When association is in terms of movement congregations rather than denominational dioceses, accountabilities sometimes become blurred and discipline difficult. While some centres such as HTB are scrupulous in fulfilling their Anglican responsibilities, others are less careful. All ridicule "rigid formality" and "stifling bureaucracy" at every available opportunity.

The second implication of the growth of Charismatic ministries has been in terms of *formation*. The activist and informal nature of their learning has left some Charismatic leaders without a solid theological foundation. Moreover, the one long-established and academically outstanding theological college with an unequivocally Charismatic orientation, St. Johns, Nottingham,[12] is clearly not sufficient to meet the level of demand for clergy to staff the considerable number of Charismatic Anglican churches.

9. www.theguardian.com/commentisfree/2013/mar/20/justin-welby.
10. www.belfrey.org.
11. www.schooloftheology.org.uk.
12. www.stjohns-nottm.ac.uk.

Warfare and Waves

New courses are now being established by large congregations, or groups of them, which combine theological study with practical experience. However, formation overall is not so well developed an element of Charismatic movement organization as it is of Calvinist.

To sum up, the Charismatic movement's organizational form is predictable, given its emphasis on evangelization and innovation. Individual congregations are highly organized and effective at attracting and retaining adherents from targeted segments of the population, especially youth, young adults, and young families. Inspired by charismatic leaders, they spin off both new church plants and also large para-church organizations. They even organize internally into "missional communities" to facilitate evangelism (see pp. 119–120) and develop extensive contacts with their local community and social agencies. The central unit of the Charismatic organizational form is thus in effect a combination of two elements: *(congregation + leader)* or *(organization + leader)*. While individual leaders do have contacts with other congregations and organizations than their own, there is not a high degree of integration and collaboration between different congregations and organizations. Each seems to concentrate more on developing its own "ministry" than on movement development. As a result, while congregations such as HTB, and organizations such as Soul Survivor and Alpha, have very considerable visibility and impact, the Charismatic movement's organizational form is a lot looser than that of the Calvinists.

A series of case studies in the rest of this chapter will provide some detailed illustration of this very summary account. The first addresses the relationship of a para-church organization (Soul Survivor) to its leader (Mike Pilavachi), and demonstrates the power of such a combination. The second examines in detail the operations of two regional hub churches, Crookes and Trinity. Finally, I consider an example of the potential hazards of the Charismatic model.

THE "BIG FAT HAIRY GREEK"

This jocular self-description,[13] together with his frequent reference to himself as one of the oldest youth leaders in the world,[14] are examples of Mike Pilavachi's ironic style. He is possibly hinting at his longevity (over twenty years) in the positions that he holds, and the fact that he did not have the

---

13. www.soulsurvivorwatford.co.uk/talks/the-me-generation.
14. www.revivalmag.com/article/interview-mike-pilavachi.

Big and Bigger

advantages of, for example, an education at Eton and Oxford in achieving them.

Pilavachi is not strictly speaking an exemplar of the (*organization + leader*) core component of the Charismatic organizational form. This is because he is not only Director of the Soul Survivor organization, but also senior pastor of the congregation of Soul Survivor Watford, a very successful church plant from St. Andrews Chorleywood. Like Nicky Gumbel, therefore, he represents a (*congregation + organization + leader*) component, so it is perhaps no accident that he is second only to Gumbel in Charismatic influence.

In 1993, Pilavachi, then a youth leader at St. Andrews Chorleywood, made a proposal to the Rector, David Pytches. It was for the establishment of a week's residential conference for youth, to complement the family conference, New Wine, which St. Andrews already sponsored. Nearly two thousand attended the first Soul Survivor conference. Two events were soon required to cope with increased demand, with a total attendance of twenty-five thousand soon becoming the norm. By 2014, four events were offered, with one in the Midlands and one in Scotland in addition to the initial two held in the West Country. Total attendance is estimated at thirty-five thousand, and in 2012 the startlingly specific total of 1,801 conversions was recorded.[15] In addition, Soul Survivor has become international, with conferences in Australia, Malaysia, Netherlands, New Zealand, South Africa, and the USA. The 2012 accounts for Soul Survivor indicated income of £3.23 million, expenditure of £3.44 million, assets of £1.05 million, and a professional staff of thirty-one.

This continued growth does not seem to have adversely affected the popularity of New Wine,[16] which continues to attract around thirty thousand to its three events. This is in contrast to the other well-known Evangelical conference, Spring Harvest, which has decreased markedly in popularity from a high point in the 1990s, when its attendances neared 100,000, and is characterized unflatteringly by Rob Warner[17] as "a gated community, a ghetto on holiday."

However, like New Wine, Soul Survivor did not merely continue as a (highly successful) annual conference. It immediately started developing spin-offs, aimed at different demographic segments and constituencies. The

---

15. www.soulsurvivor.com/about-us.
16. www.new-wine.org.
17. Warner, *Reinventing English Evangelicalism 1966–2001*, 86.

first such was youth leaders, for whom training events were soon provided, and subsequently branded as SoulNet. The "raising up" of leaders, however young, is a major pre-occupation for Soul Survivor.

Another major initiative, commencing in 2005, was Momentum, an annual conference for those in their 20s and 30s. Pilavachi distinguished this UK demographic as a segment facing very different issues from the youth. It was particularly affected by the social trends of consumerism, individualism, and a sense of entitlement, he argued.[18] As a consequence, it had difficulty in making and keeping commitments, in particular to relationships (especially marriage), career, and church. Pilavachi pointed out that only 3 percent of this cohort attended church regularly, around half the figure for the population as a whole. He called their attraction to, and retention in, church the crucial issue for the church today.

A third initiative, later named "Worship Central," trains worship leaders in the music-led element of the Vineyard liturgical model. Worship is a major activity at conferences, and albums of new and favorite songs are widely marketed after each conference.[19] More general impetus to a supernatural and ecstatic Charismatic approach is provided by another conference called "Naturally Supernatural," established in 2010. Encouragement to potential female leaders is provided at a conference called "Equal" (established 2011), perhaps in recognition of the fact that women are not yet adequately represented at the very top level in this or other Charismatic congregations or organizations. And the importance of social justice and the relief of suffering as part of the gospel is recognized by "Soul Action."[20] This initiative is partnered by Tearfund, the relief and development agency, which Soul Survivor supports and which provides short placements in development projects for Soul Survivor members. Soul Survivor also supports several other development agencies.

As if all this were not enough, Soul Survivor periodically engages in ambitious one-off projects in which large numbers of youth descend on a city (Manchester in 2000, London in 2004, and Durban in 2009) and engage in socially useful activities. How is such a high level of activity and growth initiated and sustained? One contributing factor is the close involvement in the organization Soul Survivor of the congregation Soul Survivor Watford. Many of the Soul Survivor team are members of the congregation, and the

18. www.sms.cam.ac.uk/media/1112687.
19. www.weareworship.com/uk/writers/soul-survivor.
20. www.soulaction.org/about.

Big and Bigger

offices of the organization are located in the two warehouses that constitute the church premises. These overlapping memberships allow staff to be deployed where the peaks of demand require.

A second reason for the continued growth of Soul Survivor is clearly its skill and speed in recognizing and meeting the needs of specific market segments. Pilavachi himself balks at using such terminology, responding to the interview question "How do you feel about Soul Survivor being a brand?" as follows: "Soul Survivor might be a brand now, but in the same way that New Wine would be a brand and Greenbelt would be a brand. We're not trying to be a brand, we're just trying to lead people to Jesus. What's a brand? It's a name people recognise, in that case we have not tried to build a brand."[21] Given that Soul Survivor employs at least two branding consultancies[22] this response possibly reflects Pilavachi's ambivalence about the extent to which the medium may be affecting the message.

However, it is mainly Pilavachi's own entrepreneurial abilities and drive as director, while also acting as front-of-house impresario, that have propelled Soul Survivor into the rarefied category of international ministries. For a man in his mid-fifties without children, he nevertheless possesses an ear acutely tuned into youth culture, and also a willingness to listen to the advice of those younger than himself. "Why do we have the worship music so loud that they can't possibly hear the words?" he asked his musicians. The answer was that today's youth are embarrassed to sing in public if they think they are going to be heard by others, but they will shout along happily if they cannot possibly be heard as individuals.

Pilavachi's leadership role is emphasized, both in the organization's website and also in his talks and interviews. He is clear that he rightly has authority over his worship leader Matt Redman, although "Matt has the talent."[23] He jocularly urges his HTB audience not to patronize him by their welcoming applause.[24] He differentiates Soul Survivor under his leadership from Charismatic Evangelical culture, which, he asserts, is "a million miles away from those outside the church."[25] Indeed, in a lengthy and graphic account of his gastric indisposition at a conference, he laughs at "a famous

---

21. www.Istillilluminate.co.uk/interview-with-mike-pilavachi.
22. www.visiontank.co.uk/2013/07/soul-survivor-2013-brand-roll-out.
23. www.crossrhythms.co.uk/articles/news/Pastors_and_Musicians_at_War/30324.
24. www.htb.org.uk/media/wednesday-evening-mike-pilavachi.
25. www.sms.cam.ac.uk/media/1112687.

Charismatic Christian leader" who repeatedly asked "Have sin, sickness, and Satan triumphed over you?"[26]

His talks, in a variety of settings, are all replete with self-references, although this is a common feature of all the Charismatic leaders' talks that I accessed for this book, and will discuss more fully in subsequent chapters. These "talks" (never "sermons") appear to represent a mixture of genres, ranging from a dominance of lecture mode with jokes thrown in (e.g., Alpha), to a mix of cheer leader, stand-up comedy, and Oprah Winfrey confessional. Some of these genres owe their historical cultural origin to the sermons and testimonies of old-time revivalist meetings.

However, Pilavachi also strongly distances his ministry from the excesses of the Toronto Blessing. On the contrary, he asserts "the missing gift of the Spirit which we need to rediscover is perseverance, the ability to get up and keep going one more day."[27] Worship, he affirms, is not just specific musical acts of devotion, but a lifestyle as well. It becomes mere entertainment unless it "illuminates Jesus and does not obscure Jesus." Moreover, he stresses that it is not the job of para-church organizations such as Soul Survivor to "disciple" those who are converted. This is the task of the churches, whom he values highly and wishes to help where he can. One way he has helped is to publish an accessible book about the Bible for new youth converts called *StoryLines*.

It is hardly surprising, then, that Pilavachi is now an establishment figure in the Charismatic movement, for example, being recently appointed President of St. John's College Nottingham. For an irrepressibly grandstanding pastor who led a C of E plant for nineteen years without being formally theologically trained (he was finally ordained deacon in 2012), this was a doubtless unexpected yet timely recognition of his perceived contribution to the evangelization of youth.

His perception of his career as its present phase probably nears its end is not easy to discern. To interviewers from the religious press, he tells a standard and not very revealing story. He was converted two months before his sixteenth birthday, during a tough adolescence being brought up by atheist parents. He went onto a hill (a frequent motif of conversion accounts), knelt down on the wet grass, and prayed. He didn't feel any different, but knew his life had changed. He became a bad accountant, knowing that what he was doing was not what he was gifted at, and from the age of

26. See 24 above.
27. www.Istillilluminate.co.uk/interview-with-mike-pilavachi.

Big and Bigger

twenty-one to twenty-two desperately wanted to help young people, whom he loves for their openness, honesty, and vulnerability. "Yet the Lord had me doing accountancy until I was 29. I would say to the Lord, 'This can't be it,' but then I came to a place of acceptance and I learned to be satisfied in Him. Looking back, those were not my wasted years, they were God's preparation. The Lord uses suffering to refine us and make us fruitful."

When asked about the future prospects for Soul Survivor, he says he doesn't know. "There's no grand strategy, just God's will. It's what He's doing that matters, not what we're doing. We want to serve young people for as long as He wants us to."

However, Pilavachi clearly thinks deeply about the complexities of engagement with contemporary culture. Asked the question "How does Soul Survivor stay relevant to culture but at the same time remain distinct from it?" He responds that the gospel must be presented in "the language of the people you are going to." However, "What we mustn't do is get that confused with what is the essence of the Gospel and what we're calling people to. We don't want to get wrapped up in consumerism, in sexuality. . . . The Gospel is counter cultural, but the Jesus who preached the counter cultural gospel preached it in a way others could understand. As long as we recognise the distinctive of that, I hope we will be alright." He characterizes the task as to "build a bridge into their culture and then go back across the bridge with them."

Clearly, Pilavachi recognizes there is an issue to be addressed, and, in response to a question at an academic conference,[28] he confesses that his big regret personally is the festivals. Since these are the foundation of his reputation, this is a major statement. He didn't preach the right gospel, he confesses, failing to tell the youth about the cost and commitment of the Christian life, and instead promising "revival around the corner." As a consequence, they weren't prepared for real life, which is a vale of tears. "To my shame, we preached a consumer gospel." This courageous public reflection highlights the complex issue that dominates the following chapters: *what is the relationship between the Charismatic and contemporary British secular cultures, and how will it affect the future of the C of E?*

---

28 225 [***]. See 222 [***] above.

CROOKES AND TRINITY

Holy Trinity Brompton and Soul Survivor Watford are not typical Charismatic congregations, not least because both are closely associated with Charismatic organizations, Alpha and Soul Survivor, which have a higher profile even than themselves. St. Thomas Crookes Sheffield (Crookes) and Holy Trinity Cheltenham (Trinity) are both more typical examples of large and growing Charismatic hub churches, led by their rectors, Mick Woodhead and Mark Bailey respectively.

The organizational structure of these congregations, especially of Crookes, is very complex. The first subdivision of Crookes is, confusingly, into seven "churches": Family Church, Student Church, Kids Church, Young Adult Church, Internationals Church, Youth Church, and Community Church.[29] This represents a highly developed segmentation strategy, including the separate category of young adults emphasized by Mike Pilavachi. The different "churches" have their own activities and their own leader(s), but come together on Sundays for "gatherings" (services). However, different "gatherings" are described as being oriented towards families or students. The issue therefore arises as to how the congregation as a whole can engage with members of different demographic segments so as to develop a truly congregational identity. This issue arises doubtless partly as a result of the congregation's rapid recent growth, but also of a segmentation strategy which implies that different activities and styles of worship are appropriate for different age groups.

The next lower level of organization is into "clusters." These have different labels in different congregations (e.g., HTB and Trinity), but all are intended as "missional communities," a currently popular evangelizing tactic. They consist in Crookes of between twenty and thirty people. They each have their own particular vision for mission, which they themselves have chosen, and they are led by lay people. Their aim is to reach out to various specific groups of people outside the church, and some of them may do this by planting themselves in other areas of Sheffield, sometimes in collaboration with other congregations. The relative autonomy of these clusters presents in principle an issue of control and accountability, and places a major onus of responsibility on Crookes' leaders, and on the lay leadership training systems which they provide.

---

29. www.stthomascrookes.org/welcome/staff.

Big and Bigger

Below clusters come cells, the traditional small group unit of eight to twelve people typical of churches of all sorts and of other voluntary organizations and movements. A cell is "a small group of disciples supporting each other through prayer, Bible, fun, and friendship." Each cluster has two or more cells within it which support their cluster. So "churches," "clusters," and "cells" operate both inside and outside Crookes, an organizational structure which surely implies a sacrificial level of participation and commitment on the part of members. No wonder the web page tries to reassure: "We encourage everyone to get involved in as many of these layers of church life as they can."

The size and organization of these congregations raises several issues, which I have already noted. The issue of *accountability and control* is addressed in the last section of this chapter. A second issue concerns *segmentation* and possible lack of congregational cohesion. One way in which leaders seek to mitigate this centrifugal risk is to emphasize continuously the congregational identity. At Trinity, Mark Bailey even labels a series of Sunday talks "We are Trinity."[30] In the first, entitled "The Plumbline," he quotes the testimony of a member: "Trinity is special because it opens its arms and welcomes people, even sceptics and doubters. That's the secret Trinity has, what makes it so special and makes me bring my friends along." In another talk, entitled "A New Kind of Normal," he castigates churches that have no contact with the unchurched, or that define themselves by what they are against rather than what they are for. In contrast, "We are Trinity, I am Trinity, you are Trinity. Say it to the person next to you. When people say to me 'You're Trinity aren't you, Mark? You're not normal, are you?' I love it."

Social identity is strengthened not only by emphasizing who you are as a group, but also who you are not. Bailey clearly indicates that Trinity is not a congregation which is only for the "churchy," nor zealously against error. The C of E, he observes, fails to emulate Jesus Christ, who dealt with the disreputable, brought them to church, and made them its leaders. "None of them would have been accepted by the Church of England for ministry, I can guarantee that," he promises, contrasting the C of E with Trinity, where ordinary people can lead.

Mick Woodhead of Crookes, at the age of sixty-three nearing retirement, is even more forthright. The church talks about things that don't

---

30. www.trinitycheltenham/talks&videos.

matter, insignificant rubbish, he pronounces.[31] "I don't give two hoots whether a bishop is a man or a woman or anything else," providing they are doing the work of a bishop, that is, mission, and not going up to London and chairing committees. That is a political statement, says Woodhead. He will soon get a letter, he jokes: "Dear Mick, we were going to make you a bishop but we heard your sermon!"

Clearly, to judge by these examples, the leaders of large Charismatic congregations tend to be self-confident, long-serving, middle-aged men, sometimes working with their wife as a more junior staff member (e.g., Gumbel, Bailey). They present themselves as typical of their members. That is, they are ordinary people facing many problems, but also blessed by the gifts God has given them, and active in transforming themselves, their city, and the world. In this sense they (the leaders) are the prototypical embodiment of how they wish the congregation to perceive itself ("We are Trinity, I am Trinity, you are Trinity," says Bailey). This means that the congregation can recognize and respect them as "one of us," and also get a clearer idea of who "we" are from what they say and how they behave.[32] Like its leaders, the congregation can be an active, assertive, independent, and transforming organization. So adherents' identification with the leader strengthens their identification with the congregation, and at the same time gives the leader some legitimacy and authority to introduce further changes.

As part of their representative role, these leaders ensure that clear and simple vision statements are emphasized. For Crookes this is "Meet friends, meet God, live life better" (an interesting order). Trinity is "called to make committed followers of Jesus, who change communities and nations for Him." Indeed, the very name of the congregations themselves is simplified and shortened, to "Trinity" and "Crookes." The labels are deliberately "dechurchified": services become gatherings or celebrations; priests, vicars, or ministers become pastors (who always wear open-neck shirts); sermons become talks; and Holy Communion becomes the Breaking of Bread. Once again, congregational identity is being reinforced by difference.

There has been much recent emphasis in Evangelical theology on social justice as a central component of the gospel, and therefore of evangelism. This has manifested itself in the community service component of both these congregations' programs. At Crookes, for example, "Love Sheffield mission days involve serving our local community to show God's love

31. www.stthomascrookes.org/resource/vision-2014-morning.
32. Haslam, *The New Psychology of Leadership*.

to the people of Sheffield."[33] This involves giving away chocolates, drinks, and flowers, litter picking and street cleaning, homeless outreach, and club outreach. Homeless outreach involves offering a meal and eating it together with homeless people as a missional community, reading the Bible and praying for one another. Food, hot drinks, and prayer are the staple offerings. Mick Woodhead describes these activities as "a community of beautiful people doing beautiful things for a beautiful God to beautiful people around us."[34] His mission strategy is doing beautiful things, starting by smiling at people. Trinity provides similar services to the disadvantaged, including running food and clothing banks, offering kitchen, laundry, and showering facilities, and free financial advice.

These charitable activities are based on the belief that showing love and care to needy people is an evangelical demonstration of God's love for individuals. The underlying assumption appears to be that it is the individual who is the recipient of God's love, and that enhanced justice follows from the increasing number of individuals whose needs are met. This individualist perspective plays to the organizational strengths of the congregation within its local community, as well as to the traditional Evangelical Protestant emphasis on the relationship of the individual to God. It relieves the congregation of the need to engage in political analysis and activity aimed at reducing the structural causes of inequality.

Overall, Crookes and Trinity are examples of large and growing Charismatic congregations located in cities with a considerable student population. Although they are associated with New Wine and Alpha, their powerfully led organizations are typical of the core strength of the Charismatic movement's organizational form in the UK. At the same time they demonstrate its underlying weakness: autonomous and independent organizations, congregations, and ministries concentrating so hard on their primary aims of evangelism and growth that they do not have a great deal to do with each other.

OVER THE EDGE

The C of E has very different control issues with its Calvinist and Charismatic elements. The Calvinists spend their time politically testing the limits of institutional governance; Charismatics simply fall over the edge

33. www.stthomascrookes.org/live-life-better/lovesheffield.
34. www.stthomascrookes.org/resource/commitment-2014-evening.

periodically. Such dramas always seem to catch people by surprise, but they are predictable, given the rhetoric and practice of Charismatic leaders and the inadequacy of oversight and control.

A notorious such drama historically was the scandal of the Nine O'clock Service.[35] In brief, a group of musicians led by Chris Brain established a service for youth at Crookes in the 1980s which "combined left-wing politics, a Wimberite emphasis on miracles, and hard-core electronic music." Both their explicit politics and their specific type of music were different from standard Charismatic practice, which was possibly a reason for their departure from Crookes in 1991. Brain was ordained as a priest in the C of E in 1992, and his community became the first Anglican Extra-Parochial parish. In 1995 some members of the Nine O'clock community complained about abuse of power, and Brain admitted to improper conduct with twenty female members. The leadership team resigned, the community collapsed, and Brain left the priesthood. A curate at St. Thomas Crookes from 1992–95, Mark Stibbe,[36] criticized the Bishop and the Archdeacon of Sheffield for failing to spot the growth of cult-like features in the Nine O'clock Service, but admitted that unaccountable individualism was already apparent when they were still at Crookes.

Ironically, it is Mark Stibbe who is the central figure in the following case study. The fundamental element in Charismatic structures, I argued (p. 108), is (leader + congregation) or (leader + organization). Stibbe's career demonstrates the complex nature of these relationships and how they can unravel. The story is not a relatively simple one of the abuse of power for predatory purposes, as was the case with the Nine O'clock Service, but rather concerns how a leader sought to introduce radical change in a congregation. As such, it cannot possibly be construed in terms of "rotten apples" and poor supervision, but rather has to be explained systemically as a consequence of the Charismatic culture.

Stibbe (born 1960) is extravagantly gifted. Having obtained a first-class honors degree in English at Cambridge University and a PhD in theology, he has written academic theology, popular theology, literary criticism, novels, humor, and children's books. He is also an outstandingly clear speaker. He therefore had no difficulty in understanding the rhetoric of the Charismatic movement and in working out its logical implications

---

35. Howard, *The Rise and Fall of the Nine O'clock Service*; www.independent.co.uk/news/bishop-failed-to-control-cult.

36. www.managementexchange.com/story/restoring-faith-institution . . . .

Big and Bigger

for change in congregational organization and practice. But successful and lasting implementation of change over the long term proved a bridge too far. Why this was so is a matter for conjecture. Any explanation may well include consideration of the man and the congregation, but it also has to refer to the process of the change project, and especially to the Charismatic culture, which constitutes a major element of the context.

The course of events is typically characterized in management theory as a project of organizational transformational change. Indeed, the change program at St. Andrews Chorleywood, where Stibbe was vicar, was itself reported in the management literature.[37] To start the story from the beginning, St. Andrews has historically been one of the two most influential Charismatic congregations in the UK (the other being HTB). Its vicar was, from 1977 to 1997, David Pytches, who was responsible for inviting John Wimber to England, thereby instigating the so-called Third Wave of Charismatic renewal. He also founded the New Wine festival and network, and sponsored the Soul Survivor festival and organization under Mike Pilavachi. These are currently, after Alpha, the two most prominent Charismatic organizations. Both of these were soon independent of St. Andrews. Stibbe, having been a curate at St. Thomas Crookes, was thus appointed to lead a landmark congregation in succession to a hero of the Charismatic movement, a hard act indeed to follow.

After several years of ministry at St. Andrews, Stibbe was dissatisfied with the congregation's direction. He felt that "evangelism was not in its top ten priorities,"[38] and that its new members were attracted from other local churches rather than being new converts into the faith. This was, he reasoned, because its evangelistic strategy was to attract people to a gathered church rather than going out to meet and serve them in the community: a cruise ship rather than a fleet of lifeboats. In contact with his previous church, Crookes, he decided to adopt their method of clusters (see p. 114), which he was to later rename Mission Shaped Communities (MSCs). In order to help him lead the major organizational change which this strategy required, Stibbe "hired" (his word) Andrew Williams, a former lawyer and recent ordinand, as his curate in 2003.

The accounts of what happened next are mostly written by Williams. They include the two management articles cited above, and his

---

37 www.blogs.wsj.com/management/2010/06/17/leadership-from-the-inside-out-part-ii; www.nomad.lybsyn.com/nomad_7_mark_stibbe_and_reconstructing_church.

38. www.christianitytoday.com/assets/10233.pdf.

contributions to an article in the magazine *Christianity Today* on the use of mid-size groups in evangelism. But the most detailed account is a book jointly authored by Stibbe and Williams, entitled simply *Breakout*.[39] Even allowing for his own authorship of the majority of the accounts, it seems that Williams played the major part in the events that followed. He reports "Mark asked me to take charge of developing a new church strategy," and "Looking at our current organization, I saw a gap. . . . I went searching for some 'in between' models of church, and found one in Sheffield, England" at Crookes. In November 2003 "I stood in front of a nearly full church to report on my new strategy." A month later he was telling twelve volunteer leaders of putative MSCs to set their own mission, and to take risks. When asked for advice, he responded "I don't know. Why don't you pray about it?" By January 2005, seventeen MSCs had been established.

When the church building was closed for refurbishment in 2005, Stibbe, Williams, and the full staff team decided not to hire a replacement venue, but to decentralize worship to the MSCs, meeting centrally only once per month in a school hall. The response was so overwhelming that about a thousand additional adherents signed up for MSCs, and around twenty new MSCs were formed in January 2005 alone. It was, Williams reports with uncharacteristic understatement, "quite an intense period." Stibbe stresses the huge cost to his family, and his terror when he later realized "I've just given away the whole church."

When refurbishment was completed in September, the MSC leaders almost unanimously reported that they wanted the "temporary" arrangements to continue. MSC leaders were provided with a training course, and Stibbe wrote learning guides to help them conduct worship. The mantra of "low control, high accountability" quoted by Crookes was actualized in terms of "huddles," where MSC leaders gave accounts to each other of what was happening in their MSC. By 2008, there were thirty-two MSCs operating within a radius of 25 miles from St. Andrews, with more than 1,600 adherents. Churches from Europe and North and South America were asking for advice, and St. Andrews was offering conferences and advice on how to implement this new model. They joined a learning community of fifteen European pioneer churches, and their book *Breakout* won a Book of the Year award.

But by the end of 2008 Stibbe and Williams had both left, Stibbe to establish his own "ministry," The Father's House Trust, and Williams to be

---

39. Stibbe, *Breakout*.

Big and Bigger

minister of a church in Connecticut, USA. While it is difficult to discover what happened next, there are several indications in the current St. Andrews website that things have changed yet again. A new vicar, David White, of impeccable Charismatic pedigree, has been installed. However, the number of missional communities has radically decreased. The list provided totals nine, though it is stated that "This list is not intended to be exhaustive, but gives a general overview of a number of the many missional activities in which our church and its members are currently engaged." The finances are in a rocky state, with White describing the church as desperate for injections of cash, having a focus on paying the bills, and lurching from one financial crisis to the next. "I believe the church is heading for the uplands of God's blessing," he affirms, but "after a few rocky years in the valley."

In its Mission Action Plan, submitted to the Diocese of St. Albans,[40] the congregation outlines its current perceived strengths, challenges, and changes. The strengths are primarily located in its being "church of Word and Spirit; the quality of our Biblical teaching; our prayer ministry . . ." [but not, note, "our missional communities"]. Moreover, "Our church family is aware of the various challenges we've encountered" [without specifying them]. And they are open to consider changes, "Yet we are aware, above all, of the importance of continuing to sense and prioritize God's leading, rather than forcing the direction or pace of change, and we want to avoid the temptation of becoming too programme-oriented" [a temptation to which, by implication, we succumbed under Stibbe and Williams]. Instead, the emphasis is to be on ensuring inspiring worship, welcome and hospitality, and launching a "renewed strategy for small groups in the church." Prominence in the website is given to these "Lifegroups," which, to judge by the website images, are led by Christians of mature years and experience.

Additionally, the new associate vicar has been promoted from a neighboring church. Her appointment was possibly designed to rebuild bridges after the previous regime had, on its own admission, failed to anticipate the adverse reaction of local clergy within a 25-mile radius to the sudden descent onto their parishes of MSCs from St. Andrews.

The story of St. Andrews continues to be written, as does that of Mark Stibbe. His ministry, the Father's House Trust, was based on Stibbe's own experience of being deserted by his father at a young age. Its purpose was to encourage people to receive "the Father Heart revelation" and so "heal orphan hearts." After the breakdown of his marriage, however, Stibbe

---

40. www.st-andrews.org.uk/mission-action-plan.

resigned from his post as director in 2012, and is now a "creative writer, blogger, and script doctor,"[41] offering help with the writing of books, essays, and dissertations. He describes himself as searching for the real Mark rather than the "slick religious Mark."

How are we to understand the stories of St. Andrews and of Mark Stibbe? There are several possible explanations, at different levels of analysis, none of them mutually exclusive, and all of them matters of conjecture and hypothesis. The first concerns the events from 2003 to 2008 construed as an *organizational change program*. The management literature suggests a low rate of success for programmatic interventions in which a standard recipe for change is applied to an organization regardless of its history and culture and of its surrounding context. There are indications that this was indeed the case with St. Andrews. The program was imported from Crookes, and from 2007 was promoted internationally as "the" tool for evangelism. No attention seems to have been paid to the surrounding congregations, who were certainly stakeholders, and no plans appear to have been in place regarding how to finance the MSCs. With the primary accountabilities of the MSCs being to their fellow leaders in other MSCs, the issue of control appears to have been ducked, and the identity of the church as a single congregation was probably inadequately met by monthly combined meetings.

A second possible explanation relates to *events in 2008*. Stibbe had always considered the Toronto Blessing as the possible "sea-fret" of a Fourth Wave (the "Third Wave" of Charismatic Renewal in the UK being started by the introduction of John Wimber to the UK by Stibbe's eminent predecessor, David Pytches). Perhaps searching for the Fourth Wave itself, and for an opportunity to bring it to the UK, Stibbe went to Florida in May to experience the "Lakeland Outpouring." This was led by one Todd Bentley, and was strongly focussed on the "healing" of such conditions as cancer, deafness, diabetes, paralysis, and death.[42] Bentley attributed his power to the Holy Spirit, but also to his angels, one of whom was called Emma. He was given to shouting "Bam" and "Fire, Fire, Fire," and to occasionally kicking those seeking healing in a vigorous attempt to impart the Spirit. He claimed to have raised from the dead between twenty and thirty people. He resigned from the revival in August amid financial and sexual scandals.

Stibbe returned and reported in the church website "During the meetings, deaf ears have been opened, blind eyes have begun to see, the lame

41. www.thescriptdoctor.org.uk.
42. www.churchtimes.co.uk/articles/2008/4-july/news/hype-or-fact.

Big and Bigger

have leaped for joy, and the dead have been raised. None of this is hype. It is fact." Stibbe introduced the Lakeland "anointing" to St. Andrews at weekly Sunday evening meetings, known as Fire meetings. He also supported the Dudley Outpouring in the West Midlands, led by the Revival Fires organization.[43] The Revival Fires website offers courses at its School of the Supernatural at a cost of £3,175, which will enable students to "move into supernatural signs, wonders, and miracles." Stibbe also preached internationally at conferences sponsored by Catch the Fire ministries, the new branding of the Toronto Airport Fellowship after it had been expelled from Vineyard Ministries.[44] Stibbe's support for these "Outpourings," on top of the radical and draining program of organizational change, may have been a bridge too far, either for the congregation, or the C of E hierarchy, or both.

A third and more general level of explanation for the events at St. Andrews, however, locates them within the context of the *Charismatic culture*. This culture emphasizes several value priorities, which tend to be compatible with current late-modern culture, particularly the youth sub-culture. It favors flexibility over structure, freedom over constraint, innovation over tradition, and spontaneity over restraint and rules. It values risk and excitement. Finally, it believes that all of these preferences can be achieved by taking action on one's own initiative, and it does not doubt its own capacity to succeed in this enterprise.

Echoes of these value preferences and beliefs can be seen throughout the story of the organizational change at St. Andrews. The desired change, it was assumed, could be engineered structurally, and people were perfectly capable of leading the MSCs with the minimum of training, since all were gifted and empowered by the Holy Spirit. They certainly got the flexibility they wanted, as they decided their own aims and methods and learned by trial and error. They were accountable to each other, not to the C of E hierarchy, and they acted as an autonomous congregation with little reference to their surrounding parishes.

We should remember Stibbe's story as well as that of St. Andrews. Charismatic culture maintains a biblical pre-modern worldview of reality in which supernatural events are believed to be constantly interspersed with natural events, as God determines. Hence the miraculous resurrection of the dead and the healing of physical illness is perceived to be perfectly possible today, as is God's use of one of His servants to channel the power

---

43. www.revivalfires.org.uk.
44. www.catchthefire.com.

of His Holy Spirit to achieve these ends. And if that servant is himself wounded and broken (for example, deserted by his natural father), so much the better is he qualified to heal. In Calvinists' view, God saves sinners from their sin and sanctifies them by His grace through the faithful preaching of the Word. For Charismatics, He heals sufferers from their brokenness and inspires them by His Holy Spirit so that they are gifted to lead. Perhaps Stibbe went wrong only insofar as he acted upon these values and beliefs only too faithfully. He unfortunately paid the personal price exacted from some charismatic Charismatics. The case of St. Andrews and Stibbe thus leads into the consideration of the Charismatic culture, which dominates the subsequent chapters.

CHAPTER 7

The Charismatic Self

THE SELF IN THEORY: ITS DEVELOPMENT AND PRESENTATION

CALVINISTS ARE PROUD OF the fact that they are in conflict with most of late-modern culture. As far as they are concerned, this only proves that they are on the right path: God's way, as opposed to man's. Such a posture continues to attract and retain a reactionary minority, which will always remain a minority. For Charismatics, however, the relationship with contemporary culture is much more complex.

There are some elements of culture with which they are totally in accord, while others grate alarmingly. And it does not necessarily follow that it is only the areas of agreement that attract adherents; exceptionality can also prove attractive to various different constituencies. For it is a truism that "contemporary late-modern culture" is a hard concept to justify, given the multiplicity of sub-cultures that flourish in our pluralist societies. In this chapter I will seek first to give a very general account of the social trends affecting the *concept of the self* that characterize late-modern societies such as our own; second, to review the *empirical evidence* for such trends in the UK; and third, to demonstrate that at least in this one area (the construction of the self), Charismatic and general culture are in *marked agreement*, with one crucial exception. Subsequent chapters will deal with other aspects of contemporary culture—the value placed on change, and beliefs about the nature of reality—where the coincidence may not be so close.

The late-modern societies within the globalizing world are characterized, firstly, by *increased mobility and rapid change*.[1] Increased mobility occurs between places of residence, employer organizations, occupations, and indeed, social roles of all sorts. It results in social and personal relationships becoming more temporary and provisional in nature. People have to form relationships rapidly, and consequently it becomes more important to make a good initial impression, and so gain rapid acceptance, trust, and cooperation. This rapid pace of change is often unpredictable, for some an exciting new experience, but for others risky and threatening.[2]

Second, *capitalist market mechanisms*, whether unfettered or controlled, increasingly dominate the global economy. Global and international corporations sell to tailored and segmented consumer markets. They create new "needs" not only for goods, but also for services, experiences, and life-styles. These are all commodified, giving the appearance of value and usefulness, but only meeting in temporary ways people's real social, psychological, and spiritual needs.[3]

Third, *late-modern societies are being "hollowed out,"* with many of the institutions and associations of public civil society losing their attraction and giving way to increasingly private and personal modes of interaction.[4] In place of roles voluntarily played out in public and structured interactions, intimate personal relationships become more central to one's life.[5] Anthony Giddens terms these relationships "pure," in the sense that they serve no other purpose than the relationship itself; they do not support kinship groups or satisfy obligations or support a social or political cause. Such relationships are reflexive—they have to be reviewed and worked at if they are to be maintained.

And finally, there are two trends that have been widely recognized only in the last decade. The first concerns the increasing *reach and influence of the media*. Both "traditional" and social media have increased at an amazing speed,[6] making unlimited connectivity and storage of infor-

1. Scholte, *Globalization*.
2. Beck, *World Risk Society*.
3. Bauman, *Globalization: The Human Consequences*.
4. Putnam, *Bowling Alone*.
5. Giddens, *Modernity and Self-Identity*.
6. Castells, *Rise of the Network Society*.

The Charismatic Self

mation available globally. Both types of media are increasingly owned and controlled by corporations, with the consequence that views of the world and one's place within it are usually commoditized. Since the market requires new needs for new commodities to be generated, there is a constant expectation on consumers to embrace new views of themselves and the world. Overall, the ubiquity of the media and the constant switching between virtual and physical communication create many more opportunities for the development and display of one's self.

The second recent trend is the *accelerating inequality* within and between late-modern societies,[7] together with its malign consequences and the increasingly vocal and organized opposition to it. Capital is increasing at a faster rate than income, an apparently inherent feature of modern capitalism.[8]

These trends find their socio-psychological expression in the growth of *individualism*, which is usually defined in contradistinction to collectivism. Harry Triandis defines individualism as "a social pattern that consists of loosely linked individuals who view themselves as independent of collectives; are primarily motivated by their own needs, rights, and the contracts they have established with others; give priority to their personal goals over the goals of others; and emphasise rational analyses of the advantages and disadvantages to associating with others."[9] This social pattern is internalized psychologically as one's personal identity (viewing one's self as uniquely different from others), rather than as social identities (seeing one's self as a member of various categories of person).[10]

In a famous research study conducted a quarter of a century ago, Robert Bellah noted the growth of individualism in American life.[11] In their increasing urge to be independent of such institutions as the home, the church, the employer organization, and government, Americans were running the risk of personal alienation and a loss of moral anchors, asking when in doubt "Does it feel good?" rather than "Is it good?" Bellah distinguished several different forms of individualism, with religious individualists stressing their personal relationship with God.

---

7. Wilkinson, *The Spirit Level*.
8. Piketty, *Capital in the Twenty-First Century*.
9. Triandis, *Individualism and Collectivism*, 4.
10. R. Jenkins, *Social Identity*.
11. Bellah, *Habits of the Heart*.

It is in the nature of the late-modern self and the personal identity that these social trends are most clearly evident. The self is ever more reflexive[12] (although, of course, self-consciousness itself is an age-old characteristic of humankind). That is, we are increasingly aware of our self, and construct our lives as a self-narrative. We are now treating our lives as a long-term project, an account of our achievement (or failure to achieve) the plans and projects we have formed for our selves. Such a story of the self is beginning to supplant traditional narratives based on age-stage constructions, where we "naturally" fulfill particular roles at different stages of our family and working lives, with the passages between the stages often marked by rituals.

Thus our self becomes something of which we are constantly aware, and which we are engaged in finding and creating, managing, modifying, developing, and repairing. These are all important tasks, since the day-to-day function of the self is to help us regulate and direct our social behavior. The wealthier members of late-modern societies employ a whole army of professionals to aid them in these tasks: such people as personal trainers, counselors, and therapists.[13] Others, less rich, use commoditized therapies or self-help manuals. The need to have recourse to these aids points to the often fragile nature of our selves. When our personal narrative breaks down or becomes untenable, we speak of "finding our true self," and we become vulnerable to those who wish to impose their narrative upon us. There are always alternatives available.

The supposed independent nature of the self is emphasized by the late-modern concentration on *authenticity*. The authentic self was contrasted with the false self by such theorists as R. D. Laing,[14] who urged us to act true to our self rather than in accordance with a self imposed on us by others. In particular, we need to be able to express our emotions, and indeed, displays of emotion are often taken to be evidence of authenticity, courageously revealing "the true self." One way of being perceived as authentic is to act in the same way across different social situations, since such consistent behavior tends to be causally attributed to the actor rather than to the situation.[15] Acting the role appropriate to the social situation, on the other hand, risks perceptions of pretence.

12. Baumeister, "The Nature and Structure of the Self."
13. Rieff, *The Triumph of the Therapeutic*.
14. Laing, *The Divided Self*.
15. Ross, *The Person and the Situation*.

The Charismatic Self

Being authentic is more easily said than done, however, since we spend much of our time in self-presentation to and for others.[16] Frequently we present the self we think that others want or expect to see rather than the self as we believe it to be. Alternatively, we use a particular self-presentation in order to achieve our social purposes. Self-presentation is increasingly important in the light of the four major trends of late-modernity outlined above. We have to be skilled self-presenters in order to make a rapid favorable impression in the new relationships into which our *increased mobility* is thrusting us. It is our perceived personality that matters now, not our proven character.[17] We develop all sorts of social tricks to be immediately attractive personalities, for example, humorous self-deprecation and exaggerated interest in the other. Self-presentation is also a vital skill in *consumerist society*, since we ourselves become commoditized, and have to "sell ourselves" as desirable employees, friends, and group members, as well as actually selling goods or services on behalf of our employers. The *hollowing out of society* means that, being more dependent on "pure" rather than "given" relationships, we have to attract others into intimacy by skilled self-presentation. And finally, the growth of *social media* has resulted in a vastly increased opportunity to disseminate presentations of one's self in immense detail, since information capacity is now in practice unlimited and reach is global. All that is required is someone to pay attention to the resulting innumerable technicolor records of individual lives.

It is hardly surprising that this recent increased emphasis on self-presentation has led to a tendency to greatly admire the self which we are presenting: in a word, to *narcissism*.[18] Narcissism may even decrease our capacity for "pure" relationships characterized by intimacy, as we are too busy admiring ourselves to meet the needs of the other. An entirely different outcome arises from the consumerist need for self-presentation in those service industries that require face-to-face relationships with the client or customer. In such situations, employers require from staff "authentic" displays of the appropriate emotions, as customers are alleged to be able to tell when it is "all an act." The requirement to actually feel the emotion, or to pretend it with such consummate skill that no-one can tell the difference, has been aptly termed "emotional labor."[19] The self has become commod-

16. Goffman, *Relations in Public*.
17. Sennett, *The Corrosion of Character*.
18. Lasch, *The Culture of Narcissism*.
19. Hochschild, *The Managed Heart*.

itized for the consumer's benefit. This example reinforces the universality of the importance of the self and its presentation. It is not only the wealthy who are concerned about their selves (although only they can afford the professional facilitators). Those in low-paid jobs, and those who have to deal with social service agencies to obtain benefits, also have to manage and present themselves.

In sum, trends in late-modern society have increased the attention we pay to our personal identities. How we manage, and in particular, how we present, our selves has become crucial to our social and personal adjustment. What happens when these social and psychological changes impact such established institutions as the C of E, with its long-established role distinctions and requirements?

LATE MODERNITY IN THE UK

These theoretical ideas may or may not coincide with our perceptions of the social situation in the UK. Although they are derived from empirical research, that research was largely conducted in the USA, and we have to examine more local data before we can be confident that the trends described in the previous section are true of the UK. Fortunately we have recently acquired some outstandingly good evidence: the British Social Attitudes Survey has completed thirty years of polling, asking many of the same questions from 1983 to 2013, and its thirtieth report details key trends over this period.[20]

The disentangling of true "generational" trends from other forms of attitude change is a difficult task, since changes may be equally attributable to major events, for example, the global recession beginning in 2008, and the AIDS epidemic. The main method used is to distinguish respondents by the decade of their birth (which has led to the identification in popular discourse of such cohorts as the baby boomers, generation X, generation Y, and now generation Z). The major trends are as follows.

First, the percentage of UK respondents giving a *religious affiliation* of any sort has decreased from 68 percent to 52 percent over the thirty years. This decrease is largely due to the halving of those with an affiliation to the C of E, from 40 percent to 20 percent. Second, affiliation to any *political party* has decreased from 87 percent to 76 percent, but of the latter only 31 percent say they identify very or fairly strongly with a party. Third, attitudes

20. www.natcen.ac.uk/our-research/research/british-social-attitudes.

to *sexual behavior* have radically changed, with those thinking homosexuality is always wrong decreasing from 50 percent to 22 percent. Fourth, a woman's *right to choose* whether to have an abortion was supported by 37 percent in 1983, but by 62 percent in 2013.

Interestingly, these attitudinal changes apply to those expressing a religious affiliation nearly as much as to the unreligious, emphasizing that these are society-wide generational changes. Other widely recognized changes cannot be confidently attributed to generational effects, however. For example, the percentage of people thinking unemployment benefits are too low is lower in 2013, and there is higher agreement with the statement "If welfare benefits weren't so generous, people would learn to stand on their own two feet." However, the Survey's authors attribute these findings more to the hard line on social benefits adopted by New Labour than to generational change. Indeed, 97 percent of 2013 respondents believe that it is the government's duty to provide health care as required, and to ensure a decent standard of living for the elderly.

Changes that cannot with confidence be attributed to generational change, but which are certainly noteworthy, concern trust in various societal institutions. There is a declining level of trust in politicians, bankers, the press, and the police, but this decline does not apply to institutions in general. The royal family, the National Health Service, and trade unions have not suffered equally, although all have had ups and downs along the way. On the other hand, the institution of marriage certainly seems to have decreased in popularity, according to the Office for National Statistics.[21] There were 405,000 marriages in 1971, but only 232,000 in 2009. Marriages occurred at a later age, and 40 percent of all marriages were remarriages.

Returning to the attitudes of the religious, an Ipsos MORI poll of 2011[22] found that those identifying themselves as Christians in the UK census of 2011 (54 percent of respondents) were not in favor of many policies which apparently favored the church. For example, the majority of these respondents did not believe religion should exercise a special influence on public policy; they were not in favor of an official state religion; and they did not think that religious education should teach students to believe in Christianity. And, incidentally, they approved of homosexuality, abortion, and euthanasia. It should be noted, however, that when asked why they had identified themselves as Christians, 72 percent said it was because they had

21. www.ons.gov.uk/ons/dep171778_258307.pdf.
22. www.ipsos-mori.com/researchpublications/researcharchive/2921/religious.

been baptized, whereas only 28 percent cited belief in the church's teaching. Annual attendance at any services other than baptisms, weddings and funerals was zero for 49 percent. Nevertheless, these findings reinforce those of the British Social Attitudes Survey that general trends also apply to the religious.

Clearly, there is a major leap from these UK survey findings to the general social psychological theorizing regarding the self that I outlined in the first section of this chapter. However, this gap is reduced a little by a recent UK government citizenship survey entitled *Future Identities: Changing Identities in the UK*.[23] Its aim is "to consider how changes over the next 10 years will affect identities in the UK," and it projects from the longitudinal data described above to likely future scenarios for personal and social identities.

It identifies several of the same drivers of change as those reviewed in the first section, but places particular emphasis on what it terms "hyper-connectivity," and on increasing social plurality. *Hyper-connectivity* is defined as "the use of multiple communications systems and devices to remain constantly connected to social networks and streams of information." Connectivity is constant and everywhere, easily accessible, information-rich, interactive, and with unlimited storage capacity. One of its consequences is the blurring of identities, for example, between the public and the private (which politician now has a private life?); and between work and home (work intrudes on home at will). *Social plurality* increases as a result of increased immigration and the growth of virtual communities, thus potentially causing problems for social integration. The report also predicts continuing decrease in trust of authorities (but not of all institutions); on the other hand, trust in those known personally is maintained or increased.

In sum, the evidence specifically derived from the UK gives some support to the general theoretical analysis regarding personal identity and the self. People are becoming more likely to develop detailed narratives about themselves and to disclose them freely, with virtual disclosure potentially increasing their audience exponentially. Their relationships of all sorts are more temporary, but personal intimacy and friendship are valued and friends are trusted. Nevertheless, people understandably feel vulnerable and insecure in the face of change and unpredictability. Individuals consider they and everyone else has a right to "be themselves" (for example, if they are gay), and to "choose" (abortion).

23. www.gov.uk/...../future-identities-changing-identities-in-the-uk.

The Charismatic Self

The Charismatic movement in the C of E is closely in tune with these social trends in general, but with a few specific exceptions. In the following sections, I will look in detail at some specific sub-cultural artefacts that clearly evidence this coincidence of cultures. The first is a talk by Charlie Mackesy, a professional artist and frequent contributor to HTB Alpha courses.

CHARMING CHARLIE

The context for this talk,[24] which repays careful textual analysis, is the Holy Spirit weekend. This is an element of the Alpha course located near its end, where members go away for a residential weekend at which it is expected that they may have a spiritual experience of an ecstatic nature, possibly speaking in tongues (glossolalia). Course members may be feeling apprehensive or curious about the weekend, having signed up for a fairly orthodox exploration of the Christian faith but now being faced with something unfamiliar. The talk is one of several which are preparatory to the opportunity for the experience. It therefore mirrors the usual pattern of Charismatic worship, where the talk precedes the "prayer ministry."

The talk is a polished and carefully crafted performance that nevertheless succeeds in giving the impression of informality and spontaneity. Mackesy is disarming, self-deprecatory, and giggles a lot. His performance expertly speaks to the personal identities of the members through Mackesy's own self-disclosure. Indeed, in this respect it resembles all the Charismatic addresses that I reviewed, which contain a degree of self-reference unfamiliar and astonishing to anyone from another Christian tradition.

Mackesy begins by recalling his own first time at a Holy Spirit weekend, twenty years before. He was horrified, he claims, and made a quick exit for a smoke [Implication: I'm just like many of you, wary of what's going to happen, and, like you, I'm a little bit naughty too]. A "prayer leader" asked him if he could pray for him, but he refused, standing on the fringes and wanting to go to the pub [Like you, I don't like feeling coerced, and I'm still a bit naughty]. The prayer leader once again asked his permission to pray for him, and this time he agreed in order to shut him up [Wouldn't we all]. He looked down at the carpet, and smelled the kippers on the leader's breath ("note to leaders: eat mints after breakfast") [We're not po-faced

---

24. www.youtube.com/watch?v=NRMIXjcXLBE/who-is-the-holy-spirit-HTB-alpha-weekend.

Warfare and Waves

and religious here at Alpha, we can make fun of ourselves]. Nothing much happened, a person cried, then it was Amen, experience over. He himself sat down, and felt a strange sense of peace [This is a perfectly normal experience, I can assure you, as an ordinary person like you]. I have a fear of being controlled, explains Mackesy, and then gives a hint of further self-disclosure to come by attributing this independent streak to his physical and sexual abuse at his boarding school between ages seven and thirteen [I have confided my vulnerability to you; it is ok to admit vulnerability, and we can trust one another if we do so]. Anyway, he reassures them, God does not control us, but is gentle and respects us, bringing a quiet liberation.

Just to ram home the absence of coercion, and to dispel the bad associations of the words "Ghost" and "Spirit," Mackesy pokes fun at proselytizers, to whom, he suggests, the appropriate response is "I've got diarrhoea!" He also ridicules those who go round shouting Hallelujah—"we don't do that here" reassures Mackesy. "But I've found joy." "You didn't find it here."

Having presented himself as similar to his audience, reassuring them that both he, and what is going to happen, are perfectly normal, he then enters the main body of his address, which runs through the references to the Holy Spirit in the Bible, from beginning to end. He asks his audience to follow the references in the Bible with him, but gives them the option of reading *Hello* magazine instead. Don't worry, he reassures them, his mind's as chaotic as his hair [but he, like them, can still make sense of the Bible]. After two humorous stories about himself, he gets down to the creation story, where God breathed His spirit into man to make him a living soul.[25] This prompts a story about a girl he met at a conference when he was a teenager. She said she was an occultist, and asked for prayer. "We did, there and then. 'Thank you' she said, but nothing happened." When they met her next morning, she looked at them, her hair was different, and she smiled. "You could tell—she had been given life."

The Holy Spirit inspires craftsmen and artists[26] such as Handel—indeed Mackesy himself started off painting on the streets of London. The Spirit inspired Gideon to fight for God's people though he was weak,[27] and here is he, Charlie, no good at "doing this mic[rophone] bit," but quoting Martin Luther King to the effect that fears pass [I'm just as nervous as you

---

25. Gen 2:7.
26. Exod 30:31.
27. Judg 6:14 & 34.

The Charismatic Self

would be about standing up here performing, i.e., I'm not a professional]. Next, he tells the story of his father's death.

His father was an ardent atheist, but Charlie prayed with him for ten seconds per day. He died in Charlie's arms peacefully, praying "the Lord bless you and keep you," and had added the words "and give you peace" to Charlie's card on the mantelpiece. After his father's death, he did "some bad, crazy stuff (Sorry, I'm ranting on)," and wished he himself had asked for prayer [Prayer can work powerfully for my father, for me, and for you if you ask for it]. You certainly don't have to be religious—I swear at people in traffic, he admits, but prayer works for me even so.

Mackesy's exposition is now into the New Testament. As multiple stories attest, Jesus was filled with the Holy Spirit. He (Mackesy) has always struggled to trust people as a result of the sexual abuse he suffered as a child, and the first person he trusted was Jesus [You too may be damaged, but there is someone you can trust]. Finally, he arrives at the end of the biblical story, the account of the day of Pentecost in the Acts of the Apostles, and the arrival of the Holy Spirit in fulfillment of the prophecy of Joel[28] ("I will pour out my Spirit upon all flesh; and your sons and your daughters shall prophesy, your old men shall dream dreams, your young men shall see visions"). Mackesy tells the story of Mozart and Allegri's Miserere. The Vatican heard the Miserere for the first time and decreed that it was so holy that it should only be played once a year in the Sistine Chapel. Mozart heard it, memorized it, notated it later, and released it to the world, just as Christ released the Holy Spirit to the world at Pentecost.

Having completed the biblical story, Mackesy returns to the beginning of his own story, how "Bushie," bad breath and all, prayed for him at his first Alpha, for which he will be eternally grateful. You may feel awkward, he acknowledges to his audience, but go for it [I felt awkward, and look how it's helped me. I'm no different to you, so it can help you too]. The Holy Spirit is for everyone. He himself prayed with a sick friend—"it's about softening your heart" [And like me, you too can pray with others, bless them and be blessed].

As my bracketed commentary suggests, Mackesy's talk uses his acute understanding of contemporary identity in several ways. He is extremely anxious to avoid any hint of difference between himself and his hearers. He is certainly not the teacher or the authority, nor they the learners and the beginners. Time and again he engages in self-deprecatory banter, thereby

---

28. Joel 3:28.

disarming any resistance to his message and perceptions of manipulation, and generally attracting people to his personality. He also engages in self-disclosure of personal damage and its consequences for his life, enlisting sympathy and trust. At the same time, his account of his subsequent salvation through the Holy Spirit suggested that many of his audience may have similar problems, with the same solution available. In sum, he presents himself as authentic, intimate, and emotionally literate, three key themes of late-modern personal identity. But he also identifies himself strongly with his audience, with the implication that they could be even more like him than they already are. It's not a big step to take.

Mackesy's talk was only one of several leading up to the worship event. An atheist blogger attending the course perceived it as "just the opening salvo in a day-long spiritual assault that was to climax with those attending being induced into speaking in tongues."[29] Nicky Gumbel, who spoke later in the day,[30] also recognized the potential hostility to perceptions of being manipulated. The autonomous and authentic self is indeed a powerful element of contemporary identity, as Gumbel appreciates keenly. From various accounts in the Acts of the Apostles, Gumbel notes the physical manifestations of the believers' experience of the Holy Spirit. He plaintively pleads that he's damned if he mentions them, and damned if he doesn't. If he does, he's accused of "auto-suggestion," and if he doesn't, people complain "Why didn't you warn us in advance that this sort of thing was going to happen?" He then goes on to reassure his hearers that the physical manifestations are unimportant. They are like the tingling of the spine felt by some, but only some, when they are falling in love. Not everyone who receives God's love, poured in by the Holy Spirit, experiences them, and they are really only an unimportant by-product.

Having sought to reassure the course members, Gumbel invites them to ask the Holy Spirit into their lives that very night. Nevertheless, they must not pin everything on tonight or tomorrow morning, for the commitment is throughout their lives and into eternity. Having received God's love, they are then released to express their own love for God. We can reciprocate His love in whatever way suits our personality, and in the way that we would express it to other human beings, however emotional this may be. [Gumbel goes on to a detailed account of speaking in tongues, to

29. www.simonclare.co.uk/site/?tag=nicky-gumbel.

30. www.youtube.com/watch?v=ZxfxaV59rB0/nicky-gumbel-how-can-I-be-filled-with-the-holy-spirit.

which I will refer in chapter 9.] The point to note here is that his appeal features many late-modern attributes of the self. The audience is treated as *autonomous* decision-makers: they invite entry, God does not require it. The relationship involves the *intimacy* of lovers, who should express their love with the full *emotionality* they feel. But they can express it in whatever way suits their *unique personality*; it is between each *individual* one of us and God Himself.

Of course, it does not follow that because Mackesy, Gumbel, and others whom I will quote, demonstrate an acute understanding of the basic elements of the modern self, they are therefore using that knowledge to manipulate people. They are not operating from some position of their own located entirely outside those people's culture. On the contrary, it seems clear that these Charismatics themselves embrace many of contemporary culture's underlying beliefs and values, at least those relating to the self. The origins of their adherence to these beliefs and values may lie as much in their Christian convictions as in their allegiance to contemporary culture. Older leaders such as Pilavachi, Gumbel, and Woodhead may doubtless sometimes find themselves referring to some currently popular cultural artefact in which they have to pretend an interest, but this is mere surface detail. The Charismatic culture, to which they are so devoted and which they express so eloquently, and the contemporary cultural emphasis on the individual self, are in essence largely of a piece. The Charismatic leaders are probably practising what they sincerely believe and value, which entails the obligation to share it with others.

BROKEN BETH

I have described the talks by Mackesy and Gumbel at length because they illustrate the extent to which the contemporary culture of the self in general permeates Charismatic teaching and practice. One particular element that features strongly is the *therapeutic* turn, the self as damaged, and how it may be healed. The following talks by Beth Redman illustrate the prominence of this trend, but examples could just as easily have been taken from similar talks by, for example, Christy Wimber or Mark Stibbe.

Beth Redman "has her own ministry." She is an evangelist, songwriter, singer, and author of several books including *Soul Sister* and *Beautiful*. In 2010 she wrote *God Knows My Name*, which is autobiographical in content. She is devoted to the charity A21, which combats the trafficking of women.

She is married to Matt Redman, a noted worship leader and musician, and has five children. The two talks that I will sample were delivered to Free to Be, a conference for women sponsored by HTB,[31] and to Focus, a residential conference for members of HTB.[32]

Very early in both her talks, Beth introduces the idea that her audience may be feeling vulnerable. She then refers to her own story, which involved, and still involves, very difficult relationships with her parents. She confides (to the women), "There has been a period of my life I haven't spoken about yet. We disclose only when we come to a place of healing." Quoting the biblical story of the healing at the pool of Bethesda, she confides that she too, like the sick man, felt that she had nobody. Her husband was away, and she had no family she could call on. But Jesus said to her, as He said to the man, "Get up." He is here, she tells her audience, to scatter healing, refreshment, and revival. She is proud to be needy of Jesus. Your name is on God's hand, she affirms. She wrote that sentence to her father, signed "yours sincerely, Beth Redman" [whoops and applause from the audience].

The Holy Spirit, she affirms, can transform us from brokenness to beauty, from the ashes of mourning to the celebration of marriage. Walking with her husband in California, she passes by artists painting what could have been a boat. The couple sit and talk about her story, the death of her baby and her miscarriages, and Matt tells her that "remembering leads to rejoicing." On the walk back, the artists' canvases now looked amazing. Jesus is painting for us, healing and comforting us and walking amongst us unseen. "I thank God that He has allowed me to come and tell my story. He knows your story too. The teacher is here. Amen, amen."

Beth's story dominates her talks. She expects others to be equally personally vulnerable as she herself is, and she seeks to reassure them that God can comfort and heal them as He has healed her. The dominance of her personal story is reminiscent of the testimonies of the old time revival meetings. The difference is that those stories were about sin and redemption, holiness and service, whereas hers is about vulnerability, damage, healing, and support.

This perception of, and emphasis on, vulnerability in oneself and others is not limited to a few of the prominent Charismatic speakers, however. As I will also demonstrate from the extremely professional Alpha website, it is a generally emphasized element of the Charismatic culture. The stories

31. www.htb.org.uk/podcast/5837/m4v.
32. www.htb.org.uk/focus.

of various previous Alpha course members are presented in the website,[33] chosen so that a variety of potential members might identify with one of them. The first is entitled *Beautifully Broken*. While the other stories are presented as interview questions and responses, *Beautifully Broken* is simply a personal story. It is the story of Naomi Trenier, who is a speaker at various Alpha and HTB courses, and is brilliantly written and carefully crafted.

Naomi had had unfortunate experiences of church. Whether the preachers were stern and judgmental, or charismatic with slick lights and music, God was hidden. Her compulsion to search for God she attributes to her father: "my dad and his love for me had an awful lot to do with that." On the other hand, she often argued with her mother, usually as a result of her mother's religiosity. Then "my dad would sit beside me on my bed. Once he knew I would let him, he would put his arm around me and pull me really close and tight. He would stroke my hair and say 'There, there pet. I know, I know.'"

Thus she had two voices in her head, the voice of the God telling her she was going to hell, "and then this other quieter voice calling me to love and adventure. . . . I prayed 'I need you to take it all away because I don't know what's real. I don't even know if you're there because I am so indoctrinated and the trauma is so deep.'" She felt that "though I was in the middle of this vast desert I was actually in the centre of his massive hand." Several years later, she found God. "He was right there in the desert . . . . He was everything I'd hoped He would be. He was love and compassion and grace. It was as if He stroked my hair and said 'I know, I know.'"

Naomi advises readers not to be afraid of questions. "You have to struggle and fight, because what you have at the end of it is a completely authentic and audacious faith. . . . Always be beautifully broken and desperately in need of grace because He's not to be found in 'having it together'; He's found in the desert and in the chaos."

The themes of vulnerability and trauma pervade this account, and, rather than being healed, the readers are advised to continue to be beautifully broken in the desert and the chaos, for that is where God is to be found. But the story rehearses the (good) father and (bad) mother psychological split for all to see, and God's persona as the good father is reinforced by the simile of the hair stroking and comforting words. Therapeutic narrative is never far from the surface.

33. www.alpha.org./journal/stories.

Sophie, another Alpha graduate, says, "When I read about all the people in the Bible who were broken down and built back up, I feel like I'm in the middle of this major restoration programme." Charlene, having received the Holy Spirit at the Holy Spirit weekend, says "My mind had been buzzing—full of worries, distractions, fears, and noise—but suddenly it went quiet. I felt completely loved by God and completely accepted. I had a peace that has never left. For the first time in years I was able to sleep at night and my addictions left almost instantaneously." And for Neil, "Once you realise that there is a God and that there is more to life than what you see here, you become more relaxed. I am not as anxious now about earning more money or getting a better job." All of these respondents *feel* better after their encounters with the Holy Spirit. Is this therapeutic outcome central to the Charismatic project, or is it a valued but serendipitous benefit?

INTIMACY AND EMOTION

While the language and ideas of therapy are frequent elements of Charismatic discourse, the *intimacy* of the believer's relationship with God is absolutely central. Just as intimate relationships are of immense importance in late-modern social life, so the one-to-one closeness and emotional intensity of their spiritual experience of God permeate the lives of Charismatic believers. And just as "the idea that love is an intense form of subjectivity is impossible to budge" from contemporary culture,[34] so Charismatic culture is centered upon individualistic expression—telling God how much you love Him in response to His own love for you, and expressing this feeling in whatever way seems right for you.[35]

Two main artefacts of the culture will be adduced to illustrate this emotional intimacy: the worship element of the typical Charismatic service, and a few of the talks that usually follow, but sometimes precede, this worship element. As Martyn Percy has shown,[36] the songs used in the "time of worship" develop from praise of God in His kingship and holiness at the beginning through to intimate "love songs to Jesus": a "journey to intimacy." From the theological perspective, this represents the paradox of God as being simultaneously both transcendent and immanent. However, the journey is always in one direction: towards intimacy, rather than towards

---

34. Fraser, *Guardian*, 2/7/2014.
35. Steven, *Worship in the Spirit*, 115.
36. Percy, *Words, Wonders, and Power*.

The Charismatic Self

awe and wonder. Perhaps this is because the final element in the service, to which it is building up, is "prayer ministry," when most ecstatic experiences occur.

The journey is signalled not only by the words of the songs, but also by their ballad format, the tempo of the music, and the rapturous expressions and closed eyes of the worshippers. They appear to be entirely cut off from their surroundings, concentrating on their own inner experiences. As intimacy progresses, the "worship leader" speaks less, so as to decrease external signals. The amount of repetition of the same musical and verbal phrases increases. Thus the journey towards intimacy is also a journey from the public and corporate praise of God to the privacy of whispered love. In case this sounds over-dramatic, two not untypical songs refer to laying (sic) in Jesus' arms and withholding nothing,[37] and being forever secure in the Father's embrace.

The love expressed in the second song is for God the Father, where the lordship of God and His fatherly love are in potential contradiction. However, it is always emphasized that the Father does not force His love upon His children, although once the latter have accepted of their own free will, their attitude is always one of submission and passivity in His loving arms. In the Alpha website's *Beautifully Broken* piece quoted above (p. 139), we may note the telling phrase "once he knew I would let him" of Naomi's father's physical expression of his affection, repeated in the image of God stroking her hair. Agreement is followed by submission.

In the first song mentioned above, God the Son in the person of Jesus is the object of desire. In this case, the only familial relationship with the worshipper which could be adduced is that of sibling, since both Jesus and the worshipper are children of God the Father. Furthermore, of course, Jesus is construed as a human being, just like us. In a highly sexualized culture, where frequently sex is either itself a commodity or is used to sell other commodities, the use of romantic, if not erotic, imagery in a spiritual context clearly has its difficulties. Apart from anything else, the traditional allocation of God to the male gender makes the analogy a little difficult for heterosexual male worshippers.

If the analogy with romance is difficult to maintain convincingly in the poetry of the songs, it is even harder in the demotic prose of the talks. Intimacy is indeed a prominent theme in many of the talks, although these are construed more as having a teaching function than as worship or prayer.

---

37. Steven, *Worship in the Spirit*, 122 and 152.

To select but a few examples, in an HTB conference for women, Arianna Walker tells the story of her adventurous sky-dive.[38] She wasn't afraid, she asserts, but God told her not to be afraid to be strapped to a strange man ("some random Welshman"). The aforesaid Welshman instructed "Do as you're told, I've done this 1500 times." God is like the Welshman, says Arianna. He says "strap yourself to me, don't fear the intimacy." You're not jumping out on your own, says God, I'll land you safely.

Preaching at the beginning of 2014, Mike Pilavachi urges his congregation at Sole Survivor Watford to say, with him, "Jesus, I want to press into you. I want to make you my everything. . . . Lord Jesus, I'm so sorry, I want to flee from that [my bullying]; I want to have intimacy with you. Jesus wants to have a unique relationship with Mike, his special friend."[39]

And preaching on "commitment Sunday," Mick Woodhead tells his hearers at St. Thomas Crookes to feel the love of Jesus, rather than hearing some clinical theological statement.[40] "I don't go to my wife and say 'I love you and here's a treatise on it.' No, I say 'let's have a snog.' Ooh, radical statement! It's ok, I'm married and have been for forty years [applause]. Forty years practice at snogging, me and Tricia. Christianity should be experienced."

All of these examples of Charismatic worship and teaching point to the extent to which various features of late-modern culture are central to Charismatic values in the UK. Simple intimacy, rather than the necessarily complex relationships that operate within organizations and institutions, is the preferred social mode. Emotional is preferred to rational expression, since it is supposedly spontaneous and authentic rather than calculated and masked. Individuals may respond informally according to their own unique preferences, rather than following some formal rules or procedures. All of these value preferences are common to both late-modern and Charismatic cultures.

However, we should not forget that these intimate moments with God are not in fact private. They take place in a social context. Individuals are both seen by, and see, others while intimacy takes place. Moreover, the context in which intimacy occurs is itself subject to certain social rules: the rules and expectations, however flexible, of the Charismatic liturgical

38. www.htb.org.uk/podcast/5837/m4v.
39. www.soulsurvivorwatford.co.uk/talks/cfm/reconciliation.
40. www.stthomascrookes.org/resources/commitment-2014.

ritual.[41] For example, it would be unexpected and probably unwelcome if most of the worshippers engaged in noisy ecstatic behavior during the talk, which is primarily designed to teach the faith. But it is confidently expected that the Holy Spirit will come when planned, during the "prayer ministry."

THE ONE BIG EXCEPTION

Being lesbian or gay is an archetypal identity issue. Scientists may argue about the relative effects of genetics, intra-uterine environment, and family context as predictors of sexual orientation, but the overwhelming popular consensus is that this is simply how some people are. Moreover, the extent to which their orientation is determined or chosen appears to be a matter of indifference to most people in the UK. By definition, their sexuality is a part of their individual identity, and should be respected and welcomed as such. The idea that, while people may have a gay orientation, they should not act accordingly is strongly counter-cultural. It contradicts the high value placed on the honest expression of who one is and how one feels, and prevents the gay person being authentically true to their selves. Furthermore, it may damage the person psychologically, resulting in the need for therapy.

While these specific values and attitudes are not explicitly assessed in any of the recent large scale surveys conducted in the UK, there is sufficient survey evidence to support them as a reasonable inference from the data. The British Social Attitudes Survey and the Ipsos Mori polls reviewed on p. 131 indicated a trend towards more liberal attitudes regarding sex in general and homosexuality in particular. The BSAS demonstrated that numbers of Christians believing that homosexual relations were always or almost always wrong had steadily decreased over thirty years, but still exceeded significantly those who said they were of no religion. Comparing respondents from 1981 with those of 2008 for its British sample on a similarly general question, the European Values Study found that by 2008 there was only a relatively small difference between the responses of Anglicans and Catholics and those of no religion. The overall picture is of Christians following closely, but not leading, an overall sea-change in attitudes towards homosexuality, dating possibly from the cultural revolution of the 1960s.

These general findings are supplemented, however, by more detailed analysis of the attitudes of those of particular theological persuasions. The

41. Steven, *Worship in the Spirit*, 50–54.

first of these[42] analyzed responses regarding homosexuality to a much more general questionnaire distributed in 2001 to readers of *The Church Times* who were regularly worshipping Anglicans. The survey asked about homosexual practice, same-sex marriage, the ordination of gay clergy, and the consecration of gay bishops. Theological orientation was assessed along three dimensions: liberal vs. conservative, catholic vs. evangelical, and non-charismatic vs. charismatic. All of the three dimensions predicted a different and additional amount of the variance in the responses, showing that high scores on the conservative, evangelical, and charismatic end of the dimensions each separately, and for different reasons, were related to disagreement with the homosexual line on the four issues assessed.

A recent poll by YouGov[43] analyzed the responses of 2,381 practising Anglicans to the issue of same-sex marriage. Of respondents under the age of thirty, 64 percent believed it to be right; under fifty, 53 percent; under sixty, 46 percent; and over sixty, 22 percent. Age was indeed the single most powerful predictor of attitude, but gender also predicted significantly, with men more likely than women to believe it to be wrong. Interestingly, those who said they had a certain belief in God and those who took their authority from religious sources were also more likely to believe it wrong. Only 7 percent of respondents responded in the affirmative to both these beliefs, but of this 7 percent, 65 percent opposed same-sex marriage. Supporters of same-sex marriage justified their attitude in terms of beliefs in equality and faithful love, opponents on the grounds of traditional marriage, family, and gender roles.

The general inference from these latter two surveys, then, may be that the great majority of Christians are in agreement with the trend towards more favorable attitudes regarding homosexuality, but that those of a conservative, evangelical, and charismatic persuasion remain less favorable. But there is a major difference between Calvinist and Charismatic Anglicans in terms of public profile. While the Calvinists could not be noisier about sexuality, Charismatics tend to avoid comment where they can. In an interview,[44] Nicky Gumbel carefully responds that Alpha's and his own attitudes are the same as those of the Christian church in general, and in particular those of the Anglican church, which he is under authority to

---

42. Village, "Attitude towards homosexuality among Anglicans in England."

43. www.faithdebates.org.uk/wp-content/uploads/. . . . ./WFD-Pilling-press-release.pdf.

44. www.theguardian.com/commentisfree/belief/2009/aug/28/religion-christianity.

maintain. This response seeks to disassociate the Anglican Charismatic movement (or at least its most prominent and influential element) from any degree of disapproval of homosexuality over and above that expressed in the official doctrine of the church. The latest pronouncement prohibits same-sex marriage for clergy (a prohibition which has already been disobeyed[45]).

The doctrinal distinction between orientation and practice is, however, nearly as counter-cultural as a blanket condemnation of homosexuality. It is likely to be generally perceived as an attempt to prevent individuals from acting authentically in accordance with their "real selves," their "true nature," their "personal identity." To be prevented from expressing in words and actions one's real self is to be forced to be untrue to that self and hence to "live a lie." The church may thus be portrayed as officially encouraging inauthenticity and hypocrisy. In fact, it may be perceived as taking a reactionary position on a keystone issue of our time. For Charismatics this may be important, since, as this chapter has demonstrated, on all the other major aspects of individuality and identity they have shown themselves to be closely in accord with contemporary cultural trends.

However, concern with the self (the "inward turn"[46]) is not the only element of contemporary culture to which Charismatics have paid careful attention. Another is current discourse about change.

---

45. www.charismanews.com/world/43022-gay-clergy-defy-church-of-england-s-stance-on-traditional-marriage.

46. Taylor, *Sources of the Self*.

Chapter 8

Change
Rhetoric and Reality

THE ORGANIZATIONAL CHANGE MODEL

THE DISCOURSES OF INDIVIDUALISM and of change each reflect a different element of the Charismatic identity. The former relates to the adherent's personal identity, their unique self, while the latter more concerns their social identity, their membership of a category of adherents. The discourse of *individualism* is dominated by the freedoms to be oneself, to be authentic, to be different, and to express oneself. It frequently makes such distinctions as pretence vs. authenticity; reserved vs. intimate; formal vs. informal; private vs. disclosing; and reserved vs. expressive, generally favoring the second of these binary opposites.

The discourse of *change*, on the other hand, is more concerned with the collective. Of course, *personal* change in terms of conversion and continuing transformation is central to Charismatic and Evangelical belief. However, here the emphasis is more on change in the church and the world, and chimes with the secular pre-occupation with change, especially change within organizations and institutions. It emphasizes the adherent's membership of his or her congregation, and, less often, of the Charismatic movement itself. It stresses a powerful social identity rather than a unique personal one. Once again, a set of binary distinctions permeates this

Change

discourse: continuity vs. transformation; tradition vs. innovation; structure vs. flexibility; rules, order, and restraint vs. freedom, chaos, and spontaneity; boring and safe vs. exciting and risky; and dead and moribund vs. alive and renewed. Again, the Charismatic discourse favors the second alternative in each case, with the congregation and the movement characterized as changing for the better. The C of E, explicitly or implicitly, is frequently identified by the first alternative, as badly needing to change. Of course, a central purpose and aim of movements is to change institutions, so this emphasis is hardly surprising.

The discourse of change is ubiquitous in late modern society. Its dominant presence in Charismatic narratives is another example of a convergence with the contemporary culture. The secular narrative is complex, but exhibits certain general themes. Change is often seen as a seemingly inevitable external process, outside our control. It is increasing in pace and degree, an environmental given to which we all have to adapt or perish in a social-Darwinian survival of the fittest. Hence, runs the rhetoric, it is the task of leaders to actively intervene to change institutions and organizations so that they adapt, survive, and flourish in the social jungle. It needs outstanding leadership skills to turn an organization around; indeed, the story goes, it needs transformational leaders, since only root and branch reform is generally sufficient.

Furthermore, runs a stream of management theory from the 1980s and 1990s which has now become popular discourse, it is of little use changing merely the structure of organizations. Structural change is just a cultural artefact, "re-arranging the deckchairs on the Titanic." It is the entire culture that needs to change, the underlying beliefs and values, for it is these that are holding the organization back and resulting in dysfunctional behavior by employees. And how is organizational culture to be changed? By the symbolic actions and stories of the charismatic leader, who thereby challenges the implicit assumptions of employees, expressed in the existing entrenched organizational myths and ritual practices.[1]

But a major gap was soon discovered between this managerial rhetoric and bitter reality. Organizational culture is by definition complex, with origins in specific histories and contexts. Furthermore it usually subsumes different sub-cultures, rooted in occupational and status differences. It is notoriously difficult to change, and indeed the very attempt to do so in a conscious way may be a delusion of modernity: not everything is amenable

---

1. Bryman, *Charisma and Leadership of Organizations*.

to social engineering. However, leaders did not give up, but rather sought to augment any effect of their own symbolic actions and "stage management" by sponsoring programmatic change initiatives. Management consultants were hired to help employees appear to generate for themselves organizational vision, mission, and values. The product was usually a prominently displayed set of prescriptive statements that tended to bear an uncanny similarity to other such statements, regardless of which organization has produced them.[2] Instead of organizational transformation, the outcomes were often disillusion and cynicism on the part of employees, and power-hungry narcissism from top management.[3]

The Charismatic narrative of change bears a close resemblance both to the recently dominant model within organizational change theory, and to popular use of the same discourse. Indeed, since many of the terms of the secular discourse are derived from the vocabulary of Christianity (e.g., "singing from the same hymn-sheet"), this is hardly surprising. Furthermore, the leadership of the movement and many of its adherents have themselves had, or still have, daily experience of secular late-modern organizations and their programmatic efforts to change. Given the wealthy nature of many Charismatic congregations, adherents are often in secular leadership positions themselves. Indeed, much of the organizational practice in the Charismatic movement resembles the secular model of transformational organizational change. Charismatic leadership is dominant and charismatic in nature, with explicit transformational ambitions. The search for, and development of, potential leadership talent is a constant preoccupation. And programmatic interventions, each one the current dominant Evangelical method, are popular for a period.

In the remainder of this chapter I will explore various Charismatic arenas in which the rhetoric of change is proclaimed, but the reality may or may not match up. First, I consider the discourse of *leadership* and its transformational aims and artefacts. Second, I explore the nature of Charismatic *worship* and the contrast of the rhetoric of freedom with the reality of control. Finally I present a brief account of recent attempts to *moderate* the movement's change rhetoric, perhaps in an attempt to "detoxify the brand,"[4] but more likely as an adaptation to ongoing secular cultural change.

---

2. Jackson, *Management Gurus and Management Fashions*.
3. Noon, *The Realities of Work*.
4. *The Guardian*, 4/19/2014.

Change

TRANSFORMING THE NATIONS

One of the products of programmatic attempts at change is to be found in Charismatic congregations' and organizations' statements of vision, mission, and values. Once again, the contrast with the Calvinists is noteworthy: *their* statements are dominated by lists of doctrinal beliefs. Charismatic congregations and other organizations certainly do not lack ambition for change. Trinity Cheltenham is "a church called to make committed followers of Jesus, who change communities and nations for him."[5] Holy Trinity Brompton seeks to "play our part in the re-evangelisation of the nations and the transformation of society."[6] St. Michael le Belfrey's vision is "to play our part in serving God's transformation of the North."[7] St. Paul's Hammersmith lives "to glorify God by becoming a transforming community for London and beyond. Our strategy is the formation of dynamic, urban, missional disciples or *cityshapers*. We give ourselves to be shaped by God to shape the city."[8]

This grand vision of the transformational change of communities, cities, regions, nations, and society is also sometimes echoed in the talks of the "lead pastors" to their congregations. However, their emphasis is more usually on the transformation of the congregation. Mick Woodhead of Crookes specifies a Vision Sunday at the beginning of each church and academic year, with his vision for 2013/14 being "Increase."[9] He reviews the new opportunities for training and development that are being introduced during the year, and contrasts Crookes with the church in general, which is failing and has no vision for change.

At Trinity, meanwhile, Mark Bailey too marks the new university term with high expectations.[10] Things have been building up here over August, he says, and this is also true at HTB, as Nicky Gumbel has been telling him personally. Mike Pilavachi has been filling the hall twice over at Soul Survivor. God is on the move. We're going to move in this church, and it's towards a greater connectivity with others—New Wine, HTB, Focus, Vineyard, and Hillsong.

5. www.trinitycheltenham.com/lead-pastors-welcome.
6. www.htb.org.uk/about-htb/welcome-from-the-vicar.
7. www.belfrey.org/vision.
8. www.sph.org/about-us/our-vision.
9. www.stthomascrookes.org/resource/vision-2014.
10. www.vimeo.com/29316758/mark-bailey/close-encounters/18-09-11.

These talks represent congregational and movement change as happening constantly and excitingly. The sense of the extraordinary and the radical that they seek to impart is best illustrated by a more detailed examination of a talk by Bailey entitled "A New Kind of Normal."[11] He leads with the story of his recent car crash, in which his car was damaged and remained stationary in a dangerous position as cars continued to pass at speed. Another motorist stopped and wanted everything to be kept as it was so that the details of the crash could be recorded, whereas the right thing to do was go back down the road and slow the traffic down. Bailey felt like head-butting him, he recounts, for he was playing it by the rule book. He was being "normal," obeying the norms.

Normal people scare and frustrate me, confesses Bailey, and so do normal churches. They too play by the rules, unaware of the current emergency situation of 97 percent of the local population having no contact with the church. That's not life, that's death. Jesus was a revolutionary who didn't play by the rules either, for example, healing the sick rather than keeping the Sabbath.

Bailey continues with an account of a television program about home makeovers. The resident family is sent off to Disneyland while their house is refurbished. They return to find a bus parked in front of it. Then the bus is driven away, revealing a stunning new vision of their home. The family is predictably overwhelmed and ecstatic. But what if they had shrugged their shoulders nonchalantly? They would be considered crazy for failing to recognize what they had been given. Yet the church is shoulder-shrugging to God. God can't be very interesting, conclude bystanders. This is perfectly reasonable, given the normal church's reaction to the stunning reality of God—to "park a bus" in front of God, normalizing Him. Here at Trinity we're trying to move the "bus" of church tradition out of the way and show God to people. Organized religion has changed the Lord's Prayer "thy kingdom come" to mean heaven, but God wants heaven to invade earth, and that's our purpose, for this community, this country, and the world.

A final example of transformational organizational change discourse is provided by Mike Pilavachi, in an important article published in *Revival* magazine and entitled "Naturally Supernatural."[12] A vicar wrote to Pilavachi telling him how he struggled to see his church move on, and that he

---

11. www.trinitycheltenham.com/talks-videos/we-are-trinity/a-new-kind-of-normal.

12. www.revivalmag.com/article/naturally-supernatural.

Change

was worried people were becoming comfortable with their faith. His youth group returned from Soul Survivor, and he asked them to share what they had learned with the congregation. The group talked of God's love and their experience of the Holy Spirit. They then asked everyone to stand and invited the Holy Spirit to come ("Come, Holy Spirit" is a well-established Charismatic invocation). After fifteen minutes everyone was weeping. "Everything changed in our church that day," wrote the vicar. "What I hadn't managed to do in 3 years, the Holy Spirit managed in 15 minutes. Six months later I can write and say I have a different church."

Now Christianity is a transformational religion, so it is hardly surprising that transformational change is a key element in its discourse. What is of note, however, is the close resemblance to current narratives of organizational change, particularly in terms of their interventionist and activist assumptions. For example, all those Charismatic churches that established Missional Communities (by that or another name) believed that by establishing a new church structure to include medium-sized groups they would further their aim of turning inward-looking congregations to become focussed on mission instead.

Other features held in common with management theory are clearly evident. The inspirational leadership recommended by some management theorists is present in the Charismatic discourse in double guise. The true inspiration is from the Holy Spirit, who "raises up" leaders. So, for example, when David Pytches invited John Wimber to England, it was because he was simply observing where the Holy Spirit was at work in the world (in this case in California) and responding accordingly.[13] Of course, the difficulty with such an attribution of divine authority is how one is to judge whether the source is indeed divine or all too human. It is particularly difficult when the divine source is the Holy Spirit, characterized as like the wind which unpredictably and spontaneously "blows where it chooses."[14] The story of Mark Stibbe and the Lakeland Revival (see pp. 122–123) suggests how difficult such a judgment can be. Leaders who are charismatic in their self-presentation and are celebrities within the movement may feel confident that they are directing inspired and transformational change, particularly when their favorite "gifts of the Spirit" are amply evidenced in the behavior of adherents.

13. George, *The Origins of the New Wine Movement*.
14. John 3:8.

Indeed, one of the key emphases of the movement is that it is not just the famous movement leaders who possess the gifts of leadership. On the contrary, even in early youth, leadership can be developed and practised. Pilavachi's story (above) of the youth group rather than the vicar transforming their church is typical. Again, there is a connexion between this Charismatic emphasis on youth, and the general cultural association of societal and organizational change with the young. The story of the Charismatic organization Onelife provides an example.[15]

The founder and Director of Onelife, Pete Wynter, says he was "'born again' into a culture of leadership" in his school Christian Union. As he matured, he was "privileged enough to find myself surrounded by Christian leaders who believed in raising up the next generation, and were willing to take risks on over-passionate, under-experienced individuals like myself." He arrived at St. Andrews Chorleywood, and "knew that I wanted to give the young people the same chance to lead that I had enjoyed." A missional community that was aimed at reaching teenagers in Chorleywood gave young people the chance to lead worship, lead services, preach, head up various teams, and explore their gifts on a weekly basis. "Amazingly, young people began to be doing the kind of things that you would expect from a fully trained youth worker."

This experience led Wynter to establish Young Leaders Conferences while still employed as youth leader at St. Andrews. These multiplied across the country, and St. Andrews released him from his youth work but paid him full-time to establish Onelife, whose vision is "to raise up a generation of transformational leaders (14–21 year-olds) who will grow up together to lead and influence in every sphere of society. . . . May our faltering efforts become the foundations for great things in the years to come as we see business, media, politics, education, medicine, the church, families, young and old, all impacted by a level of Godly leadership that transforms this country."

So the discourse of transformational leadership and change permeates the Charismatic movement, and carries strong echoes of the secular narrative. As with the secular narrative, however, the rhetoric sometimes falls short of the reality, and consequently has some unintended outcomes. For example, charismatic leadership can tip over into excessive power or celebrity cults, as exemplified on p. 118. And the stress on the development of youthful leadership does not seem to have permeated to the top

---

15. www.onelifeonline.org.uk/about/history.

Change

positions in congregations and organizations, which are largely led by middle-aged men. Furthermore, the number of Charismatic C of E worshippers did not increase significantly between 1998 and 2005.[16] However, several of the largest congregations and organizations have certainly grown and flourished, but a detailed analysis of why each of these have expanded while some others have contracted would doubtless reveal differences of approach in different contexts. In general, congregations and organizations that are located in proximity to student populations have expanded, as have those associated with a single "product" (e.g., Alpha).

A specific potential arena for change is the C of E. The Calvinist movement within the C of E openly challenges the authority of that institution, supporting alternative structures such as GAFCON, and undermining the authority of bishops of whom they do not approve. Charismatics, however, offer no such overt challenge. The more outspoken "pastors" of large congregations sometimes engage in knockabout humor at the hierarchy's expense, with Mick Woodhead joking that he has finally blown his chances of an episcopal post by criticizing bishops for going up to London, chairing committees, and talking about insignificant rubbish like the issue of woman bishops. But concerted and organized political opposition such as is offered by the Calvinists is absent. Rather, the Charismatics *inadvertently* offer a potential threat to the C of E.

This threat lies in their emphasis on *the congregation*. Rather than talk about being Anglicans, or being Reformed Anglicans (like the Calvinists), they concentrate on their local congregational identity—"We are Trinity," shouts Bailey. Given that the adherents of a church such as Trinity are likely to come originally from a range of denominations or from none, this congregational emphasis is understandable. An informative comparison with the Calvinists is provided by the sermons of Nicky Gumbel and Phillip Jensen, the Calvinist Sydney Anglican, on John's letters to the seven churches in Asia Minor in Revelation chapter 2.[17] Both preachers entitle them "The Jesus Letters." Jensen employs John's admonitions to the churches to castigate the recalcitrant hierarchy of the Anglican Communion and the C of E for its heretical teaching and sinful practice. Gumbel, however, applies the text solely to Holy Trinity Brompton. "What does Jesus think about HTB?" asks Gumbel. Jesus, he says, is wandering around asking, "How are you

---

16. Brierley, *The English Church Census of 2005*.

17 www.htb.org.uk/talks-and-videos/nicky-gumbel/the-jesus-letters; www.sydney-cathedral.com/resources/sermons/the-jesus-letter.

doing here?" In the Revelation text, every church has its own angel—so has HTB. Then Gumbel applies the text at length to the individual's relationship with God, quoting an Alpha attender's warmth inside as she felt safe in God's arms, unconditionally loving her (was her name perhaps Naomi?). Finally, he returns to HTB, emphasizing that he wants it to be a place where everyone experiences God's love.

Congregationalism can lead to local power bases that may dominate parishes and dioceses and even provinces. Not for nothing is Gumbel described as one of the two most powerful people in the C of E.[18] However, the success of big Charismatic congregations in terms of their size, outreach, wealth, and media profile is evidently perceived by the C of E as a source of strength, vitality, and potential growth, rather than as a threat. The institution believes it needs the movement while being wary of its power. It has therefore incorporated it by promoting eminent Charismatics to prominent positions, and by including unthreatening elements of Charismatic worship in its liturgy.

In any event, the narrative of organizational change is enormously attractive, offering as it does the prospect of actively intervening personally to bring about an exciting new reality. The reality may not match up to the rhetoric, but the prospect is alluring.

THE NORMALIZATION OF ECSTASY

While *organizational change* discourse in both secular and Charismatic arenas has focussed on the ideas of transformation and leadership, the changes in *modes of worship* that the Charismatic movement has introduced are rooted in other ideas. In particular, they are promoted and justified in terms of the change from a rigid structure of liturgy to its flexibility; from rules, order, and restraint in worship to freedom, chaos, and spontaneity; and from boredom and safety to excitement and risk.

The account on the Alpha website by Cris Rogers gives a snapshot of these rhetorics in use.[19] "We sit around on a Sunday night—often it's wild and silly, but I love it." In his sermon "The Plumbline,"[20] Mark Bailey spells out, and then answers, a question which he says he is often asked—

---

18. www.theguardian.com/comment-is-free/2013/mar/justin-welby-powerful-evangelical-church.

19. www.alpha.org/journal/stories/a-radical-church.

20. www.trinitycheltenham.com/talks/we-are-trinity/the-plumbline.

Change

"Why aren't you more reverent, holy, and worshipful?" This question really means, according to Bailey, "Why aren't you more churchy?" "Churchy" is typified by language such as "redeemed, sacrifice, sanctified, propitiated, constipated . . . ," whereas here we have a band, dim lights, visuals, and off-the-wall humor. The reason is accessibility: Jesus too dealt with the disreputable and brought them to church by using the popular idioms of His day. None of them would have been accepted for ministry by the Church of England. Or again, "I'm wearing a suit," Mike Pilavachi apologizes to youth leaders, "but I haven't sold out. I've got to go to another event where I simply have to wear a suit."

The rhetoric is not only evidenced in the contents of the talks, but also in their style. They are overwhelmingly "spontaneous" and informal. Speakers banter with their audience, asking rhetorical questions demanding an answer, then requiring a louder answer. In jest, they promise rewards such as chocolate biscuits or CDs for "spontaneous" interjections of "amen." They frequently ask whether their time is up yet, as though they are in a free flow of unpremeditated inspiration. They refer to a gesture they find they have just made inadvertently. And they sometimes lapse into mumbling incoherence. Talks by Christy Wimber,[21] Mike Pilavachi,[22] Beth Redman,[23] and Mark Bailey[24] each exemplify different elements of this style.

However, the most obvious apparent demonstrations of freedom, spontaneity, and risk are not to be found in talks but in the other two key elements of Charismatic worship: the "worship" period, usually located at the beginning of the "meeting" or "gathering," and the "prayer" element, at the end. In the *time of worship*, a worship leader directs the band, choosing and presenting, and sometimes performing, songs. This is done in the freewheeling style of the disc jockey at a club, or the presenter at a pop concert, performers who continuously adapt the program to the ongoing responses of the audience. It is, however, in the "prayer ministry" that the most apparently spontaneous events occur.

The *prayer ministry* is construed as the time towards the end of the service when God is said to be actively present in the person of His Holy Spirit. It is often introduced with the invocation "Come, Holy Spirit," the

---

21. www.new-wine.org/resources/free/ministry-themes/church-leadership/christy-wimber.

22. www.soulsurvivorwatford.co.uk/talks/mike-pilavachi/on-singleness.

23. www.htb.org/talks&videos/beth-redman/beauty-for-ashes.

24. www.vimeo.com/29316758/mark-bailey/close-encounters.

words with which the Toronto Blessing is reported to have initially got under way. The prayer leader manages the process, and prayer ministers work on a one-to-one basis with worshippers who move forward. Worshippers have been prompted to do so by "words of knowledge." This is when the prayer leader mentions various ailments or other problems from which worshippers may be suffering, usually by saying that they themselves have a vision of the problem or are physically experiencing symptoms of it themselves. This enables the worshipper to identify with them.

Worshippers are then encouraged to go forward into a space cleared of chairs. On the first occasion they ever do so, it will be an exciting and risky adventure into the unknown, a journey on which a prayer minister will accompany them, pray with them, and lay hands on them. The various forms of ecstatic behavior that may result include speaking in tongues, falling to the floor, laughing uncontrollably, lying prone, jumping up and down, trembling and jerking, and weeping and wailing. These behaviors are taken to be the evidence of the Holy Spirit working on the worshippers, so that, for example, falling prone onto the floor is described as "being slain in the Spirit."

This rhetoric of spontaneity and abandonment to the Spirit and the reality are some distance apart, however. If the Holy Spirit "blows where He chooses" it might appear presumptuous to assume that His presence can be predicted at 9.45 pm on a Sunday evening, or arrive conveniently at the Alpha Holy Spirit weekend, as scheduled. And it is not so much predicted, as organized and managed, again a possible contradiction in terms. As James Steven observes,[25] the prayer leader and prayer ministers do not engage in ecstatic behavior themselves. They are busy facilitating it, for example, by suggesting that it is about to happen, making funneling gestures to enable the Spirit to enter their worshipper client, and clearing the floor of chairs to make ecstasy safe (and more likely). The intimate devotional music with which the "time of worship" concluded may be repeated during the prayer ministry. This level of control by people who are definitely in control of themselves and what they are doing raises the issue of the unequal distribution of power in the relationship.

Furthermore, the individual's intimate ecstasy is choreographed to be visible to all, since it occurs in a public and visible place and is watched by others who are not participating. Again, the question of the inequality of power and its possible exploitation arises. The theological justification

---

25. Steven, *Worship in the Spirit*, 144–56.

Change

proposed by John Wimber was that all can see the Spirit at work, a physical manifestation of the divine. Yet suppose ecstatic behavior does not occur. Does this indicate the absence of the Holy Spirit, or something much more prosaic?

In fact, such ecstatic behavior is normalized as part of regular Charismatic ritual, a ritual that is in tune with current cultural values of immediacy, spontaneity, visible authenticity, excitement, and novelty. The processes of normalization and legitimation are partly established by the Charismatic appropriation of terminology for their own purposes. The words "worship," "prayer," and "Holy Spirit," for example, are given meanings that are restricted relative to their customary usages. "Worship" is used of a period of singing to a band rather than of the general activity of praise and adoration of God. "Prayer" is used of an opportunity for ecstatic behavior rather than of communion with God. And the Holy Spirit is treated as the source of ecstatic behavior as referenced in the Acts of the Apostles and St. Paul's letter to the Corinthians,[26] not, more generally, as God working in people's lives.

All of these restricted usages give legitimation to ecstatic religious behavior, since they use words which have a more general meaning and acceptability in the Christian church as a whole, and in general discourse. Ecstatic behavior becomes normal and indeed expected in the context of Charismatic worship, enabling worshippers and prospective adherents to confidently engage in activities that, if they were exhibited regularly elsewhere, might be considered to be symptomatic of mental illness.[27] Ecstasy is a potentially creative and normally healthy experience,[28] but its Charismatic behavioral expressions are liable to be misunderstood. Hence their normalization is crucially important to the Charismatic movement, for otherwise potential and existing adherents might fear ridicule or have doubts about their own mental health.

In summary, Charismatic worship appears to accord well with contemporary cultural values of spontaneity and informality, and also employs popular cultural forms. However, the contemporary rhetorical narrative by which it is described and justified fails to reflect the degree to which it is in fact managed and controlled.

---

26. Acts 2; 1 Cor 10:12–14.
27. Claridge, "Spiritual Experience: Healthy Psychoticism?"
28. McBride, "Secular Ecstasies."

CHANGING THE NARRATIVE

But the Evangelical wing of the C of E has historically survived better than some other parts of the church because it has changed and adapted to its situation. There is evidence that the Charismatic movement within the Anglican Evangelicals is engaging in just such a process of adaptation and change. Perhaps it recognizes that there is no evidence of recent increase in the numbers of Charismatic adherents, in contrast to the growth of the 1980s and 90s. Perhaps it realizes that it is impossible to rely on yet another "wave" of the Holy Spirit's power from across the Atlantic, given the scandals of the Lakeland Revival of 2008 (see p. 122). Or perhaps, more profoundly, it is becoming aware of certain changes in contemporary culture, and seeking to adapt its rhetoric and its practice accordingly. The Charismatic narrative of individualism and change may itself be changing.

Change is immediately apparent in the current website of New Wine, the main association of Charismatic congregations, which underwent a major revision in 2010.[29] There remains the traditional Charismatic vision statement of "Christians experiencing the joy of worshipping God, the freedom of following Jesus, and the power of being filled with the Spirit" and thereby (somehow) changing the nation. But to it are added the more explicit and interventionist aims "to see churches renewed, strengthened, and planted, living out the word of God in every aspect of life, serving God by reaching the lost, broken and poor, and demonstrating the good news of the Kingdom of God to all."

A similar makeover has been applied to the New Wine statement of values. These are now each expressed as a balance between two elements, for example, continuity and change, leadership and every-member ministry, mission and community, and natural and supernatural. Clearly this binary structure is an attempt to counteract the perception of Charismatics as characterized by one of the pair of features to the detriment of the other: in fact, as favoring change, leadership, community, and the supernatural. They may be perceived as obsessed with *change* to accommodate the culture, to the detriment of the unchanging gospel; as concentrating on charismatic *leadership* at the cost of everyday faithful service; as providing a safe *community* for spiritual experiences rather than love and justice to the dispossessed; and as concentrating on their *supernatural* gifts from the Spirit but ignoring their equally God-given wisdom and reason.

29. www.new-wine.org/home/about-us.

Change

John Coles, the National Director of New Wine, appears to have been the driving force behind this changed narrative, which may have several strategic purposes. The first is to firm-up relationships with other elements within the Evangelical wing of the C of E. We Charismatics have failed to give sufficient emphasis to biblical theology, the values statement admits, holding out an olive branch to the highly critical Calvinists and to mainstream Evangelicals. This is in contrast to the brusque statement to be found on the websites of some Charismatic congregations and organizations that their "beliefs are those of the Evangelical Alliance (see website)."

The second purpose of the changed narrative is to build bridges with the C of E in general. We have been too concerned with celebrity leaders at the cost of the ordinary faithful worshipper, the new statement of values implies. We have over-emphasized the gifts of the Spirit at the expense of the other sources of authority recognized in the mainstream Anglican tradition. And we have failed to do enough of what we are supposed to be doing as Evangelicals: getting out from our churches and preaching and living the gospel.

The wording of this "Mission and Community" value is significant. "Community" refers to the "insider" community of the congregation, with all the benefits of relationship, healing, faith, hope, and love that it can bring to adherents. "Mission" does not mean simply venturing outside into the evil secular world and making converts, but "to love and reach the lost, to care for the poor, and to bring justice to our homes, neighbourhoods, workplaces, and nations . . . ." New Wine is affirming by this wording that social action in favor of the poor and those suffering injustice is an essential part of the gospel. The C of E is not the only intended audience to this affirmation; so are all people of faith, and the secular media to boot. Indeed, under the headline "Evangelicals Take to the Streets to Buff up Their Tarnished Image: Help for Poor and Needy as Christians Seek to 'Detoxify the Brand,'" the *Guardian* reports on examples of social projects that are filling some of the gaps "as the welfare state retreats."[30]

Now many sociologists would see this development as an example of the inevitable normalization and incorporation of the untamed power of charisma into the constraints of institutional life, as theorized by Weber. Ardent Charismatics might, less theoretically, consider it a sell-out to the establishment. However, it might more usefully be construed as a far-sighted attempt to re-align the Charismatic movement within the C of E with

30. *The Guardian* 4/19/2014.

current and future changes in general cultural values. When we examine more closely two recent talks by Coles and Pilavachi, and relate them to the social interventions of Justin Welby (see pp. 6–9), this interpretation gains plausibility.

In a talk on Charismatic meetings (services)[31] Coles emphasizes, first, that monologue is not an appropriate model of teaching. Theologically speaking, it is the Holy Spirit who is the real teacher, and he can speak to the congregation as well as through the preacher. Hence, adult spiritual learning occurs more properly through dialogue rather than monologue, and interpretation and application of the Bible should be a community rather than an individual activity. In worship ministry and prayer ministry, there should be no attempt to manipulate God to be present, nor to manipulate people. All are learning to minister together. On the other hand, the term "dialogue" implies a willingness to change one's beliefs and values through openness to the other, in this case the church as "the whole people of God." The existing Charismatic opportunity to learn and practise various "ministries" does not appear to incorporate this radical degree of openness.

However, Coles' recommendations clearly critique charismatic celebrity and emphasize the gifts of ordinary adherents. They therefore mesh with the growing current distrust of many experts and authorities, including politicians, and public figures in general.

Pilavachi[32] echoes the critique of "excessive claims" and "messy manifestations" by "the charismatic celebrity with the white suit on the platform" (despite his own celebrity status). He questions "what the point of it all is when there's a world outside our church doors that needs concrete love, hope, and action." But he equally doesn't want "charismatic lite," but a church that is "naturally supernatural," with "the whole church involved in the whole ministry of Jesus." Like Coles, Pilavachi is criticizing celebrity cults and emphasizing the ability of every adherent to engage successfully in Christian social action.

Pilavachi also critiques some aspects of individualism, asserting that we now have the most self-confident and self-assertive but also the most miserable generation.[33] The narcissistic individual is the product of consumerist society—every commodified experience, for example the Grand Canyon or the Great Barrier Reef, is only complete if I take a picture of

---

31. www.freshexpressions.org.uk/on-demand/john-coles.
32. www.revivalmag.com/article/naturally-supernatural.
33. www.bible-reflections.net/sermons/the-me-generation/3713.

myself enjoying it, he notes. Consumerism, individualism, and entitlement all inhibit any form of social commitment: to relationships, career, and church.[34] Pilavachi partly blames himself for this state of affairs, for at the Soul Survivor festivals he too preached a consumerist gospel of spiritual experiences and revival just around the corner. He should, he now realizes, have told them about the cost and commitment involved in discipleship.

So Charismatic Anglicans, especially the large congregations, are becoming heavily involved in social action. In addition to earlier symbolic gestures, such as brushing shoes or giving out sweets, they are now supporting food banks, debt counselling, refuges and shelters, job clubs, ex-offenders centres, and many other crucial charitable services to those in need. This degree of involvement at a time of recession and growing inequality will raise important issues for Charismatics with regard to their relationship with government. For example, to what extent are they prepared to provide services that many might believe are the responsibility of government itself? How far are they to go in patching up the damage caused by what many perceive as unjust government policies?

Which, of course, leads to the most difficult issue of all: how to "bring justice to our homes, neighbourhoods, workplaces and nations," as the New Wine values statement puts it. Charitable works and the alleviation of suffering are uncontroversial duties of all people of faith, but justice is a wider and more difficult concept. Issues of distributive and procedural justice necessarily involve questioning the basic power structures and political processes of our society. Justin Welby was addressing such issues when he attacked Wonga. To what extent do current Charismatic beliefs regarding the nature of reality and the social world permit the issues of justice to be properly explored? The next chapter examines these beliefs at length.

However, whatever the issues that the Charismatics have to address for themselves, their turn towards increased social action chimes in well with growing public dissatisfaction with the outcomes of unregulated free market capitalism and the consequent increase in inequality.

---

34. www.sms.cam.ac.uk/media/1112687.

CHAPTER 9

The Days of Miracles and Wonders

"NATURALLY SUPERNATURAL"

THE CHARISMATICS ARE IN tune with contemporary culture with regard to individualism (chapter 7). They also share the popular enthusiasm for change (chapter 8), and appear willing to change their own vision and values to accord with changes in cultural attitudes and values that they see emerging over the horizon. However, there is a third, more fundamental, element of Charismatic culture where the coincidence with the current *zeitgeist* is more problematic. The most fundamental component of all cultures is their *assumptions about the nature of reality*. What do they believe to be the causes of events and actions? What authority or justification do they have for these beliefs? What is their perception of the world in which they live? I will seek to show that in some respects at least, late-modern and Charismatic accounts are likely to be at odds with each other.

Detailed consideration of two texts suggests some of the answers to these questions. The first is a talk by Tim May at the HTB Summer Nights programme "Worship, Teaching, and Prayer" entitled "The Miraculous Power of God."[1] May begins disarmingly by admitting that he has problems with miracles. Indeed, he feels awkward and embarrassed about them, for example, about "what happens at the front" [of the church in the prayer ministry]. But at the time described in the Acts of the Apostles, May in-

---

1. www.htb.org.uk/media/miraculous-power-god-21-august-2013.

The Days of Miracles and Wonders

sists, miracles were normative, and they also happen today. People find this problematic, for two reasons, he suggests. First, they seem scientifically implausible. But, he claims, miracles do happen. Indeed, a blind woman was healed at New Wine, and at Focus [the HTB conference] a woman with ¾-inch-thick glasses was healed, he reports. A second difficulty that people have is that miracles seem spooky and weird. But God works miracles in order to demonstrate His love and compassion [a reassuring motive that further normalizes prayer ministry].

Those with the first problem (perception of implausibility) have no hope of a miraculous blessing, since miracles can only be experienced by the non-cynical [assumption: doubts about plausibility are cynical]. Those fearing the "spooky and weird" need to put healing into the context of cosmic history and future. The great miracle of the resurrection of Christ ushered in the end-times of history, during which a little bit of heaven can come down in the form of miracles, a foretaste of the coming kingdom of God. We get to partner with God to bring a small part of the perfect future into the present [this echoes the eschatological theology of John Wimber: the kingdom now but not yet].

May returns to his own "cynicism," and says that letting go of this meant that he was letting God heal him. A feeling of desperation is a magnet for God's power. Miracles happen for us when our level of desperation is greater than our fear of failure or ridicule. Be amazed, like children, be bold, go for it and don't hold back, do a little bit of shouting, May urges. Say to yourself: this stuff is available, I want this [a spiritual commodity to be consumed]. He then tells his audience to pray exactly where they are, and stay sitting. "Holy Spirit, fill this place now," he says. Then he asks the audience to do a bold thing: to stand up where they are. He concludes by thanking God for those who are standing, and prays "that we reject the voices of cynicism and pain and that we are up for this—you're a miraculous God." [Possibly, further "prayer ministry" occurs now, but is not recorded.]

The second text of interest is the article by Mike Pilavachi in *Revival* magazine entitled "Naturally Supernatural,"[2] already referenced on p 150. He first tells of his horror at the treatment of a man with no legs who failed to be healed and so could not obey the evangelist's command to walk in faith. He was ignored at the end of the meeting, and sadly wheeled himself out. Pilavachi "desperately wanted to see more of the miracles and healings that had taken place that night, but not at the price paid by that man . . .

2. www.revivalmag.com/article/naturally-supernatural.

no-one knows what to do with those who are still broken" [the occurrence of some healing is taken as given]. How do we explain to ourselves when someone isn't healed, asks Pilavachi. We [who is this "we"?] surmise they may suffer from a lack of faith, a secret sin, or a demon. True, faith is associated in the Synoptic Gospels with healing, but healing certainly isn't totally dependent on it: God's love plays a major part. Anyway, Pilavachi "knows of many people who have immense faith, have confessed all their sins, definitely don't have a demon [the existence of demons is assumed], and still struggle with illness and injury."

He explains this absence of healing in terms of the "kingdom now and not yet" doctrine of Wimber. For now, we must pray for healing and deliverance, and some are gloriously set free, but some are not. In the early church, as described in the Acts of the Apostles, healings, miracles, signs and wonders occurred in abundance, but yet Paul had bad eyes and a "thorn in the flesh," Timothy had a poorly stomach, and Epaphroditus nearly died [it happened sometimes in the early church, at the beginning of the church era, the "last days," so it sometimes happens now].

Pilavachi now condemns certain excessive claims and manifestations—roaring and shaking and laughing inside the church [typical features of the Toronto Blessing]—as insular and immature. However, he urges Charismatics not to settle instead for a "charismatic lite" version of raising hands, singing modern songs, clapping, and having altar calls. Rather, he wants "the whole church to be involved in the whole ministry of Jesus." He dreams of a "church that is 'naturally supernatural' and walks in the manifest presence and power of the Spirit, without being weird." Every adherent can become like waiters and waitresses in a restaurant. "We take the order from the customer and then take it to the chef. Only the chef can make up the order. But we get to play. We get to be involved" [Any faithful believer can seek to heal others, but God decides if they are to succeed in doing so].

Pilavachi then emphasizes the importance of using healing to reach the broken world with God's love. He tells three stories, one already reported above, and the other two about his "friend called Matt" (could his surname be Redman?). The first of these runs as follows. Matt was having a drink in a pub "when he felt like God spoke to him about a woman who'd just entered the bar, saying she had a problem with her toes [this seems a very specific piece of divine information to 'feel']. . . . Matt obediently [obeying his 'feeling'?] approached the woman and her group of friends, explaining he was a Christian and that he thought God had told him to ask her if she had a problem with her toes. The woman was amazed. There was no way Matt could have known [inference: so it must have been supernatural], but as she pulled off her shoe and sock, she revealed what Matt described as 'very skanky toes.' She let him pray, and the toes visibly improved."

Then one of the woman's friends told Matt he had a problem raising his arm above 90 degrees, and was, after prayer, able to raise it fully. "They were amazed. They told Matt they were atheists who were now having a rethink!" Pilavachi concludes "If we can learn to invite the Holy Spirit into the very mundane, everyday aspects of our lives—if we can learn to be naturally supernatural—then I have no doubt that we'll see our churches, and the lives of people we meet, completely transformed."

These two texts are somewhat different. Tim May simply rehearses the orthodox Charismatic position on miracles and healing. Mike Pilavachi is trying to develop the revisionist sentiments expressed by John Coles and described in the final section of chapter 8. In particular, he emphasizes the ministry of all believers and their capabilities for evangelism and healing. In an interview with *Revival* magazine,[3] he gives an example of this happening at Soul Survivor. He had been coaching adolescents in how to exercise prayer ministry by laying their hands on their friends who had problems. Those prayed over were invited to come to the front and give their testimony. A youth with a broken ankle stands at the front weeping, takes the cast off his ankle, and runs around jumping over people. He'll tell everyone, says Pilavachi.

While the two texts differ in some respects, they both suggest the same assumptions about the nature of reality. In order to illustrate that these do not relate to healing alone, but to all the Charismatic phenomena typically observed, here is an example about the use of foreign tongues from Nicky Gumbel.[4] In his talk to Alpha delegates about the various ecstatic experiences that have occurred in the past, he says that the use of a foreign tongue (xenolalia) has been observed six or seven times at Alpha. On one occasion, Penny was praying over Anna. Anna, who spoke Russian, asked "Why are you praying for me in Russian?" Apparently, Penny was saying "My dear child" in Russian. This word must have been supernaturally given by God, since Penny knew no Russian. Anna concluded that God was speaking to her.

3. www.revivalmag.com/article/interview-mike-pilavachi.

4. www.youtube.com/watch?v=ZxfxaV59rB0/nicky-gumbel-how-can-I-be-filled-with-the-holy-spirit.

Among the assumptions that appear to be made in these texts, are, first, that events and behavior that cannot easily be explained in other ways are supernaturally caused. Second, that these supernatural causes are in some sense persons, such as God the Holy Spirit, Satan, and devils. And third, that human history is divided into cosmic periods, the last of which we presently inhabit, and that this location in cosmic history prevents God from fully bestowing His supernatural love on humankind—hence failures to heal.

ATTRIBUTIONS: EVERYDAY THINKING ABOUT CAUSATION

Discussion of the construction of reality and of the worldview implied in the previous section could come from several different perspectives. The most obvious is *theological*, where mainstream theologians might criticize the Charismatic emphasis on the immanent over the transcendent aspects of God, and its concentration on the ecstatic evidence of the Holy Spirit's work rather than His fruits in daily life as biblically described.[5] They would also query the cosmic worldview of historical "dispensations"[6] in the last of which we are, according to the Charismatics and others, presently located. *Philosophers* might observe that the binary ontological distinction between the natural and the supernatural that permeates Charismatic discourse is impossible to justify and maintain today, while *scientists* would criticize the quality of the evidence cited for miraculous events and the nature of the inferences drawn from it. They would argue that such events are in principle explicable in natural terms.

However, this book is written from a *social scientific* perspective, and seeks to understand Charismatic beliefs about reality in terms of the social context in which they are produced. Two key ideas dominate the following discussion: attribution, a primarily psychological construct, and differentiation, a sociological one.

Attribution refers to ordinary people's attempts to make sense of human behavior by explaining it in terms of various causes.[7] In general, people do not feel the need to explain frequent, expected, everyday behavior, treating it in a common-sense way as "taken-for-granted." It is only for unusual,

---

5. Gal 5:22–23.
6. Boyer, *When Time Shall Be No More*.
7. Ross, *The Person and the Situation*; Trope, "Attribution and Person Perception."

unexpected actions and events, or ones that evoke strong emotions, such as terror or awe and wonder, that they search for an explanatory account. This search for an explanation is motivated by the human need to understand, make sense of, predict, and control the environment.

Of course, what is usual, normal, and taken-for-granted behavior differs across cultures, both geographical and historical. For example, the vast majority of the technologically-based activities of modern societies are taken-for-granted (although not often fully understood) by their users. Those alive in the period described in the Acts of the Apostles would, on the other hand, have urgently required causal explanation for such, to them, extraordinary human activities as aviation or telecommunication, had they observed them. Or, travelling backward in time rather than forward, late-modern people might seek explanations for ritual behavior such as animal sacrifice.

The range of causes that modern people adduce by way of explanation for unusual actions or events is immense. We attribute them to individual *persons*, especially to their motives; to immediate emotional states such as anxiety, fear, intimacy, or anger, or to more stable dispositional motivations such as need for power, recognition, or affiliation. We might attribute the willingness of an adherent to go to the front at prayer ministry time to their immediate anxiety about an ailment, but their attendance at the service itself to their general need for affiliation.

Alternatively, we may make an attribution to the *situation* in which the action occurs, for example a natural situation such as a disaster, or a social situation such as a quarrel, personal poverty, or a totalitarian government. An adherent's entire behavior during a Charismatic meeting might simply be attributed to the fact that it was a meeting, and that's what people do in services.

Frequently we use a *combination* of personal and situational attributions:[8] "that's what a person like her would do in that situation." Or an adherent might explain "She needed healing and the Holy Spirit was present." The number of potential explanations available is clearly of great importance, since if there are several convincing alternatives, we are more likely to discount the immediately obvious one.[9] Instead of observing that Mike is doing a lot of angry shouting, and immediately concluding that he

---

8. Jones, "From Acts to Dispositions."
9. Kelley, "Attribution Theory in Social Psychology."

must be a grumpy person, we might take into account the facts that he has been drinking and that a group of youths is ridiculing him.

Psychological research has demonstrated some interesting general features of attributions (at least as practised in late-modern societies). For example, we don't behave like impartial scientists when inferring the causes of behavior. Rather, a variety of "biases" affect our judgments. For example, the form of attribution that we decide to use is affected by our own motivations. We are (hardly surprisingly) more likely to attribute favorable events to ourselves, but unfavorable ones to others, or to the situation.[10] However, this self-serving bias is only typical of individualistic cultures; in more collectivist oriental cultures, the bias is, rather, a self-effacing one, and people attribute their success to luck or the help others have given them.[11]

Moreover, we generally fall into the "fundamental attributional error" of attributing too much causality to the person and too little to the situation (evidenced in experimental situations designed to allow objective indices of causality). This bias is due to the person's unusual behavior capturing the observer's attention, rather than the situation in which it occurs; it is the person who is salient. So the more unusual and inexplicable is the behavior, the more likely we are to pay attention to the person him or herself, and the more likely to attribute it to some special feature of their mood or personality. When it nevertheless becomes difficult to imagine why anyone could possibly laugh uncontrollably for no apparent personal or situational reason, people may accept a supernatural explanation (e.g., it must be the Holy Spirit).

Finally, attribution theorists direct our attention to the determinants of which of the varied explanations of behavior available to them people may choose.[12] Who are the observers, for example, and what hat are they wearing? (Or, putting it in psychological terms, which of their social identities is salient in the situation?) In order to make this rather abstract account more relevant, here are some possible causal attributions that might be made by different observers for ecstatic behavior in the "prayer ministry" phase of Charismatic worship:

By an adherent: the worshipper has surrendered to the Holy Spirit, and it is the Holy Spirit who has entered the person and is causing the behavior.

10. Miller, "Self-serving Biases in Attribution of Causality."
11. Smith, "Honoring Culture Psychologically When Doing Social Psychology."
12. Trope, "Attribution and Person Perception."

By a student of religion: the worshipper is fully engaged in a Charismatic service, and this form of worship includes ecstatic behavior as a part of its liturgy.

By a clinical psychologist: the worshipper is more suggestible than most, and those leading the service have been suggesting ecstatic behavior and inducing it by rhythmic repetition.

By a popular journalist: the worshipper is emotionally needy or unstable, and the leaders are exploiting them for their own power-crazed purposes.

All of the above causal attributions are interactive, that is, both the person and the situation are implicated in the explanation offered. Some attributions, however, may be simple ones, either to the person or to the situation alone; for example: "she's deranged"; or "the Holy Spirit has come"; or "that's happy clappies for you"; or "taking them away for the weekend made all the difference." Simple attributions are perhaps the ones we rely on more when we fail to consider the range of possible explanations. There are indeed many attributions available to late-modern people.

DIFFERENTIATION: THE ESSENCE OF MODERNITY

The key defining feature of modernity is the *differentiation* of the social system into several different functional systems, whereas before it had operated largely according to the norms imposed by religious institutions.[13] Each such system now has its own culture, which has developed in such a way as to facilitate its primary purpose. So, for example, *belief* in the possibility in principle of empirically investigating everything, a high *value* placed on evidence, transparency, and rationality, and accepted *norms* of experimental practice and replicability characterize the culture of the social system of science in its basic aim of understanding the world. Different basic aims, beliefs, values, and practices are to be found in different systems, for example, government, business, religion, education, the arts, the legal system, and so on. The basic aims of religion are, arguably, first, to connect with the transcendent, and second, to dialogue with other systems regarding the outcome of that connexion.[14]

Differentiation of social systems is a continuous process, but it is in a dialectical relationship with their integration. Thus, for example, new

13. Casanova, *Public Religion in the Modern World*.
14. Beyer, *Religions in Global Society*.

scientific sub-disciplines are continuously being created (differentiation), but at the same time, science in general has now become globally integrated, in the sense that the same investigatory practices are accepted worldwide. In the modern world, the different social systems are each credited with their own expertise and sphere of operation. It could be argued, however, that the avowed and explicit aims and purposes of each of the global social systems is only part of the story. Science may seek to understand and explain, business to create wealth, government to acquire and use political power, and so on. But all systems are also implicitly concerned to reproduce themselves. Scientists are constantly citing the need for further research, business people urge the exploitation of new sources of profit, artists proclaim the continuing necessity of pushing back the boundaries of what's possible, and vicars count bottoms on pews.

Such focus on their own aims, and desires for self-generation and replication, suggest a degree of self-interest on the part of each of the global social systems. However, while they may desire independence, they are in fact dependent on each other for the necessary opportunity to achieve their aims and purposes. At the level of global society and at far more local levels also, different systems have to relate. Science and business corporations, or science and government, collaborate in developing technologies, for example. Education enables other systems to operate by developing people capable of developing and using them, while the legal system provides a regulated and orderly context in which they can flourish. Religion encourages other systems to consider the transcendent as well as the immanent, together with its ethical implications.[15] Such interdependence constitutes the overall global social system.

Different systems may seek to influence how others operate: governments may regulate business, and religion may argue for ethical norms of behavior to operate in a variety of other systems, for example. But such inter-systemic processes are seldom permitted to take the form of a complete takeover of one system by another: boundaries are generally maintained. Theocracies, for example, are rare and generally disapproved of, since they involve a takeover of government and the legal system by religion, a reinstatement of pre-modernity.

For religion is now merely "one among others." It can no longer claim the right to control such functions as law, health, politics, or science, since these are now independent, though also interdependent, systems. It cannot

---

15. Luckmann, *The Invisible Religion*.

The Days of Miracles and Wonders

even claim to be the exclusive adviser of moral practice and ethical principle to other systems, since morality is not now the sole preserve of religion. As a consequence, the religious system tends not to evaluate itself in terms of the degree of its influence on other systems. Rather, it concerns itself with the numbers of adherents who, and the activities which, further its basic aims of achieving connexion with the transcendent and the passing on of its content. Its success criteria are more internal rather than external, and hence other global systems may have difficulty in discovering its potential value for them. Yet in principle, the application of a transcendent perspective to the concerns of the other systems could perform an immensely important integrative role.

Global social systems clearly differ in terms of their power and centrality vis-à-vis the total global social system itself. Many would argue that business corporations are now the most powerful global system, with nation states trailing in their wake.[16] However, power and reputation are possibly negatively related, with government and business currently enjoying relatively low public esteem, while science, medicine, the law, and the arts are much more highly respected, according to surveys of occupational reputation.[17] These systems all have the sort of outcomes that can be easily recognized and attributed to them. Government incompetence or corruption have immediate and visible effects, as have unregulated corporate power, improved medical treatments, and profound artistic products. Religion's effects, however, are harder to discern.

Some commentators, for example Jose Casanova,[18] suggest that religion may increasingly be seeking to influence "civil society," the public sphere, in respect of such values as respect for human rights to freedom, security, and respect. These are flagship values of the Enlightenment and hence of profound importance in the development of modernity. Thus, this form of involvement of religion in other global systems, particularly in government and markets, is seeking to hold modernity to its prospectus. It is certainly not reacting against it in principle, but rather critiquing the operation of some of the dominant systems. And the fact that religion is indeed a truly global system enables such promotion of universal societal values irrespective of national or regional location. The common good is a global concept.

16. Ohmae, *The End of the Nation State;* Drucker, *Post-Capitalist Society.*
17. www.gallup.com/poll/1654/honesty-ethics-professions.
18. Casanova, *Public Religions in the Modern World.*

ATTRIBUTION AND DIFFERENTIATION

The connexion between the psychology of attribution and the sociology of differentiation is now evident. Differentiation of functional social systems, the essence of modernity, makes available a great number and a wide range of possible explanations for people's actions. The different worldviews, belief systems, and practices typical of several of the global social systems are available to modern people as sources of explanations. This is because they operate within these systems, and are familiar with, and maybe internalize, their cultures. And they are certainly likely to search for explanations for behavior as unusual as people "speaking in tongues," "being slain by the Spirit," laughing uncontrollably, and disregarding their medical symptoms.

The sorts of explanation they come up with depends upon which of their social identities is salient at the time. If they are Charismatic adherents, they are unlikely to need any explanation for themselves, since they have become socialized into accepting such behavior as normal in the church situation. However, they may give a Charismatic explanation, attributing the behavior to the Holy Spirit, if they are asked by a non-adherent to explain what is going on. Different social identities may be salient in the context, for example, a social scientist writing about the Charismatic movement, a music lover looking for the latest CDs, a student scanning the promotional literature distributed to sophomores, a marketer searching for new niche markets for products, or a politician looking for new constituencies. All of these people coming into contact, either direct or mediated, with ecstatic Charismatic behavior, will have either salient at the time, and/or central to their view of themselves, a social identity. And that identity will incorporate an internalized set of beliefs that constitute part of the culture of the social system concerned, and that will generate explanations. Indeed, because we late-moderns are reflexively conscious of the different social systems, of the different "hats we wear," then we can actually use the systems themselves as satisfactory explanations: "That's what some religious people do in church" is all we need to know.

The contrast with pre-modernity could not be greater. Then the social system was little functionally differentiated. People tended to need no explanation for their customary behavior, but when they were surprised or astonished by events or actions, they invoked the supernatural. During the Axial age (800–200 BC),[19] a distinct formal system of priestly functionaries

---

19. Jaspers, *The Origin and Goal of History*.

The Days of Miracles and Wonders

developed so that religion was clearly distinguished from the mundane, the sacred from the secular.[20] The Bible is full of accounts of human life in which the writers did not feel the need to invoke God, Satan, angels, or demons. But frequently they did. According to the biblical writers, God spoke through the prophets, for example, and performed miracles when they invoked His power. Demons possessed those whom we would today call mentally ill, and Christ, and later His disciples, called them out and banished them. God raised Christ from the dead, and sent His Holy Spirit, who inspired the disciples to speak in foreign tongues and in "the tongues of angels," and to heal those who were sick. Attributions to the supernatural were numerous indeed. The supernatural was the only way to explain actions and events that were unusual, and furthermore there was a religious language and binary worldview already available to provide and express such attributions.

It is, however, this pre-modern biblical language and worldview that Evangelical Christians in general, and Charismatics in particular, use in their religious practices. Their binary distinction between the natural and the supernatural is derived from the mundane vs. transcendent duality of biblical times. So extraordinary, so miraculous is the event of Penny apparently praying in Russian when she did not know that language that, concludes Nicky Gumbel, it must have been the Holy Spirit at work (see p. 165). Of course, the use of this binary distinction ultimately results in a "God of the gaps." That is, if we infer God when no other explanation is likely, there is an obvious danger that as more alternative explanations are constantly becoming available, God comes to have less and less scope. Interestingly, the same binary distinction is dismissed by atheist scientists such as Dawkins, who wish to argue that everything can now be explained in terms of the natural (i.e., is amenable in principle to scientific investigation).

The Charismatics' adoption of pre-modern language and thought forms for their religious practice is buttressed by a particular theological worldview that divides cosmic history into a series of eras.[21] As previously noted, we are now supposed to be located in the church era, the last before Christ returns to establish His kingdom. The present dispensation started with the resurrection of Christ and the gift of the Holy Spirit at Pentecost. Hence, runs this account, the miracles and wonders which the early dis-

---

20. Eisenstadt, *Fundamentalism, Sectarianism, and Revolution*.
21. Boyer. *When Time Shall Be No More*; Wojcik, *The End of the World As We Know It*.

ciples were able to perform remain within our own capacity, we who live later in this same last period of human history.

Now clearly the beliefs and practices of many late-modern Christians are internally constructed and consistent. They can also be happily embraced by people who conduct the rest of their lives using markedly different beliefs and practices in different social situations, where the norms of other global systems than religion operate. They have also internalized the beliefs, values, and norms of several other systems, for example, the arts, medical, and education systems. They may, indeed, be happy to incorporate elements of these other cultures into their religious culture (e.g., musical forms), and to influence them in turn in accordance with some Christian beliefs, values, and practices. However, what they are likely to balk at is the assumption by their religion of the fundamental aim and purpose of another system whose beliefs and values they also hold. In the case of medicine, this is the cure of physical disease. It is an entirely different claim to provide holistic spiritual healing than to cure a broken ankle, make a blind person see, or resurrect someone from death. And it is a further category confusion to explain failure to effect physical cures by the fact that the kingdom of Christ has not yet arrived (see p. 164). To accuse those who are disturbed by these trespasses onto the core territory of other systems of being "cynical" (p. 163) is to utterly miss the differences between modernity and pre-modernity.

AUTHORITY AND THE SOURCES OF KNOWLEDGE

Functional differentiation of systems points up another issue regarding our construction of reality. It forces us to ask not just what we think we know, but also how we think we know it. What is the authority for our beliefs? How are we to decide whether they are true or not? Different social systems legitimize their beliefs in different ways. There are, in other words, several accepted but very different truth criteria, unless, of course, one only accepts one social system as legitimate. Economic value is a business criterion, empirical verifiability and falsifiability a scientific one, and divine revelation a religious one, for example.

If religion deals with the transcendent, then how the transcendent reveals itself to humankind is therefore a key issue. Disputes about claims of revelation have dogged religions, especially Christianity. Has God revealed Himself through the church, or the Bible, or Jesus Christ, or the natural

The Days of Miracles and Wonders

world, or human reason or virtue, or individual spiritual experience, or all of these, or some of them, or predominantly one only? Or is it even appropriate to speak of revealing to humankind the essentially transcendent and unknowable?

For Calvinists, the answer to this question is clear: *sola scriptura*, the Bible alone, reveals God's truth. For Charismatics, there are somewhat different emphases. They repeatedly affirm their adherence to the historic evangelical statements of creedal belief, but their emphasis is much more on the experience of the Holy Spirit as the source of truth. They believe that since any Christian can experience the Holy Spirit personally, and many do, then the truth is revealed to many individual adherents. The Holy Spirit is the ultimate authority, not the church or its representatives. It is adherents who are empowered by his Holy Spirit to know and do God's will. They may exercise a variety of the Spirit's gifts, such as speaking prophetic words, healing the sick, etc. There is no need for any priestly expertise: the Holy Spirit has empowered them. Being gifted is what is important, not being qualified.

Now most are willing to allow religions to work out their own beliefs, values, norms, and practices for themselves, so long as they do not violate legal or moral constraints (as for example in the cases of child abuse and female genital mutilation). However, other issues are currently being debated, such as equal opportunities in ecclesiastical employment with respect to gender and sexual orientation, the freedom of girls to grow up and then to choose for themselves whom they marry, and the content of religious education in schools receiving state finance.

For Charismatics these concerns of other social systems about religion may appear irrelevant. They are not especially involved in any of the issues mentioned above, but on the contrary are increasingly concerning themselves with socially approved community work. On the other hand, in principle their beliefs and practices with respect to the sources of legitimacy and authority may lay them open to difficulties. There are three fundamental issues here. The first is in respect of the Holy Spirit as the primary personification of the source of divine revelation. His work is characterized, they believe, by immediacy, spontaneity, and power, not by reflection on principles and consideration of possible consequences. How do they avoid being carried away by the excitement of it all? Second, all believers can receive revelation from the Holy Spirit and are encouraged to communicate them. How are truly divine messages to be distinguished from others, and how are these others, and their proponents, dealt with? And third, the concentration upon flagship congregations and organizational ministries enhances the power of charismatic leaders. How can they guard against abuse of such power (an occasional but damaging consequence)? Charismatics would doubtless respond that they check the authenticity of revelation against the Bible, and that they are subject, together with the Calvinists and others, to the disciplines of the Church of England. However, a popular perception of "weirdness" is not the only issue facing Charismatics; authority and legitimacy for their beliefs is another.

In sum, the pre-modern nature of the Charismatics' *beliefs and language regarding the nature of reality and the causes of action* may result in difficulties for modern people with their multiple social identities and system memberships. However, the *values* of the Charismatic culture are in considerable agreement with many elements of contemporary culture, as I argued in chapters 7 and 8. It therefore attracts many, particularly the young. It succeeds in subsequently retaining them by providing them with powerful personal and social identities. The former is derived from the intimate and unique relationship the adherent enjoys with the Almighty, and the latter is formed in the local congregation: "We are Trinity" indeed.

CHAPTER 10

A Global Institution

CALVINISTS AND CHARISMATICS: DIFFERENT BUT SIMILAR

So what are we to conclude about the Calvinist and the Charismatic movements and their present and future relationship with the institutional C of E? And what, as a result, is the likely future for that institution?

First, any lingering notions that the two movements are really only slightly different siblings in the Evangelical family must now be banished for good. Their cultures are different, in terms of their basic aim, their beliefs, their value priorities, and their practices. Calvinists exist to fight for the Reformed faith while Charismatics wish to inspire the church and convert the world. Calvinists assume that doctrinal belief is the core of the faith, while Charismatics insist that the power of the Holy Spirit is the key to renewal. Calvinists maintain a stern dichotomy between the sacred and the secular, while some Charismatic values reflect those of contemporary British culture. And while both movements aspire to informality of liturgy and practice, only Charismatics aim for miracles and ecstasy.

They do have certain things in common, however. First, *they are both very effective* in their own terms. The Calvinists have succeeded in waging a continuing and very public struggle against the C of E and the Anglican Communion, skillfully using these institutions' structures and processes to their own advantage. They have chosen the issues on which to fight, and they have made the most of their political opportunities. While the C of E has survived the onslaught, it has suffered major opportunity costs and reputational damage as a result. And the Anglican Communion appears to be falling to an alliance of British Calvinists and African conservatives, an outcome which the C of E may come in time to welcome as a means of escape from an unwanted position of leadership.

The Charismatics, too, have been successful in their own terms. They have developed a considerable number of large and influential congregations. They have planted new churches where none previously existed or where congregations had previously failed. They have developed nationally and internationally effective methods of evangelism through such organizations as Alpha. As far as their emphasis on the Holy Spirit in their theology and their liturgy is concerned, their influence has been felt across the C of E, although usually in a much attenuated form. And finally, they wield considerable influence within that institution, partly because of the size and wealth of their big congregations and the prominence of some of their leaders.

A second commonality between the movements is one of the reasons I have adduced in previous chapters for their success: *both are extremely well organized.* As I have demonstrated in depth, both have developed a dynamic organizational process consisting of four elements: controlled formation of leaders, large and influential congregations, able and media-savvy leaders, and organizations/pressure groups/ministries. This enables their own continued reproduction as movements, and also the successful management of the context on which they depend. The Calvinists' political skills have hitherto ensured that they have an enemy to oppose and their own preferred issues to contest. The Charismatics' adaptability enables them to select and spiritualize elements of contemporary culture and find new ways of relating to their local community. In sum, both movements are well organized at the congregational, organizational, and movement levels of analysis. They both have sophisticated marketing and media techniques, and are adept at political manoeuvring (Calvinists) and acquiring influence (Charismatics). And they have able leaders and committed followers.

MOVEMENTS AND INSTITUTION AGAIN

What, then, are some tentative answers to the questions that I posed at the beginning of the book? First, what might be the relationship between the

A Global Institution

two movements and the institution? I argued in chapter 1 that movements and institutions are mutually dependent, bringing different strengths to the party. The C of E brings an organizational framework, using tried and tested and legally supported structures and processes to coordinate activities and allocate resources. It provides connexions with other social systems, and continuity, authority, legitimacy, and recognition. It also provides a media profile and platform without which the movements could not promote themselves. The two movements, on the other hand, bring passion and commitment to the particular aims upon which they are focussed. Their adherents have a strong social identity as movement members, since the movements are clearly differentiated from other movements and institutions. They wish to change the institution in ways which support their aims.

I also specified in chapter 1 some of the possible forms of relationship between movements and institution. Movements can achieve their aims to a degree and then become incorporated into the institution (thereby losing their driving commitment to change). Alternatively, moving in the opposite direction, they can split from the institution, lose the benefits it brings, but, as a new sect, have the potential to develop as they wish. Thirdly, the institution can seek to nullify the movement, or attempt benign indifference. Or, finally, movements can use the institution as a base from which to achieve their aims elsewhere, or they can actively attack the institution from within, seeking to replace its framework with their own.

What are the implications of the accounts I have given of the Calvinists and the Charismatics for the future of the relationship between these two movements and the C of E? Any answer to this question depends upon the aims of the C of E. If we can discover these, then we can ask whether the aims and cultures of the Calvinists and the Charismatics are compatible with them. Taking careful note of the actions of its new leadership, and assuming that the institution will follow their lead, then the C of E's shorter-term strategy seems likely to demonstrate the following elements. First, an overall redirection of the balance of attention and emphasis away from the internal institutional, and towards the external societal, context. Second, a concentration on issues of justice and poverty, not only in terms of their mitigation by charitable actions but also by addressing their causes. Third, an emphasis on evangelism and the promotion of the kingdom of God, of which justice is an integral part. Fourth, a concentration on the C of E rather than on the Anglican Communion and its struggles. And finally, a necessary reform of the C of E's internal structures and processes so that they are fit for these purposes.

Given these strategic aims, what do they imply for the C of E's relationship with the two movements? Are the C of E's and the movements' aims mutually compatible? Are continued close relationships with the movements likely to be beneficial or prejudicial to the achievement of the C of E's aims? Are the costs of maintaining such relationships simply too great to make any benefits worthwhile? The answers to these questions differ profoundly for the two movements.

CALVINIST PROBLEMS AND CHARISMATIC POSSIBILITIES

My analysis of the Calvinists paints them overall as sectarian absolutists. They will not be satisfied until the C of E as an institution formally adopts their own culture, with its doctrinal belief system, its values, and its practices. This being as likely as pigs flying, they will never achieve their aim. They will, however, gain great satisfaction from the struggle to do so, which will motivate them and maintain a core support for the foreseeable future. Their movement's organizational effectiveness ensures continued and highly visible conflict if their present relationship with the C of E continues as it is.

The Calvinist posture is highly detrimental to the C of E leadership's aims. It focuses attention and effort on the internal rather than the external context. It relates to issues of justice only in terms of the supposed persecution of Calvinists. It treats evangelism primarily as a means of producing more Calvinists. And its politicking in the Anglican Communion is a major diversion and challenge. Its present relationship with the C of E is, in sum, incompatible with the new leadership's aims, and an insupportable cost in terms of time, energy, patience, and, above all, reputation.

What sort of relationship, then, might the C of E seek to establish with the Calvinists, and how might it set about doing so? It doubtless already appreciates that the movement is entirely dependent on the existence of the institution and its organizational processes. Without an enemy, the Calvinists would have no-one to fight against. Without their opportunity to select issues for debate and force them onto the agenda, they would be deprived of the oxygen of publicity. And since their struggle is waged primarily on the mediated battleground, they would be unable to maintain any appreciable level of conflict, their reason for existing.

A Global Institution

The C of E will therefore seek to reverse the two-decade process of the conciliation and appeasement of the Calvinists, which was based on a noble but futile effort to maintain formal unity of the Anglican Communion and the C of E. From the adoption of a formal statement on homosexuality to the agreement to appoint "flying bishops," this process has had disastrous outcomes, as do most organizational decisions made under duress. The particular tactics employed to achieve its reversal will include revision of the voting system of Synod to ensure that a minority of one section of Synod will never again stand in the way of the will of the vast majority of the C of E.

The form of relationship with the Calvinists will therefore remain one of conflict. Hitherto the Calvinists have called the tune, by threatening schism and establishing alternative authorities in order to extort concessions. Now the C of E will seize the initiative. It will use its institutional resources to ensure that it determines what the issues are and how they are decided. And it will call the Calvinists' bluff by making it clear that keeping them within the fold is of much less importance than addressing the needs of the world and promoting the kingdom of God.

The relationship with the Charismatics will be entirely different. In terms of alignment of strategic aims, the Charismatics are far more in tune with the new C of E leadership than are the Calvinists. They too are now predominantly outward facing, having recently reemphasized their commitment to evangelism and included within that concept social interventions in local communities. These interventions may be derived from charitable and evangelistic motives rather than from a fundamental desire for justice, but they are certainly a move towards the latter. The Charismatics are thus aligned with the third C of E emphasis, evangelism. As for the fourth, (concentration on the C of E rather than the Anglican Communion), the Charismatics concentrate on neither at present, but rather on their own congregations and ministries. The public denigration and ridicule of the C of E in some Charismatic quarters, and its continued characterization as the dead hand of bureaucracy actively preventing the workings of the Holy Spirit, is a clear area of contention. But such a stand-off will become less tenable if the C of E persuades the Charismatic leadership that it is committed to making its structures and processes fit for purpose.

The C of E leadership will seek to emphasize to the Charismatics how important their contribution will be to the achievement of its aims. They will welcome the Charismatic enthusiasm for local evangelism and the creation of new congregations. They will support local initiatives such as that in the North sponsored by large Charismatic congregations. However, they will urge Charismatic congregations, "ministries," and organizations to re-affirm their Anglican identity and to contribute to the revised strategic direction. This will necessarily involve an increased Charismatic understanding that neither individual conversions nor acts of charity are themselves sufficient. Charismatic leadership courses might profitably devote some of the time currently spent in consciousness-raising to developing a more sophisticated understanding of the modern world.

And finally, Charismatics will need to understand and admit that the resources of the C of E as a whole are vital to their own development. This includes the variety of high quality theological and pastoral training available in the C of E. It also includes the institutional requirements of, and processes for, transparency, accountability, and discipline. Scandals concerning the abuse of power, or claims of resurrection of deceased people and physical healing of incurable conditions, will not sit well in an institution now consciously relating to the rest of society.

So the C of E's relationship with the Charismatics will certainly not be one of conflict, as it will continue to be with the Calvinists. Rather, it is likely to be one of greater incorporation, with the former valuing the latter's evangelistic energy sufficiently not to snuff out the inspiration and enthusiasm, and the latter recognizing that other parts of the C of E, and indeed the institution itself, have roles to play in the establishment of the kingdom of God. The movement will have achieved its own objectives—and movements do not go on for ever.

INSTITUTION AND CULTURE

There remains, however, one major issue that arises from the likely continued prominence of Charismatics in the church. It is that of the C of E's relationship to contemporary culture. Calvinists, for their part, disapprove of it entirely as secular and therefore sinful. Charismatics, however, use its artefacts freely, express some of its values, but disagree with its beliefs about reality. To what extent, then, should the C of E leadership maintain a counter-cultural stance, and in what particular respects?

First, it will clarify its attitude regarding the use of specific *artefacts* of contemporary culture, for example in Charismatic worship. The romantic words of the love songs to Jesus, the celebrity status of the worship leaders, the stand-up comic style of the talk, and the individualized and self-contained ecstasy of the prayer ministry are all similar to forms of popular entertainment. The justification given for their use is that these current modes of communication present the eternal message of salvation in a format that modern people can understand. Whatever the medium, the same message is received, runs the justification. While the cliché "the medium *is* the message" is doubtless an overstatement for purposes of effect, the Charismatic justification of the opposite position is unlikely to hold much water. Entertainment is a commodified product, chosen by its consumers for their enjoyment and satisfaction, and its presentation is such as to ensure their attraction and gratification. It is part of the market-based economy. Is it compatible with the values of God-centered worship?

Second, the C of E will consider whether the *value* priorities demonstrated in Charismatic discourse and practice are compatible with its aims. The concentration on the individual, their healing and their experiences, again relates closely to individualist secular culture. On the other hand, the Charismatic emphasis on the congregation and on the local community demonstrates that other priorities are collectivist in nature.

Finally, the C of E will urgently seek to present to late-modern people a *theological* narrative that does not ask them to reject their social identities. To define faith as choosing the supernatural over the natural as an explanation of events and behavior is to ask them to deny who they are—people who live in a functionally differentiated late-modern world, not a pre-modern society with a binary worldview of natural and supernatural.

In sum, the C of E will use its own aims and purposes as the criteria for which elements of contemporary culture it embraces and which it rejects. Its increasing focus on the external social world rather than the internal religious one, and its concern for societal justice and survival, suggest that its criteria will be consciously chosen with these aims in mind. In particular, relationships will be cultivated with those social systems which are likely to prove allies in addressing these issues.

DOOM, GLOOM, AND NOSTRUMS

Current commentaries on the C of E do not, of course, base their views merely on a consideration of two of the movements within it, as I have done so far. They instead address urgent and pressing issues, which, according to some commentators, threaten its continuing existence.[1] Should it, for example, treat the downward trend in its attendance figures overall as the central evidence for its impending demise and the need for drastic overhaul?

If it does adopt this criterion of failure or success, then it might be interested in discovering how it is that the Calvinists and the Charismatics maintain or enhance their attendance figures, whereas those of other elements of the institution are on the slide. Any such investigation is likely to come up with explanations and recommendations at the organizational level of analysis. This is partly because the two movements are well organized and numerically relatively successful, and partly because a question couched in organizational terms is likely to come up with organizational answers.

By way of example, we may consider a recent research project sponsored by the C of E,[2] which follows a well-established methodology within the management literature: to discover the pockets of "success" within an institution or organization, and isolate the features that differentiate them from the "failing" remainder. These distinctive features are termed "success factors," and are typically recommended as solutions for the organization as a whole. Against an overall backdrop of a decrease of 9 percent in terms of regular attendance over the decade 2002–12, the research question was what factors characterize "successful" and "failing" elements of the church, using multi-method investigation techniques. Archbishop Welby argues that such data should help the C of E to "stop doing things that help accelerate decline and focus on things that develop growth."

The research indicates that successful growth results from different strategies in different contexts. However, "fresh expressions" of church which seek to attract new converts by meeting informally outside church buildings are one frequent success factor. So are the peaceful and reflective ambience, worship, music, and friendly atmosphere in cathedrals, which increased their weekly attendances by 35 percent over the decade. As for congregations themselves, the key success factors are those predicated in the general management literature as important for every type of organization: leadership; mission and purpose; willingness to continually reflect, learn, and adapt; involvement of all the members; prioritizing growth; and recruiting and developing new and existing members.

---

1. www.telegraph.co.uk/news/religion/18nov2013.
2. www.anglicanink.com/article/church-england-reports-signs-growth.

A Global Institution

But of course these success factors are themselves dependent upon having motivated congregations, including able lay and ordained leaders. The chicken and egg nature of the problem is only too clear. And such Christians may not be attracted to an institution and to congregations that do not stand for and act out their own beliefs and values. Further analysis of the attitudinal data in terms of age cohort and values might yield more understanding than the discovery of "success factors" alone.

Indeed, when we consider the responses of Anglicans of different age cohorts, whether regular attenders or not, there are major age-related differences on ethical issues, especially those relating to gay marriage, euthanasia, and abortion.[3] The percentage of Anglicans under thirty who are liberal on these issues is typically 20 percent higher than those in their fifties, sixties, and seventies. It is hardly surprising that an institution with a leadership in its fifties (and those are the younger ones, as the average age of bishops is sixty-two) is out of step with its incoming members. Partly no doubt as a consequence, the C of E has only 10 percent of adherents in their twenties, as opposed to 50 percent composed of the over sixties. When asked why they are hostile to the church, the most frequent reason young people give is that it is sexist and homophobic.

This age effect is also evident in the crucial matter of ordained leadership.[4] The number of ordained clergy who are paid a salary for their work (in other words, those for whom it is both a vocation and a career) has dramatically declined between 2002 and 2012, a decrease only partly offset by the ordination of women. Now, two thirds of C of E licensed clergy are unpaid. In other words, a crisis in professional staffing has been averted by volunteer replacement. But the majority of both salaried and unpaid clergy are aged over fifty. There are less than 100 full-time salaried clergy under thirty, and the total loss of clergy exceeds new recruitment. The number leaving the ministry for other reasons now exceeds those who are leaving to retire. Neither the volunteer nor the female recruits can mask this leadership crisis. Linda Woodhead remarks, "there are no longer enough troupers left to keep the show on the road, and the show will have to change."

There is no shortage of suggestions about how to keep the show on the road, or turn the ship around, or whatever metaphor for change appeals. Andrew Brown, an influential commentator on the UK religious scene,

---

3. www.churchtimes.co.uk/articles/2014/7-january/features/time-to-get-serious.

4. www.churchtimes.co.uk/articles/2014/7-february/features/not-enough-boots-on-the-ground.

argues that the C of E should give up pretending it is a coherent entity with clearly defined opinions and policies.[5] It should stop its "grand gestures, speeches, proclamations and debates." Indeed, "The General Synod and the 'Church of England' as a body capable of having opinions or policies on anything need to shut up." The local congregation is the key unit about which churchgoers care, and that is where the effort needs to go. "What matters is not doctrine, but the way that faith plays out in everyday life." In this "unglamorous and local future," it is "only by admitting it has already been disestablished can the church hope ever to re-establish itself." So the *local congregation* is the institution's key component.

The centrifugal forces exerted by the two movements, and by others, now render impossible the idea of a C of E based on unity as uniformity, maintains Linda Woodhead.[6] She argues that the Church could be a model of how a religious body can embrace genuine pluralism, but she stops short of deconstructing to congregational level. Rather, she imagines a possible future in which there is a form of franchising of the C of E "brand," to which various "branches" would retain loyalty and enjoy the benefits of its central services. She describes six relatively independent franchises based on the present diversity of the C of E, and suggests that they be allowed to flourish on their own terms, in open competition with one another, and largely responsible for their own finances, functioning, and governance. While the parochial system will continue to be reshaped into something more appropriate to an urbanized, mobile society, bishops will remain as the system's cement, organized into colleges representative of all of the franchises.

Woodhead argues that the C of E must recover a sense of itself as a church for the whole of society rather than chiefly for regular churchgoers. Its strengths are its schools, chaplaincies, and other forms of outreach into society—not just congregations. It must enter into a much more open, reciprocal, and post-paternalistic relationship with UK society and its own members, with duties and responsibilities on both sides.

Michael Hampson, a former priest, proposes a mix of these two approaches.[7] Congregations should be in charge of their own finances, he argues, and the various factions will form networks that congregations

---

5. www.theguardian.com/commentisfree/andrewbrown/2013/dec/26/church-of-england.

6. www.churchtimes.co.uk/articles/2014/28-february/features/a-remedy-for-an-ailing-church.

7. Hampson, *Last Rites*, 200.

A Global Institution

will choose between and join. These will have "their own bishops, clergy, structures, policies, liturgies, and life," with the Church of England finding a role as little more than an estate-management quango.

Yet others prescribe a complete disestablishment of the C of E. They argue that the offence establishment causes in a multicultural society is currently a millstone round the C of E's neck, and that the entire policy of the state's relationship with religion needs to be rethought. It is perhaps a moot point, argues Adrian Hamilton, whether establishment is holding the C of E back or propping it up.[8]

A principled alternative, however, is to hope that the institution can maintain its historic inclusive character by the practice of dialogue, as the organization "Modern Church" urges the newly appointed Archbishop of Canterbury.[9] "The Classic Anglican tradition of maintaining diversity within unity . . . has recently come under pressure, with demands for uniformity of belief accompanied by schismatic acts. In our view, diversity of belief should be accepted as a normal part of church life and the process of seeking truth in matters of faith. . . . It is in the interplay and the conflict between . . . the common mind of the church and the common mind of a culture that the meaning of the Gospel for a particular time and place is to be discerned." Unfortunately, the practice of dialogue and the holding of absolutist belief are mutually incompatible, as the C of E has learned to its cost.

The number and variety of these recommendations reflect the perceived urgent need of radical change within the C of E. Several commentators date the time of absolute crisis to within the next ten years. Clearly, some basic reforms, for example in finance and organization, are a necessary condition for the institution to continue into the twenty-first century. But while they are certainly necessary, they are not sufficient in the longer term.

THE ELEPHANT IN THE CRYPT—AGAIN

All of these proposals and prophecies are essentially *local* in nature. In this respect, they resemble my accounts of both movements and of the institution, which have been resolutely local throughout. One cannot get

---

8. www.independent.co.uk/voices/faith/will-the-last-person-to-leave-the-church-of-england.

9. www.modernchurch.org.uk/resources/mc/2012-8.htm.

much more local than the sermons of a vicar to his (sic) congregation, but this book is full of them. I have construed the Calvinists as located within Britain's religious and imperial past, and the Charismatics as reflecting the values of the 1960s counter-culture and free-market consumerism. *Any policy recommendations for the C of E based on the relative success of these two movements, or derived from the current debate on its future, are therefore likely to be based on a local, and therefore incomplete analysis. This is because the implications of globalization for any religious institution, especially a national one, have not yet been fully discussed.*

From a social scientific perspective, globalization is an ongoing social process with three fundamental features (see pp. 20–21). To recapitulate, the first is the global connectivity of people, finance, and information within and between social systems; the second, the constant dialectic between each of the global social systems and their local instances (so-called "glocalization"); and the third, global consciousness of these systems, and the social identification with humankind, or with the entire natural and social world, which follows from it.

The implications of each of these features for the C of E are profound indeed. First, consider *connectivity*. The institution cannot ignore or discount the global religious context, limiting its concern, for example, to Anglicanism, or to Christianity. The symbolic actions and nascent ecclesiastical reforms of Pope Francis have global reach, influencing what people think about the appropriate role of church leaders. The attempts of Muslim clerics to deal with extremist Islamic elements point to the universal difficulties of reconciling absolutist with mainstream religion, and the dangers of being associated in the public perception with absolutism.

More important still, global connectivity points up the various relationships between religion and the other global social systems. For example, there is globally a plethora of religion's different connexions with the *nation state*, ranging from theocracy through to total separation. Any informed discussion of the disestablishment of the C of E cannot conceivably ignore these ongoing developments in the political arena elsewhere. And what of global religion's relationship with *global corporations*? As labor becomes increasingly mobile, for example, how can religious leaders effectively intervene to secure just treatment for local migrant workers unless they collaborate globally? And how can the C of E on its own possibly hope to exercise any ethical influence on the nature of *scientific* research and its technological development? Science and technology are global, but

A Global Institution

a religious institution, associated in global perceptions with a single nation-state, is irredeemably local.

Finally, the fact of global connectivity must surely focus any institution's attention on its global reputation. That reputation primarily depends on mediated representations, and while such representations cannot be so managed as to consistently portray the reality convincingly, the need for a global media strategy that embraces both traditional and social media is inescapable. Any such strategy will, of course, be informed by an appreciation of the sort of institutional action which is likely to be picked up as a story by the media, and of the probable effects of such coverage on reputation. The worst recent example of Christian failure in this regard is the case of child abuse, where the scandal was compounded by the churches' attempts to conceal the truth, and then by their failure to anticipate the global reputational damage suffered as a consequence both of the criminal acts themselves, and of the global reach of the media reporting them.

The second basic feature of globalization is the dialectical relation between *the global and the local*. What each congregation of the C of E does locally is both informed by, and also informs, the global religious system. This extraordinary claim has been rendered yet more extraordinary by the recently rapid progress of globalization itself. For that progress has increased the gap between the local and the global. In its early days the effective context of the C of E was "Christian Europe," and its local exemplar was the bishop's diocese. Today, the gap is considerably wider, but the task of bridging it is made infinitely easier by connectivity of information and people.

So, for example, the model of inter-faith relations embraced by the leaders of global religions informs the relationship of the local C of E congregation with its multi-cultural urban neighbors. The specific internal church structure for mission developed at St. Andrews Chorleywood becomes a model for practice in evangelical churches world-wide (see p. 119). The mission partners sent out to Africa by a large C of E congregation collaborate there with international non-governmental organizations, learn from them, and inform the congregation when they return on leave. A foreign student in Britain informs their British congregation of a group of people in their native country suffering religious persecution. The congregation engage with the issue by involving other congregations, lobbying parliament, mounting a press campaign, and flooding the social media. The image of one particularly brutal attack trends worldwide on Facebook, and citizens of many countries demand action from their governments.

But most important of all is the third element of globalization: the *consciousness of belonging* to the global social system of humankind; to at least some of the global functional systems of which it is constituted; and to planet Earth. This shared consciousness makes possible such concepts as human solidarity, human rights, distributive and procedural justice, and the common fate of life on earth. Furthermore, the awareness of several differentiated global systems, and the perception of personal membership of them, implies a level of cognitive complexity and flexibility in one's worldview. It leads to the recognition of the validity of different perspectives, and their appropriate fit to certain types of situation. And it results in complex personal and social identities for individuals which embrace and reconcile the membership of these sometimes incompatible social categories. Has the C of E even begun to explore the complexities of late-modern identities?

Given the ubiquity of this global consciousness, the C of E cannot ignore its implications for its own culture. Potential and actual adherents will increasingly be concerned with human rights, justice, and the survival of the planet. They will not entertain the possibility of absolutist positions regarding belief and doctrine, nor of exclusive membership of sectarian groups. They will regard many of the issues that absorb the time and attention of the Church as self-obsessed, exclusive, and utterly irrelevant to their concerns. They will lose patience with the Church's preoccupation with maintaining and reproducing itself. Rather, they will expect the C of E to engage with other religious groups and with other social systems in an effort to address the existential issues which they perceive the world to be facing. These issues they will construe in systemic terms: they certainly will not believe that they can be solved simply by increasing the number of individuals whom they bring into the church.

It is not as though the C of E does not have available the inspiring theological ideas that can bring a transcendent perspective to these issues. It has theologies of creation, of all humankind as the children of God, and of the possibility of redemption and hope for all. As a local institution within the global religious system, the C of E also possesses valuable specific emphases and resources to bring to the global table. For example, as Michael Hampson observes, "it occupies a unique position between a billion Roman Catholics on one side, and half a billion Protestants on the

A Global Institution

other."[10] But unless it recognizes the implications of its global context and adapts accordingly, local social connexions, organizational skills, and cultural fit will not secure its survival in the long term. The latter are necessary, but not sufficient conditions.

TOWARDS A STRATEGIC DIRECTION

So what might be the bones of its long-term global strategy, and what narrative could it use to inspire the world? Any tentative suggestions must be based on the two fundamental purposes of the global religious system: to relate to the transcendent, and communicate and act out what it derives from that relationship. But, to reiterate, any part of the global religious system will only succeed in these aims if it appreciates the implications of the three key features of globalization: connectivity, glocalization, and global consciousness.

I have argued that the global social system is differentiated, and that it and its components are reflected in the conscious social self-identification of late-modern people as human beings first, and then as citizens, parents, business people, Christians, scientists, teachers, and so on. This global consciousness makes people more aware of global issues, particularly since they will recognize them being played out not only globally, but in their local manifestations also.

The two most compelling global issues are existential in nature, threatening the very future of the global social system itself. They are climate change and injustice. Both are likely to disrupt, if not destroy, global society as it seeks to develop increased connectivity and a greater attention to human rights and security. *Climate change* will initially threaten the survival of those living in the areas most affected. These are already likely to be poor, and they will require resources which the institutions and citizens of less affected regions may be unable or unwilling to provide. Increased social conflict is a likely outcome.

Distributive injustice both within and between nations is also menacing. The gap is widening between the richest and poorest, threatening social connectivity and shared identity through the existence of so-called "failing families" and "failing states" (for "failing," substitute "poorest").

Given the urgency and importance of these issues, their salience in global consciousness, and their existing presence in the theology of

---

10. Hampson, *Last Rites*, 197.

Christianity and other religions, the strategic choice of issues for the C of E to address appears clear enough. But how best to address them is of course the hard part. This is where the differentiated global systems become vital. Modern religious adherents recognize that such global issues will only be meaningfully engaged with if the other global systems are involved also. While some of the most obviously powerful players (the oil industry, investment banks, and totalitarian nation states, for example) are usually unwilling to engage, softer power enabled by global connectivity might prove a major asset. Non-governmental organizations such as development agencies, professional associations, trans-national agencies, social movements and single-issue pressure groups in civil society, other denominations, and other religions may all prove collaborative partners and powerful allies. But it will be impossible to go it alone and hope to have any long-term effect. Recognizing and valuing the contributions of other systems is one of the necessary conditions for establishing collaborative relationships.

While the leaders of the C of E will be seeking to establish such collaborative relationships at the global level, they have at the same time to speak and act locally. They have to explain why they believe these two issues to be important, and demonstrate in local practice their ability to address them in collaboration with allies. They have to choose specific instances to target, and ensure that these are both of concern to people in general and offer some hope of progress. Only when leaders have demonstrated their ability to create the necessary changes at local level can they have credibility globally and start to inform global strategy. Somehow the C of E's leaders have to persuade the vicars of the big and visible Anglican congregations of all theological persuasions that climate change and injustice are the key gospel issues (and are of course related), and that they will not be successfully addressed by acts of Christian charity alone.

Archbishop Welby has already made a start on this strategic approach with his attack on pay-day lenders (see pp. 6–10), involving local congregations in the proposed solution to this acute problem of injustice and the exploitation of the poor. It might be argued, however, that he did not recruit enough allies before beginning his campaign. Archbishop Sentamu sends a similar message with his Living Wage Commission,[11] involving the Trades Union Congress, British Chamber of Commerce, local government, the National Council of Voluntary Organisations, a public health expert, an employer (KPMG), and a representative of low-paid workers. However,

---

11. www.livingwagecommission.org.uk/about.

it remains to be seen whether this initiative will exercise a major impact on the outcome of the current debate on this issue, which, like pay-day lending, directly impacts poverty. More recently, in the run-up to the General Election of 2015, both archbishops have emphasized the scandal of poverty as exemplified by the growth of food banks. Emphasizing the structural causes of poverty, they have, more controversially, criticized the ever-increasing inequality between the rich and the rest. They have also urged the C of E and other organizations to divest their shares in fossil fuel companies.

While such initiatives serve as local instances which could inform global practices, there is also the other direction of "glocalization" to consider: the influence of the global on the local. While both archbishops have extensive international connexions, they cannot yet match the facility of Christian leaders such as Pope Francis in exercising global influence by his symbolic acts for the poor, or Archbishop Desmond Tutu, by his part in the struggle against apartheid, his leadership of the Truth and Reconciliation Commission, and his defence of persecuted gays and lesbians. Both these leaders have made injustice and poverty their targets, and the Roman Catholic Church and, to a lesser extent, the Anglican Communion have consequently been associated in the public mind with their struggles.

The strategy of the C of E will also be closely related to the essence of globalization: *connectivity*, in particular of people and ideas. The worldwide migration of labor and of refugees from poverty and conflict has resulted a multi-cultural population in the UK, a partial reflection of global society. The C of E thus has the opportunity to model locally how religion might operate as a global system. Interfaith collaboration in fighting injustice in the UK will therefore be a high priority, in particular, injustice experienced by minorities of other faiths as well as Christianity, and by economic migrants and refugees. The C of E will always stress inclusively its commonalities with minorities and immigrants as brothers and sisters in God, rather than concentrating only on injustices suffered by Christians.

Connectivity of information and ideas again challenges the C of E to act inclusively rather than exclusively. The media, the internet, and social media can all be used to differentiate the C of E from other Christians, other religions, and other social systems than religion. Of course, such differentiation can be of use to show what it is that the C of E in particular can contribute to addressing global issues. For example, its extensive historic connexions with African Christians is one such unique contribution and its position straddling Protestantism and Catholicism another. However, its main effort will be to direct attention to *areas of commonality between global religious movements and institutions*, since these relate to the key global issues. It will, in other words, concentrate more on integration than on differentiation. Among these commonalities are the golden rule for ethical behavior, respect for human beings and human life, awe and wonder at the universe, a striving for justice and peace, an over-riding concern for the poor, an awareness of the transcendent, and the abiding hope of salvation for humankind.

Clearly, the present leadership of the C of E appreciates the importance of globalization and its implications for the institution. Whether it can persuade and inspire its warring factions, its celebrity vicars, and its overstretched rank and file to do the same is a matter for conjecture. It has already made a promising start by choosing its own, and the right, issues, and by playing down those with which the C of E has saddled itself for the last twenty years.

A full appreciation of the global perspective is indeed a necessary condition for the longer term survival and success of the C of E. But it is impossible to preach global social justice if the Church does not fully support justice and equality for women, gays, and the poor within its own structure and UK society. And it is impossible to do either effectively with an ageing and diminishing leadership and membership. Internal reform and external influence are both necessary conditions for these happy outcomes to occur. If faith and hope continue to be its guiding lights, the Church of England will yet succeed.

Bibliography

Ammerman, Nancy T. "Religious Identities and Religious Institutions." In *Handbook of the Sociology of Religion,* edited by Michele Dillon, 207–24. Cambridge: Cambridge University Press, 2003.
Ashforth, Blake E., and Fred A. Mael. "Social Identity and the organization." *Academy of Management Review* 14 (1989) 20–39.
Balmer, Randall. *Mine Eyes Have Seen the Glory: A Journey into the Evangelical Subculture in America.* 3rd ed. New York: Oxford University Press, 2000.
Bartlett, Annie, Glenn Smith, and Michael King. "The Response of Mental Health Professionals to Clients Seeking Help to Change or Redirect Same-sex Sexual Orientation." *British Journal of Psychiatry* 179 (2009) 545–49.
Bates, Stephen. *A Church at War: Anglicans and Homosexuality.* London: I.B. Tauris, 2004.
Bauman, Zygmunt. *Globalization: The Human Consequences.* Cambridge: Polity, 1998.
Baumeister, Robert F. "The Nature and Structure of the Self: An Overview." In *The Self in Social Psychology,* edited by Robert F. Baumeister, 1–20. Hove, UK: Psychology, 1999.
Beck, Ulrick. *World Risk Society.* Cambridge: Polity, 1999.
Bellah, Robert N., and Phillip E. Hammond. *Varieties of Civil Religion.* New York: Harper & Row, 1980.
Bellah, Robert N., Richard Madsen, William N. Sullivan, A. Swidler, and Steven M. Tipton. *Habits of the Heart.* 2nd ed. Berkeley CA: University of California Press, 1996.
Benedict, Philip. *Christ's Churches Purely Reformed: A Social History of Calvinism.* New Haven CT: Yale University Press, 2002.
Benn, Wallace, Gerald Bray, Roger Beckwith, and Michael Ovey. *A Way Forward.* 2005. Online: www.fows.org/index.php?option=com. . .id. . .way-forward
Beyer, Peter. *Religions in Global Society.* London: Routledge, 2006.
Boyer, Paul. *When Time Shall Be No More: Prophecy Belief in Modern American Culture.* Cambridge: Harvard University Press, 1992.
Brewer, Marilynn, and Caporael, Linnda R. "Social Identity Motives in Evolutionary Perspective." In *Social Identities: Motivational, Emotional, and Cultural Influences,* edited by Rupert Brown and Dora Capozza, 135–52. Hove, UK: Psychology, 2006.
Brierley, Peter. *The Tide is Running Out: What the English Church Attendance Survey Reveals.* London: Christian Research, 2000.
Brown, Callum. *The Death of Christian Britain.* Abingdon: Routledge, 2001.
Bryman, Alan. *Charisma and Leadership of Organisations.* London: Sage: 1992
Casanova, Jose. *Public Religions in the Modern World.* Chicago: University of Chicago Press, 1994.

Bibliography

Castells, Manuel. *The Rise of the Network Society.* Oxford: Blackwell, 1996.
Claridge, Gordon. "Spiritual Experience: Healthy Psychoticism?" In *Psychosis and Spirituality: Consolidating the New Paradigm,* edited by Ian Clarke, 75–88. London: Wiley-Blackwell, 2010.
Coleman, Simon. *The Globalization of Charismatic Christianity.* Cambridge: Cambridge University Press, 2000.
Cox, Harvey. *Fire from Heaven: The Rise of Pentecostal Spirituality and the Reshaping of Religion in the Twenty-first Century.* Reading, MA: Addison-Wesley, 1995.
Davie, Grace. *Religion in Britain: A Persistent Paradox,* 2nd ed. Chichester, UK: Wiley-Blackwell, 2015.
———. *Religion in Britain since 1945: Believing without Belonging.* Oxford: Blackwell, 1994.
———. *Religion in Modern Europe: A Memory Mutates.* Oxford: Oxford University Press, 2000.
Drucker, Peter F. *Post-Capitalist Society.* Oxford: Butterworth-Heinemann, 1993.
Durkheim, Emile. *The Elementary Forms of the Religious Life.* New York: Free, 1965.
Edwards, David. *A Concise History of English Christianity.* London: Fount, 1998.
Eisenstadt, S. N. *Fundamentalism, Sectarianism, and Revolution: The Jacobin Dimension of Modernity.* Cambridge: Cambridge University Press, 1999.
Fukuyama, Francis. *The End of History and the Last Man.* London: Penguin, 1992.
Furlong, Monica. *C of E: The State It's In.* London: Hodder & Stoughton, 2000.
Furre, Berge. "Crossing Boundaries: The 'Universal Church' and the Spirit of Globalization." In *Spirits of Globalization: The Growth of Pentecostalism and Experiential Spiritualities in a Global Age,* edited by Sturla J. Stalsett, 39–51. London: SCM, 2006.
George, Philip. *The Origins of the New Wine Movement.* 2013. Online: www.wtctheology.org.uk/wl/?id=im&filename=wtc%20Conf%20paper.
Giddens, Anthony. *Modernity and Self-Identity: Self and Society in the Late Modern Age.* Cambridge: Polity, 1991.
Goffman, Erving. *Relations in Public.* London: Allen Lane, 1971.
Gordon, Bruce. *Calvin.* New Haven, CT: Yale University Press, 2009.
Hampson, Michael. *Last Rites: The End of the Church of England.* London: Granta, 2006.
Hart, Darryl G. *Calvinism: A History.* New Haven CT: Yale University Press, 2013.
Haslam, S. Alexander, Stephen Reicher, and Michael Platow. *The New Psychology of Leadership: Identity, Influence, and Power.* Hove, UK: Psychology, 2011.
Hassett, Miranda K. *Anglican Communion in Crisis: How Episcopal Dissidents and Their African Allies are Reshaping Anglicanism.* Princeton NJ: Princeton University Press, 2009.
Hastings, Adrian. *A History of English Christianity 1920–1990.* 3rd ed. London: SCM, 1991.
Heinze, Rudi, and David Wheaton. *Witness to the World: A History of Oak Hill College 1932–2000.* Carlisle, UK: Paternoster, 2002.
Herriot, Peter. *Phillip Jensen, Bible Believer: The Psychology of Fundamentalist Leadership.* Kindle Direct, 2013.
———. *Religious Fundamentalism: Global, Local, and Personal.* London: Routledge, 2009.
———. *Religious Fundamentalism and Social Identity.* London: Routledge, 2008.
Hilborn, David. *Charismatic Renewal in Britain: Roots, Influences, and Later Developments.* London: Evangelical Alliance, 2003.

Bibliography

Hochschild, Arlie R. *The Managed Heart: Commercialisation of Human Feeling.* Berkeley: University of California Press, 1983.

Hogg, Michael A., and Dominic Abrams. "Intergroup Behavior and Social Identity." In *Handbook of Social Psychology,* edited by Michael A. Hogg and Joel Cooper, 407–31. London: Sage, 2003.

Hogg, Michael A., and Barbara-Ann Mullin. "Joining Groups to Reduce Uncertainty: Subjective Uncertainty Reduction and Group Identification." In *Social Identity and Social Cognition,* edited by Dominic Abrams and Michael A. Hogg, 249–79. Oxford: Blackwell, 1999.

Howard, Roland. *The Rise and Fall of the Nine O'clock Service: A Cult within the Church?* London: Mowbray, 1996.

Huntington, Samuel P. *The Clash of Civilizations and the Remaking of World Order.* New York: Simon and Schuster, 1996.

———. "The Clash of Civilizations?" *Foreign Affairs* 72, (1993) 22–49.

Issues in Human Sexuality: A Statement to the House of Bishops. London: Church House, 1991.

Jackson, Bradley. *Management Gurus and Management Fashions.* London: Routledge, 2001.

Jaspers, Karl. *The Origin and Goal of History.* New Haven, CT: Yale University Press, 1965.

Jeffery, Steve, Mike Ovey, and Andrew Sach. *Pierced for Our Transgressions: Rediscovering the Glory of Penal Substitution.* Wheaton IL: Crossway, 2007.

Jenkins, Philip. *God's Continent: Christianity, Islam, and Europe's Religious Crisis.* Oxford: Oxford University Press, 2007.

———. *The Next Christendom: The Coming of Global Christianity.* 2nd ed. Oxford: Oxford University Press, 2007.

Jenkins, Richard. *Social Identity.* 3rd ed. New York: Routledge, 2008.

Jones, Edward E., and Keith E. Davis. "From Acts to Dispositions: The Attribution Process in Person Perception." In *Advances in Experimental Social Psychology* 2, edited by Leonard Berkowitz, 220–65. New York: Academic, 1965.

———. "The Rocky Road from Acts to Dispositions." *American Psychologist* 34 (1979) 107–17.

Juergensmeyer, Mark. "Religious Antiglobalism." In *Religion in Global Civil Society,* edited by Mark Juergensmeyer, 135–48. New York: Oxford University Press, 2006.

Kelley, Harold H. "Attribution Theory in Social Psychology." In *Nebraska Symposium on Motivation* 15, edited by David Levine, 192–240. Lincoln, NE: University of Nebraska Press, 1967.

Kim, Sung-Gun. "Pentecostalism, Shamanism, and Capitalism within Contemporary Korean Society." In *Spirits of Globalization: The Growth of Pentecostalism and Experiential Spiritualities in a Global Age,* edited by Sturla J. Stalsett, 23–38. London: SCM, 2006.

Kings, Graham. "Canal, River, and Rapids: Contemporary Evangelicalism in the Church of England." *Anvil* 20.3 (2003) 167–84. Online: www.fulcrum-anglican.org.uk/news/2003/20030930watercourses.cfm?doc=2.

Laing, Ronald D. *The Divided Self.* Harmondsworth, UK: Penguin, 1965.

Lasch, Christopher. *The Culture of Narcissism: American Life in an Age of Diminishing Expectations.* London: Abacus, 1980.

Legge, Karen. *Human Resource Management: Rhetorics and Realities.* London: Macmillan, 1995.

Bibliography

Lehmann, David. *Struggle for the Spirit*. Cambridge: Polity, 1995.

Lienesch, Michael. *Redeeming America: Piety and Politics in the New Christian Right*. Chapel Hill, NC: University of North Carolina Press, 1993.

Luckmann, Thomas. *The Invisible Religion: The Problem of Religion in Modern Societies*. New York: Macmillan, 1967.

MacCulloch, Diarmaid. *The Reformation: A History*. New York: Viking, 2003.

———. *Thomas Cranmer: A Life*. New Haven: Yale University Press, 1996.

Maltby, Judith. *Prayer Book and People in Elizabethan and Early Stuart England*. Cambridge: Cambridge University Press, 1998.

Martin, Bernice. "From Pre- to Post-modernity in Latin America: The Case of Pentecostalism." In *Religion, Modernity, and Postmodernity*, edited by Paul Heelas, 102–46. Oxford: Blackwell, 1998.

McBride, Ray. "Secular Ecstasies." *The Psychologist* 27.3 (2014) 168–70.

McGillion, Chris. *The Chosen Ones: The Politics of Salvation in the Anglican Church*. Crows Nest, NSW: Allen and Unwin, 2005.

McGrath, Alister. *Christianity's Dangerous Idea: The Protestant Revolution—A History from the Sixteenth Century to the Twenty-First*. New York: HarperOne, 2007.

Miller, Dale T., and Michael Ross. "Self-serving Biases in Attribution of Causality: Fact or Fiction?" *Psychological Bulletin* 82 (1975) 213–25.

Naim, Moises. *The End of Power*. New York: Basic, 2013.

Noll, Mark A. *The New Shape of World Christianity*. Downers Grove IL: IVP, 2009.

Noon, Michael, and Paul Blyton. *The Realities of Work*. London: Macmillan, 1997.

Norenzayan, Ara, and Scott Atran. "Cognitive and Emotional Processes in the Cultural Transmission of Natural and Nonnatural Beliefs." In *The Psychological Foundations of Culture*, edited by Mark Schaller and Christian S. Crandall, 149–70. Mahwah, NJ: Erlbaum, 2004.

Ohmae, Kenichi. *The End of the Nation State*. New York: Free, 1995.

Percy, Martyn. *Catching the Fire: The Sociology of Exchange, Power, and Charisma in the "Toronto Blessing."* 1996. Online: www.latimertrust.org/downloads/Publication%20Downloads/pdf%20books/Is53pen.

———. *Words, Wonders, and Power: Understanding Contemporary Fundamentalism and Revivalism*. London: SPCK, 1996.

Piketty, Thomas. *Capital in the Twenty-First Century*. Boston: Harvard University Press, 2014.

Porter, Muriel. *Sydney Anglicans and the Threat to World Anglicanism*. Farnham, UK: Ashgate, 2011.

Putnam, Robert D. *Bowling Alone: The Collapse and Revival of American Community*. New York: Simon and Schuster, 2000.

Redman, Beth. *God Knows My Name: Never Forgotten, Forever Loved*. Colorado Springs CO: Cook, 2001.

Rieff, Phillip. *The Triumph of the Therapeutic*. Harmondsworth, UK: Penguin, 1966.

Roberts, Vaughan. *Battles Christians Face: Tackling Big Issues with Confidence*. 2nd ed. Milton Keynes, UK: Authentic Lifestyle, 2012.

———. *Daring to be Different in an Indifferent World*. Milton Keynes, UK: Authentic Lifestyle, 2000.

Robertson, Roland. *Globalization: Social Theory and Global Culture*. London: Sage, 1992.

Rokeach, Milton. *The Nature of Human Values*. New York: Free, 1973.

Bibliography

Ross, Lee, and Richard E. Nisbett. *The Person and the Situation: Perspectives of Social Psychology.* New York: McGraw-Hill, 1991.

Schein, Edgar H. *Organizational Culture and Leadership.* 2nd ed. San Francisco: Jossey Bass, 1992.

Scholte, Jan A. *Globalization: A Critical Introduction.* 2nd ed. Basingstoke, UK: Palgrave Macmillan, 2005.

Sennett, Richard. *The Corrosion of Character: The Personal Consequences of Work in the New Capitalism.* New York: Norton, 1998.

Smith, Peter B., and Michael H. Bond. "Honoring Culture Psychologically When Doing Social Psychology." In *Handbook of Social Psychology,* edited by Michael A. Hogg and Joel Cooper, 43–64. London: Sage, 2003.

Steven, James H. *Worship in the Spirit: Charismatic Worship in the Church of England.* Milton Keynes, UK: Paternoster, 2002.

Stibbe, Mark, and Andrew Williams. *Breakout.* Milton Keynes, UK: Authentic Media, 2008.

———. "This Is That: Some Thoughts concerning Charismatic Hermeneutics." *Anvil* 15.3 (1998) 181–93.

Taylor, Charles. *Sources of the Self.* New York: Cambridge University Press, 1989.

Taylor, Shelley, and Susan T. Fiske. "Salience, Attention, and Attribution." In *Advances in Experimental Social Psychology* 11, edited by Leonard Berkowitz, 249–88. New York: Academic, 1978.

Triandis, Harry C. *Individualism and Collectivism.* Boulder CO: Westview, 1995.

Trope, Yaacov, and Ruth Gaunt. "Attribution and Person Perception." In *Handbook of Social Psychology,* edited by Michael A. Hogg and Joel Cooper, 190–209. London: Sage, 2003.

Village, Andrew, and Leslie J. Francis. "Attitude towards Homosexuality among Anglicans in England: The Effects of Theological Orientation and Personality." *Journal of Empirical Theology* 21.1 (2008) 68–87.

von Campenhausen, Hans, and J. A. Baker. *Ecclesiastical Authority and Spiritual Power in the Church of the First Three Centuries.* London: Black, 1969.

Walker, Andrew G. *Restoring the Kingdom: The Radical Christianity of the House Church Movement.* London: Hodder & Stoughton, 1988.

Ward, W. R. *The Protestant Evangelical Awakening.* Cambridge: Cambridge University Press, 1992.

Warner, Rob. *Reinventing English Evangelicalism, 1966–2001.* Milton Keynes, UK: Paternoster, 2007.

Wilkinson, Richard, and Kate Pickett. *The Spirit Level: Why More Equal Societies Almost Always Do Better.* London: Allen Lane, 2009.

Williams, Rhys H. "Religious Social Movements in the Public Sphere: Organization, Ideology, and Activism." In *Handbook of the Sociology of Religion,* edited by Michele Dillon, 315–30. Cambridge: Cambridge University Press, 2003.

Wocjek, Daniel. *The End of the World As We Know It: Faith, Fatalism, and Apocalypse in America.* New York: New York University Press, 1997.

Woodhead, Linda, and Rebecca Catto, eds. *Religion and Change in Modern Britain.* London: Routledge, 2012.

Wuthnow, Robert. *Boundless Faith: The Global Outreach of American Churches.* Berkeley: University of California Press, 2009.

Index

accountability, 106–7, 114–15, 117–24, 182
Acts of the Apostles, 135, 162, 167
affiliation, 103
    political, 130
    religious, 130–31
Africa, 22, 76–77, 82, 88, 178, 189, 193
    Pentecostals in, 35
Allegri, Gregorio, 135
All Souls Langham Place, 38, 85–86, 88, 91, 94
Alpha, 11, 41, 105–7, 114, 117, 119, 133–41, 144, 153–54, 156, 165, 178
Anglican
    Church of North America (ACNA), 59, 77, 82
    Communion, 22, 29–32, 48, 64, 67–68, 76–84, 153, 178, 180–81, 193
    Mainstream, 11, 31, 56, 58–60, 67–73, 75, 81, 90, 93–94, 98
    Mission in England (AMIE) 11, 31, 60, 77–78, 81–84, 90, 93
Anglicans for Renewal, 39
Anglo-Catholics, 29–30, 65
Arab Spring, 84
Archbishops' Council, 3
artefacts, 95–96
attitudes, 130–32, 185
attribution, 128, 166–69
    and bias, 168
    and differentiation, 172–74
authenticity, 128–29, 143, 145
authority, 64–66, 174–76
Axial Age, 173

Bailey, Mark, 114–17, 149–50, 153–55
Battles Christians Face, 56
Beautiful, 137
Beautifully Broken, 139, 141
beliefs, 96–99, 162–66, 174–76
Bellah, Robert, 127
Benn, Wallace, 49–52, 70, 76, 82, 93
Bentley, Todd, 122
Bible, 12, 33, 47, 52–55, 64, 74–77, 83–84, 87, 91, 97, 112, 134–35, 140, 175–76,
Bishop of Sheffield, 88
bishops, 2–3, 30–32, 50, 60, 82, 116, 185–86
    flying, 30–31, 47, 50, 65, 181
    gay, 54, 59
    women, 30, 32, 52–53, 65
Boddy, Alexander, 38
Book of Common Prayer, 18
Brain, Chris, 118
brand, 111, 186
Breakout, 120
Bristol University, 46
BBC, 6–7, 53, 59
British
    Association for Counselling and Psychotherapy, 69–70
    Chamber of Commerce, 192
    Empire, 21–22, 29
    Medical Association, 69
    Psychodrama Association, 69
    Psychological Society, 72
    Social Attitudes Survey, 130–32, 143
Brown, Andrew, 185–86
Burkill, Mark, 48

Index

Cable, Vince, 7
Calvert, David, xi
Calvin, John, 16, 26
Calvinists
  appeasement of, 181
  vs Charismatics, 10, 12–17, 34, 41, 57, 99, 103–4, 117–18, 124–25, 144, 149, 153, 175, 177–83
  contemporary, 28
  culture of, 95–100
  effectiveness of, 177–78
  formation of, 43–49, 63, 90–94
  history of, 16–17, 25–32, 97
  leaders of, 49–63
  organization of, 91–94, 178
Cambridge Inter-Collegiate Christian Union (CICCU) 44, 55
capitalism, 126, 161
Carey, George, 30, 40, 70
Casanova, Jose, 171
cathedrals, 184
celebrity, 160
cells, 115
Chalke, Steve, 45
change, 126, 146–61
  climate, 191
  generational 130–31, 185
  organizational, 118–22, 146–48, 151–54
Chapman, John, 74
Charismatics
  vs Calvinists, 10, 12–17, 34, 41, 57, 99, 103–4, 117–18, 124–25, 144, 149, 153, 175, 177–83
  culture of, 111–12, 118–24, 133–45, 162–66
  effectiveness of, 178
  formation of, 107–8
  global spread of, 36
  history of, 37–42
  organization of, 104–9, 178
Christ, Jesus, 33, 44–45, 61, 78, 87, 99, 112, 115, 138, 140–43, 153–55, 173
Christ Church
  Bromley, 86–88, 97
  Central, 88
  Fullwood, 86, 88, 91
  Mayfair, 86, 91
  Virginia Water, 86, 90–91
  Walkley, 88
Christenson, Larry, 38
Christianity Today, 120
church
  attendance, 4, 130, 132
  planting, 66, 83–84, 88, 105, 108, 114
Church Commission, 7, 89
Church of England
  culture of, 1–2
  future of, 177–94
  history of, 1–2, 15–18, 21–22
  membership of, 4, 131, 184
Church Society, 11, 49
Church Times, 144
civil society, 171–72
civilizations, 19
clergy, 61–62
  gay, 30–32
  recruitment of, 83, 185
climate change, 191
Coles, John, 105, 159–60, 165
colonialism, 34–35
Commission on Doctrine, 3
commodification, 127, 129, 183
Confederation of British Industry, 54
conflict, 100, 180–82
conformity, 100–1
congregations, 3–4, 11, 13, 74, 85–92, 103–8, 114–16, 153–54, 176, 184–87
connectivity, 21, 28, 188–89, 193
consciousness
  global, 21, 190–91
  raising, 182
consumerism, 19, 129, 161, 163, 183
control, 106–7, 114–15, 117–24, 156–57
conversion
  narrative, 54–55, 102, 112–13
  therapy, 68–72
Core Issues Trust, 72
Cornhill Training Course, 74
corporations, 171, 188
Cost of Conscience, 61
Cox, Harvey, 32–33
Craig, Alan, 73
Cranmer Hall Durham, 47
Cranmer, Thomas, 16

Index

creationism, 90
culture, 19
   of Calvinists, 95–100
   of Charismatics, 111–12, 118–24, 133–45, 162–66
   of Church of England, 1–2
   contemporary, 37, 113, 125–30, 146–48, 159–60, 182–83
Cunningham, Richard, 45–46
cynicism, 163, 174

Daily Mail, 7
Daring to be Different, 56
Davie, Grace, 4
Davidson, Mike, 70, 72
Davies, Glenn, 50
Dawkins, Richard, 45, 90
demons, 164, 166, 173
dialogue, 160, 187
Different by Design, 75
differentiation, 5, 13, 20, 56, 100–101, 116, 169–72
   and attribution, 172–74
   vs. integration, 5, 13, 20, 170, 193–94
disestablishment, 187
dispensationalism, 39, 164, 166, 173–74
doctrine, 26–28, 52, 81, 96–100
Dow, Graham, 46
Durkheim, Emile, 5

ecstasy, 33–34, 37–41, 106, 140, 143, 154–57, 168–69.
Emmanuel College Gateshead, 90
emotional labor, 129–30
English Church Census, 4
Enlightenment, 23, 36, 171
Episcopal Church of the USA (ECUSA) 31, 59, 76–77, 82
European Values Study, 143
Evangelical, 2, 4, 9–10, 16, 18, 29–31, 38, 41, 46–47, 50, 54, 56–58, 74, 89–90, 92, 106, 111, 116–17, 158–59, 173, 177
   Alliance, 41, 139, 159
   Council, 49
   Ministry Assembly, 74–75
evangelism, 44–45, 119, 180–81
Exclusive Plymouth Brethren, 54

Ex-Gay Movement, 71
exorcism, 34, 39

Facebook, 190
Faith in the City, 2
family, 58, 99–100
Father's House Trust, 120–21
Fellowship of Confessing Anglicans (FCA) 31, 48–49, 51, 58, 60, 78, 81, 90, 93
Financial Conduct Authority, 9
Financial Times, 6–7
flying bishops, 30–31, 47, 50, 65, 181
Focus, 138, 149
formation, 11
   Calvinist, 43–49, 63, 90–94
   Charismatic, 107–8
Forward in Faith, 65
Fountain Trust, 38–39
Free to Be, 138
Fukuyama, Francis, 19–20
Future Identities, 132

gay, 29, 47–48, 52, 55–56, 68–73, 75, 100, 131, 143–45, 181, 193
   bishops, 54, 59
   clergy, 30–32
   marriage, 58–59, 65, 144–145
Gay Myths, 72
generational change, 130–31, 185
Giddens, Anthony, 126
Glasman, Maurice, 8
Global Anglican Future Conference (GAFCON), 11, 31, 48–50, 52, 58, 60–61, 67, 76–83, 90, 98, 153
globalization, 18–24, 28, 35–36, 126, 187–94
   and connectivity, 21, 188–89, 193
   and glocalization, 20, 36, 189–90, 193
   and Pentecostalism, 35–36
   and reflexivity, 21, 190
God, Gays, and the Church, 70
Graham, Billy, 54, 92
Greenbelt, 59, 111
The Guardian, 6, 159
Gumbel, Nicky, 105–7, 109, 116, 136–37, 144, 149, 153–54, 165–66

Index

Hamilton, Adrian, 187
Hampson, Michael, 186–87, 190
Harper, Michael, 17, 38
Hart, Darryl, 28
healing, 40, 106, 122–23, 162–66
Hill, Wes, 47–48
Hillsong, 149
history
  of the Calvinists, 16–17, 25–32, 97
  of the Charismatics, 37–42
  of the C of E, 1–2, 15–18, 21–22
Holloway, David, 90
Holy Spirit, 32–33, 35–37, 39–40, 46, 61, 112, 122–24, 133–40, 143, 151, 155–57, 160, 163, 165–69, 175–76, 178
Holy Trinity Brompton (HTB) 11, 13, 39, 41, 105–8, 111, 114, 119, 133, 138–39, 142, 149, 153–54, 162–63
Holy Trinity Cheltenham (Trinity) 105, 107–8, 114–17, 149, 153, 176
Home Affairs Select Committee, 60
Hooker, Richard, 16
house churches, 39
human rights, 98
Human Rights Articles, 73
Huntington, Samuel, 19–20
hyper-connectivity, 132

identity
  nested, 102–3, 146–7
  personal, 101–3, 127, 130, 132–33, 143, 145–46, 176
  social, 13, 62, 75–76, 94–95, 99–103, 115–16, 127–130, 132, 146, 168, 172, 176, 179
The Independent, 70
indigenous religion, 34
individualism, 117, 127–28, 140, 146, 158, 160–61, 183
Industrial Revolution, 1–2, 17
industrialization, 35–36
inequality, 127, 161, 193
institutions, 1–6, 23–24
  advantages and disadvantages of, 3–4
  vs. movements, 9–10, 13–15, 178–183

integration vs. differentiation, 5, 13, 20, 170, 193–94
intimacy, 140–43
Ipsos MORI, 131, 143
Issues in Human Sexuality, 30

Jackson, Pete, 88
Jensen
  Peter, 51
  Phillip, 51, 74, 92, 95, 153
Jerusalem Declaration, 31, 50, 52, 76–77, 89
Jesmond Parish Church, 86, 90
Jesuits, 14
Jesus Christ, 33, 44–45, 61, 78, 87, 99, 112, 115, 138, 140–43, 153–55, 173
John, Jeffrey, 31, 50
Johnson, Boris, 72
justice, 5–6, 161, 116–17, 191–92

Kansas City Prophets, 40
Keller, Tim, 74
King Report, 69
Kings, Graham, 10
Knox, John, 16
Korea, 34
KPMG, 192

Laing, Ronald, 128
Lakeland Revival, 122–23, 151, 158
Lambeth
  Conference 1998, 30, 50, 58, 76–77, 81
  Palace, 7
Latimer Trust, 47–48
leaders, 11, 49–63, 108, 111, 116, 185
leadership, 49, 147–48, 151–52, 185
Leafe, Susie, 67
legitimation, 157
Lesbian and Gay Christian Movement, 30
Living Wage Commission, 192
Lloyd, Michael, 48
Los Angeles, 33
Lucas, Dick, 16, 74, 85, 97
Luther, Martin, 25, 68
Lutherans, 16, 25

Index

Machen, J. Gresham, 27
Mackesy, Charlie, 133–37
management theory, 44, 119, 184
markets, 126
marriage, 131
　gay, 58–59, 65, 144–45
May, Tim, 162–63, 165
media, 6–9, 54, 58–62, 66, 93–94, 126–27, 129, 180, 189
medicine, 68–72
mental health, 157
Methodists, 2, 14, 17, 106
Middlesex University, 74
Millar, Sandy, 39, 41, 105
ministry of all believers, 92, 95, 106, 152, 160, 164–65
miracles, 162–63
mission, 44, 82–84, 108, 114, 159
Mission-Shaped Communities, 119–123, 151
modernity, 172–74
Modern Church, 187
Momentum, 110
moral authority, 5–6
Moore College Sydney, 47
movements
　vs. institutions, 9–10, 13–15, 178–83
　organization of, 11–12, 37–38, 43, 91–94, 178
Mozart, Wolfgang Amadeus, 135
Muslims, 8, 58–59, 188

Naim, Moises, 23
narcissism, 129, 148, 160–61
narratives, 13, 54–55, 79–81, 103, 112–13, 128, 158–61
nation states, 188
National Council of Voluntary Organisations, 192
National Health Service, 131
naturally supernatural 110, 150–51, 160–66
Nazir-Ali, Michael, 70, 82
nested identity, 102–3, 146–47,
Netherlands, 26–27
A new kind of normal, 150
New Labour, 131

New Wine, 39, 60, 105–6, 109, 111, 117, 119, 149, 158–59, 162–63
Nine O'clock Service, 117
Nolland, Lisa, 70, 72
normalization, 157, 159
norms of behavior, 96, 99–100

Oak Hill College, 11, 47–49, 75, 80, 90–91, 94
Office for National Statistics, 131
organization
　of Calvinists, 91–94, 104
　of Charismatics, 104–8
　of C of E, 184–87
　of movements, 11–12, 37–38, 43, 91–94, 178
organizational change, 118–22, 146–48, 151–54
Osborne, George, 7
Ovey, Mike, 48, 76, 80
Oxford
　Centre for Mission Studies, 58
　Inter-collegiate Christian Union (OICCU) 46
　Movement, 2, 18

Packer, Jim, 16, 47, 50–51, 74, 97
parish contributions, 60, 66, 78, 88–90
penal substitution, 45, 48, 51, 57, 64, 74, 80, 97
Pentecostals, 32–36
Perkin
　Christine, 60
　Paul, 32, 49, 59–63, 70, 72, 77, 82, 89–90, 92–94, 98
persecution, 46, 50–51, 55, 72–73, 79–80, 84, 94, 99, 103
personal identity, 101–3, 127, 130, 133, 143, 145–46, 176
Pilavachi, Mike, 105, 108–14, 119, 137, 142, 149–50, 152, 155, 160–61, 163–65
Pilkington, Lesley, 70–72
Pilling Report, 78
Piper, John, 74
Pippert, Rebecca Manley, 44–45
The Plumbline, 154–55
political affiliation, 130

Index

Pope Francis, 193
poverty, 193
power, 98, 156, 161
prayer ministry, 40, 106, 133, 143, 155–57, 168–69
primal
  hope, 33
  piety, 32–33
  speech, 32–33
Proclamation Trust, 11, 55, 57, 73–76, 82, 90, 93
prototypes, 49, 52, 55–56, 63, 116
psychotherapy, 68–72
Puritans, 16–17, 27, 29
Pytches, David, 17, 39, 41, 46, 105, 109, 119, 122, 151

Reconstructionists, 27
Redman
  Beth, 106, 137–40, 155
  Matt, 106, 111, 138, 164–65
Reform, 30–31, 47–49, 51–52, 60, 64–67, 75, 81, 90, 93–94, 98
Reformation, 16–17, 24–29, 39, 97
relationships, 126, 129
religion, 19–20, 131, 169–72, 175–76
religious affiliation, 130–31
Renewal, 38–39
Revival, 150, 163, 165
Revival Fires, 123
Reynolds, Jim, 72
Ridley Hall, 47
Roberts, Vaughan, 32, 49, 55–57, 66, 68, 75, 90, 92–94
Robinson, Gene, 31, 50, 59, 67, 76
Robinson, John, 3
Rogers, Cris, 154
Roman Catholics, 8, 14, 16–18, 22–29, 34, 190, 193
Royal College of Psychiatrists, 69, 71
Runcie, Robert, 2
Rwanda, 82

St Aldates, 46
St Andrew the Great, 85
St Andrews Chorleywood, 39, 105–6, 108, 119–23, 152, 189
St Ebbes, 46, 55, 66, 85–86, 90

St Helens Bishopsgate, 11, 66, 74, 85, 87–89, 94
St Johns Nottingham, 39, 107, 112
St Johns Tunbridge Wells, 75, 86–87, 91
St Marks Battersea Rise, 11, 59, 61, 77, 86–90, 94
St Marys Walkley, 88
St Matthews Elburton, 90
St Michael-le-Belfrey, 39, 107, 149
St Nicholas Sevenoaks, 186–87
St Pauls Cathedral, 2
St Pauls Hammersmith, 149
St Thomas Crookes, 105, 107–8, 114–19, 122, 142, 149
Samuel, Vinay, 83–84
Sandom, Carrie, 75
Sants, Hector, 8
science, 20, 166, 169–70, 188–89
Scotland, 26–27
Second Vatican Council, 23, 34
secularism, 61–62, 98–99, 101
segmentation, 87, 109–11, 114–15
self
  concept, 101, 125–37
  disclosure, 135, 138–40
  esteem, 94, 103
  presentation, 129
  reference, 112, 133, 135
Sentamu, John, 192
Sizer, Stephen, 90
social
  action, 75–76, 99, 159, 161
  identity, 13, 62, 75–76, 94–95, 99–103, 115–16, 127–30, 132, 146, 168, 172, 176, 179
  justice, 116–17, 161
  pluralism, 132
  science, 9–10, 37
  systems, 169–76, 192–94
sola scriptura, 26, 45, 47, 175
Soul
  Action, 110
  Net, 110
  Survivor, 11, 39, 105–14, 119, 142, 149, 151, 161, 165
Soul Sister, 137
Southwark Good Stewards Trust, 89–90
speaking in tongues, 32, 38, 133, 136

Index

Spring Harvest, 41, 45, 109
Stacey, Nick, 3
Steven, James, 156
Stibbe, Mark, 118–24, 137, 151
Stockwood, Mervyn, 3
Stonewall, 69, 72
Story Lines, 112
Stott, John, 16, 38, 51, 74, 85, 97
Strange, Dan, 75
strategy, 12–13, 44, 179–80, 191–94
Strudwick, Patrick, 70
students, 43–44, 91–92
success factors, 184–85
Sugden, Chris, 32, 49, 58–60, 70, 72, 82–84, 93
Summer Nights, 162
supernatural, 34–36, 123–24, 160–61, 165–66, 172–74, 183
Sydney Anglicans, 27–29, 50–51, 153
Synod, 3, 32, 52–54, 59, 65, 181, 186

Taylor, William, 66, 89
teaching, 40, 106, 141–42
Tearfund, 110
Temple, William, 16
Thatcher, Margaret, 2
theology, 25–26, 37, 140–41, 166, 173–74, 183, 190–91
therapy, 137–40
Third Wave, 37
Thirty-Nine Articles, 16, 18, 50
Thomas, Rod, 32, 49, 52–55, 66–67, 90, 92–94
The Times, 51
tongues, speaking in, 32, 38, 133, 136
Toronto Blessing, 20, 37, 40–41, 105, 112, 156, 164
Total Politics, 6
Trades Union Congress, 192
Transport for London, 72–73
Trenier, Naomi, 139, 154
Trinity College Bristol, 47
Truth and Reconciliation Commission, 193
truth criteria, 101, 174–76
Turnbull, Richard, 48
Tutu, Desmond, 193

UK
    Border Agency, 74
    Council for Psychotherapy, 69
United
    States, 27, 38–40, 67, 130
    Church of South India, 23
Universal Church of the Kingdom of God, 34
University and Colleges Christian Fellowship (UCCF) 43–47, 90, 92–93

values, 44, 96, 99–100, 158–59, 176, 183
Vineyard, 39–41, 105, 110, 149
vision, 44, 116, 149, 158
vulnerability, 138–39

Wabukala, Eliud, 77–78, 81–83
Walker, Arianna, 142
Warner, Rob, 109
Watson, David, 17, 39
Weber, Max, 10, 159
Welby, Justin, 6–9, 54, 80, 83, 107, 160–61, 184, 192
White, David, 121
Williams, Andrew, 119–21
Williams, Rowan, 18, 31, 66, 89
Wimber
    Christy, 106, 137, 155
    John, 39–40, 105–6, 119, 122, 151, 157, 163–64
women, 46, 48–49, 51, 64, 66–67, 75, 81, 87, 110
    bishops, 30, 32, 52–53, 65
    ordination of, 29, 48, 65, 67
    right to choose, 131
Wonga, 6–9, 161
Woodhead
    Linda, xi, 185–86
    Mick, 14–17, 137, 142, 149, 153
World
    Council of Churches, 23
    Council of Reformed Communions, 28
    Health Organization, 69
worldview, 98
worship, 40, 106, 110–12, 140–41, 154–57
Worship Central, 110

Index

Wycliffe Hall, 47–49, 55, 60, 90, 93–94
Wynter, Pete, 152

xenolalia, 165–66

YouGov, 144

www.ingramcontent.com/pod-product-compliance
Lightning Source LLC
Chambersburg PA
CBHW070256230426
43664CB00014B/2554